D1219106

# Faith and Politics in Iran, Israel and the Islamic State
## *Theologies of the Real*

Religious faith has been gaining in reach and influence throughout global politics over the last three decades, most prominently in the Middle East, and theologies of this nature are based on the understanding that faith in God is to be based, primarily and predominantly, on the realness of God's presence. The West, accustomed to its own discussion on religion and politics emphasizing democracy and individual freedoms, has been at a loss to explain and engage these rising religious polities. Through an innovative approach to the role of faith in politics, *Faith and Politics in Iran, Israel and the Islamic State* considers political theologies of the real formulated during the twentieth century and proposes that, while religion in the West has been committed to absolutist vision, these theologies have drawn their strength from a commitment to their concrete, divinely infused reality.

Ori Goldberg teaches at the Lauder School of Government, Diplomacy and Strategy at the Interdisciplinary Center Herzliya. He was a Fox International Fellow at Yale University, Connecticut, and a research fellow at the Shalom Hartman Institute in Jerusalem. He is the co-author of *Understanding Shiite Leadership: The Art of the Middle Ground in Iran and Lebanon* (Cambridge, 2014).

# Faith and Politics in Iran, Israel and the Islamic State

## Theologies of the Real

ORI GOLDBERG

*IDC Herzliya*

CAMBRIDGE
UNIVERSITY PRESS

# CAMBRIDGE
## UNIVERSITY PRESS

University Printing House, Cambridge CB2 8BS, United Kingdom

One Liberty Plaza, 20th Floor, New York, NY 10006, USA

477 Williamstown Road, Port Melbourne, VIC 3207, Australia

314–321, 3rd Floor, Plot 3, Splendor Forum, Jasola District Centre, New Delhi – 110025, India

79 Anson Road, #06-04/06, Singapore 079906

Cambridge University Press is part of the University of Cambridge.

It furthers the University's mission by disseminating knowledge in the pursuit of education, learning, and research at the highest international levels of excellence.

www.cambridge.org
Information on this title: www.cambridge.org/9781107115675
DOI: 10.1017/9781316336120

© Ori Goldberg 2018

This publication is in copyright. Subject to statutory exception and to the provisions of relevant collective licensing agreements, no reproduction of any part may take place without the written permission of Cambridge University Press.

First published 2018

Printed in the United States of America by Sheridan Books, Inc.

*A catalogue record for this publication is available from the British Library.*

ISBN 978-1-107-11567-5 Hardback
ISBN 978-1-107-53594-7 Paperback

Cambridge University Press has no responsibility for the persistence or accuracy of URLs for external or third-party internet websites referred to in this publication and does not guarantee that any content on such websites is, or will remain, accurate or appropriate.

*For Ifat, Avigail, Dudu and Dror*

# Contents

# Preface and Acknowledgments

This book straddles the line between essay and reflection. In it I try to frame a phenomenon that is occurring in real time, the rise of political faith in the non-Christian monotheistic world. The turgidity of the previous sentence is, perhaps, my motivation to embark on this quest. There seems to be no way to speak of these new theologies in the Middle East without enforcing a categorical separation between faith and politics. The immediate conceptual framework available is a historical one, appreciating traditions for their stable continuity and not, say, for their non-linear dynamics of ideas. The theologies of the real, motivating so many people in the here and now, appear pale and dilapidated after being curtailed by history and political theory.

I wanted to begin to suggest a different way to consider these emerging theologies. This book begins and ends by taking theologies of the real to mean what they say and to say what they mean. I approach them by reading whole texts, because whole texts are quite often the medium of choice for self-expression by theologians (and believers) of the real. The flow of the text, its moral and devotional duty to participate in the creation of the very world in which its composers and readers live, these make it a unique medium for the articulation of politics. Preserving this virtue of the text, and with it the elusive integrity of these theologies of the real, has been my top priority. The language of this book is often associative and figurative, but only because of the conviction that in the real these theologies celebrate, the associative and the figurative are as concrete at anything.

I do not offer any solutions. I certainly have my thoughts on the problems presented by Islamic State (IS), Iran and Israel to their immediate environment and to the rest of the world. Still, this book was not meant to provide recommendations and action items. My purpose throughout this endeavor is mainly to make these theologies of the real accessible, on their own terms and merits, for meaningful contemplation and (perhaps) conversation. This purpose has led me to forgo many scholarly privileges, like extensive references to the words of others. I hope my decisions have (my) desired effects on you, my gentle readers.

As for acknowledgments, they are my favorite part of any book. I would like to thank Asaf Hazani for his thoughts, his direction and his friendship. He is my partner in crime, my ideal reader and my most effective teacher. I am thankful to Major General Gershon Hacohen for his friendship, guidance and passion. Gershon represents the very best of Israel's past, present and future, and I am proud to be his student and his friend. I would like to thank Eliran Barel for his remarkable generosity of mind and heart. Shaul Setter saw me through various rough patches and offered intellectual companionship of the highest order, and for this I am in his debt.

Dave Stephenson, my brother from another mother, put many of my thoughts into the context of the world at large, as only he can. I am grateful for his friendship and his presence. I thank Professor Boaz Ganor for inspiring me to approach this project with the serious glee I hope it deserves. It is a pleasure to thank Mr. Lewis Bateman, my legendary editor at Cambridge University Press for his professionalism, his many kindnesses and his faith in me. Heartfelt thanks go out to Sara Doskow at Cambridge University Press, who saw this work through with dedication and grace.

Finally, everything I am and everything I do comes from my wife, Ifat, and my three children, Avigail, Dudu and Dror. I thank them for making me the person I am and for allowing me the time and presence of mind to write this book. It is all theirs.

# Introduction

## *Religion as a Political Problem*

Religion is a pesky problem. The "wicked problem" is now a staple of strategic discourse and social science research.[1] Wikipedia defines it as: "a problem that is difficult or impossible to solve because of incomplete, contradictory, and changing requirements that are often difficult to recognize."[2] Acknowledging the existence of wicked problems, accepting that not all problems could be reduced to a set of resolvable parameters and variables, permanently changed philosophy, social planning, mathematics and various other fields. Religion is not a wicked problem, not least for its appropriation of "wicked" in other contexts. If anything, many see religion as too complete, too stable and not sufficiently contradictory or open to critical inquiry. Religion is a pesky problem because it will not go away.

The West, and with it the international community created in the Western image, have invested significant effort in distancing themselves from religion. A separation of church and state is de rigueur for the modern nation-state. Religion is seen, ideally, as a private pastime. Faith can shape one's outlook but it cannot shape one's social or legal obligations. This barrier is enforced with differing intensities. France considers the state an alternative to the communal coherence and positive values of organized religion, and thus curtails the possibility of religious expression

---

[1] While there are different accounts regarding the coining of the term "wicked problem," it was famously used in Horst Rittel and Melvin Webber, "Dilemmas in a General Theory of Planning," *Polity Sciences* 4, 1973, pp. 155–169. It is available online at: http://urbanpolicy. net/wp-content/uploads/2012/11/Rittel+Webber_1973_PolicySciences4-2.pdf (last accessed on October 18, 2016).

[2] See https://en.wikipedia.org/wiki/Wicked_problem (last accessed on October 18, 2016).

in state-sponsored public space. Consider, for example, the debate in France over the permissibility of wearing a burkini.[3] The British state, with its tradition of civic laissez-faire, allows ritual to enter public space. In October 2016, London's Oxford Street was pedestrianized for a commemorative march on Ashura. The tenth day of the month of Muharram is the most important holiday of the Shi'i Muslim year, being the anniversary of Imam Hussein's death in AD 683 at the hands of superior Sunni forces. In Iran and Iraq, the Ashura march is known for scenes of weeping and self-flagellation. In London, the marchers carried signs denouncing terrorism and proclaiming Islam a religion of peace.[4] Despite the obvious differences, both the British and the French (and the countries on the spectrum between them) consider religion a potentially positive force if and when it affirms the avowedly non-religious social order already in place.

Still, religion will not go away. In fact, the spectrum of separation I've just described demonstrates the insistent tenacity of religion as a public force. The French, apparently, fear the potential adverse effects of religion so much that they are willing to violate basic tenets of individual freedom in their struggle to keep religion in its place. The British apply the carrot rather than the stick, but the extraordinary measure of restricting the use of public space (Oxford Street) speaks volumes on the desire to hold the line before the advancement of religion. It is indeed seen as "Religion," a somewhat monolithic entity including within it all those who find themselves reserved with regard to the potential for fulfillment offered by the modern, liberal order. Is the non-religious side of the equation as clearly definable?

Christoph Schmidt suggests, in a fascinating introductory article to a Hebrew volume on political theology and Jewish modernity, that the modern liberal order itself is based on a conflation of modernity with the coming of the kingdom of God:

While the … Church saw the kingdom of God as a transcendental kingdom, the modern revolutionaries – from Lessing to Friedrich Hegel and from Heinrich Heine to Ernst Bloch – turned it [the kingdom of God] into the purpose of human history, a utopia. In other words, the thinkers of modernity established

---

[3] See www.nytimes.com/2016/09/01/world/europe/burkini-france-us-germany-africa.html?_r=0 (last accessed on October 18, 2016).

[4] See www.standard.co.uk/news/london/ashura-day-traffic-at-marble-arch-and-oxford-street-brought-to-a-standstill-as-muslims-march-on-holy-a3367501.html (last accessed on October 18, 2016).

an "eschatological" theory, directed toward the utopian purpose of history, as the realization of the kingdom of God.

One can consider the interpretative act of modernity in a much more radical light: when modernity removes the kingdom from its heavenly birthplace and wishes to establish it as a real political kingdom, it effectively inherits the apocalyptic tradition of John in the New Testament:

1 Then I saw "a new heaven and a new earth," for the first heaven and the first earth had passed away, and there was no longer any sea. 2 I saw the Holy City, the new Jerusalem, coming down out of heaven from God, prepared as a bride beautifully dressed for her husband. 3 And I heard a loud voice from the throne saying, "Look! God's dwelling place is now among the people, and he will dwell with them. They will be his people, and God himself will be with them and be their God. 4 'He will wipe every tear from their eyes. There will be no more death' or mourning or crying or pain, for the old order of things has passed away."[5]

Schmidt frames the debate about the metaphysical heart of modernity as a struggle between eschatology and apocalypse, the peaceful resolution of history against its violent upheaval, both inspired by the growing proximity (perhaps the actual presence) of the kingdom of God. The philosophical discussion he describes in the eighteenth and nineteenth centuries took on overt political relevance during the first decades of the twentieth century. Carl Schmitt, a German jurist and political theorist,[6] reintroduced the classical term "Political Theology"[7] into Western political theory in 1922, with a slim, paradigm-shifting eponymous volume.[8] Schmidt suggested that the Western liberal state leans on weak, secularized imitations of theological-political tenets. Schmitt rejected the liberal notion that sovereignty comes from the democratic representation of the state's citizens. Instead, he suggested, sovereignty is the ability to

---

[5] See Christoph Schmidt and Eli Schonfeld (eds.), *God Will Not Stand Still: Political Theology and Jewish Modernity* (Hakibbutz Hameuchad, 2009), pp. 18–19 (in Hebrew). The translation of the passage from Revelation 21:1–4 may be found online at: www.biblegateway.com/passage/?search=Revelation%2021 (last accessed on October 18, 2016). I expanded the original quotation in the Hebrew volume.

[6] Schmitt was also a senior Nazi, teaching at the University of Berlin and fulfilling senior roles in the legal establishment of Nazi Germany before and during World War II. It is, perhaps, evidence of his stature that he was not tried after the war, but continued to teach, write and publish. For an interesting biography of Schmitt, see Reinhard Mehring, *Carl Schmitt: A Biography* (Polity Press, 2014).

[7] For a historical review of the concept, before and after Schmidt, see the introduction by Hent De Vries to Hent De Vries and Lawrence Sullivan (eds.), *Political Theologies: Public Religions in a Post-Secular World* (Fordham University Press, 2006), particularly pp. 25–47.

[8] See Carl Schmitt, *Political Theology: Four Chapters on the Concept of Sovereignty* (University of Chicago Press, 2005).

determine the occurrence of an emergency. That is, the sovereign is the one capable of severing the regular run of the mill in favor of extraordinary circumstances. This sovereign has the power to curtail the regularity of institutional order, trivializing the stability of the state before larger, violent and volatile forces. This, Schmitt proposed, is a human approximation of divine authority as it appears in scripture.

Schmitt's notion of "political theology" has, in many ways, defined scholarly approaches to religion in the political sphere. Speaking broadly,[9] the relationship between religion and institutional politics is often seen to include dimensions of deception, impersonation and misdirection. Prodding religion in politics, one may expose foundational fallacies at the core of the liberal order, describe the ultimate weakness of secularization or consider the spiritual potentialities of a virtual world. The threat of religion described above may seem clearer if religion and the state are understood to support and undermine each other in intricate, surreptitious ways. Religion must then be approached with caution, in scholarship and policy both, so as not to unravel the core of the social fabric. Of course, this understanding refers predominantly to religion as practiced in a "Judeo-Christian" world. In this world, religion and politics are elaborately woven below the surface, at the level of primeval foundations.

But the most urgent religious threats to the modern order are less elaborate. As I suggested earlier, the case of Islam, from the Middle East to the heart of Europe, is often framed dichotomously. Muslims are seen as "objectively" different, possessing different values and a potentially contentious attitude. This may be because Islam is popularly perceived as a total civilization, requiring obedience in every aspect of life.[10] It may be related to feelings of disenfranchisement among Muslims in the West, leading to anything from a demand to observe Muslim ritual in public to terrorist attacks. It may have something to do with the brutal displays of violence on the part of organizations like IS and Al-Qaeda. In all three (and other) cases, the role of Islam in the political sphere is considered distinctly, removed from the structures and essence of that political sphere itself. Islam is "religion," encroaching on a "civil" tradition, each

---

[9]  Intentionally so, in full awareness of the rich and diverse discourse on religion and politics in multiple disciplines, from sociology and political theory to literature and philosophy.

[10]  See, for example, the website politicalislam.com, suggesting that the totality of Islam creates, by necessity, a totalitarian civilization that has been engaged in subjugation since its inception, 1400 years ago: www.politicalislam.com/totalitarian-islam/ (last accessed on October 18, 2016).

bearing very different strategies and values. The project of "political theology" is irrelevant to the issues raised by the Muslim world.

This, of course, is true not just with regard to Islam. Political Judaism also provides an acute challenge to the sensibilities of "political theology." The establishment of the state of Israel was a revolution and a rupture in Jewish history. The historical evolution of Judaism as a religion had taken place mainly in diasporas, where Jews did not enjoy political sovereignty. Israel necessitated a rethinking of Judaism as a tradition of such sovereignty. Israel's 1967 victory over its Arab neighbors jumpstarted a religious-political movement that promoted legitimate nation-state interests – borders – using undisguised religious arguments for legitimacy. The settler movement installed the Israeli state in the West Bank and the Gaza Strip in fulfillment of God's biblical promise to the patriarch Abraham. The settlers and their unabashed rhetoric (and actions) drew (and still draw) attention from the spiritual components of secular Zionism. Many secular Israelis and outside observers consider the settler version of the Israeli narrative, an unfolding of divine redemption, to be an all-out challenge to Israeli civil society and to the heritage of a less apparently political Judaism.

This simplistic, dichotomous understanding breeds willful ignorance of political theologies arising in Judaism and Islam. Most significantly, a dichotomous understanding depicts these theologies as, at best, two-dimensional and less than real. Such theologies can be reduced to mere derivatives of historical circumstance or spiritual necessity, explained as mere realizations of ulterior forces. This book is an attempt to address these political theologies head-on, respecting their internal complexity and coherence on their own terms. I would like to present these political theologies not as realizations, but as theologies of the real.

I will present three such theologies, from the Islamic Republic of Iran, Israel and the Islamic State (IS). My argument is straightforward. I propose that these theologies share a profound commitment to realness. That is, these theologies emphasize their grounding in the real world, highlighting emergence, uncertainty and complexity as the main components of reality. Where they are seen by many as trite in their binary extremity, I would like to approach and engage them as elaborate, devoted celebrations of the real. I will return most frequently to the political expressions of this realness, particularly the concept of sovereignty as it is understood and practiced in physical and institutional space. The challenge these theologies present to the West is very often to be found in their conceptions of sovereignty and authority.

My method in all three cases will be similar. Following historical and conceptual introductions, I will present, and closely read, a seminal text (or texts) composed within these emerging political theologies. An English translation of the original texts will be closely followed by my analysis and interpretation. I have two main reasons for this methodological choice. First, texts are the preferred medium of articulation and persuasion in the political traditions of Judaism and Islam. Interpretation and study are prized mechanisms for producing meaning and preserving communal and intellectual memory in these traditions. The experience of closely reading a text will allow us access to the language of these theologies, language understood but also performed and spoken. Access to the experiential dimension of these theologies is, I think, important when attempting to transcend the traditionally limited scope of their analyses by others.

My second reason for choosing texts is my desire to engage with these theologies in as immediate a fashion as I could muster. The relationship between religion and politics, when it comes to Islam and Judaism, is often consigned to the realm of security and strategy. When it is not, the sentiments of faith driving these theologies are condensed into a discourse of historical/social/political context and circumstance. In both cases, those qualified to consider and analyze within both strategy and scholarship are experts. The price of entrance to these expert arenas is high, requiring detailed knowledge and disciplinary training. This emphasis on expertise, particularly the neutrality required for its effective practice, diminishes the immense relevance and vibrancy of these texts (and these theologies) for the lives of ordinary Muslims and Jews. I am not suggesting that the theological discussions in this book are similar to ones regularly held by lay Muslims or Jews. Still, my presentation of texts in their entirety (in close reading) is an attempt to provide my readers with all they need in order to engage with these theologies without the mediation, and often the restriction, of purely expert knowledge.

The cases presented are not similar, and I do not pretend to draw a comprehensive model of *a* theology of the real. These theologies are evolving, unfolding phenomena, occurring in real time in the here and now. The Israeli case is significantly longer than the Iranian and IS cases, because the Israeli theology of the real was formulated in oppositional response to powerfully dominant national narratives. I found it necessary to draw the contours of these dominant narratives, also through the reading of seminal texts, in order to situate the theology of the real and shed light on its urgency and power. The Iranian case considers a text written in 1988, in a unique situation of crisis and loss. It is formulated as a theology of mourning and coping, but also of resurgence in the face of adversity. The Islamic State's theology of the real will be the only "organizational" case, not generated by a single person in an affirming or subversive engagement with his environment.

My point, if I may be explicit, is that engagement with these theologies of the real should precede attempts to "resolve" or "handle" them. Engagement requires a suspension, as broad as possible, of biases and prejudices. I do not mean to say that one should approach IS as non-violent. It is an extreme organization, violent and (pardon the unscientific language) scary. Not dismissing this perfectly understandable fear, I would like to chip at the solid conviction that phenomena like IS, or like Israel and the Islamic Republic of Iran, are simple reactions against the progressive complexity of the non-religious order and are thus easily understandable if not easily resolved. Reading nearly whole texts from beginning to end, I've chosen to provide these theologies with a comprehensiveness that is, almost by its very nature, complex and dynamic. The book rarely provides "answers," because I believe the need to ask proper questions with regard to these theologies is much more urgent. Proper asking can and should, with further application and development, lead to effective answers.

I

# THE CRISIS OF THE REAL

# I

# Khomeini at the End of the Iran–Iraq War

## *The Necessity and Frustration of Faith*

On July 3, 1988, the USS *Vincennes* fired two SM-2MR surface-to-air missiles at an Iranian Airbus 300, Iran Air's Flight 655 from Bandar Abbas to Dubai. All 290 persons on board the flight died, among them 38 non-Iranians, 16 crew members and 66 children.[1] The tragedy gave impetus to ongoing attempts to end one of the most brutal wars fought in the last half-century, the eight-year-long war between Iran and Iraq. The war was waged between September 1980 and August 1988. In terms of casualties and destruction, it was one of the most brutal wars fought during the second half of the twentieth century. In terms of spoils, it was one of the most futile wars ever fought. Neither side managed to acquire additional territory or significantly undermine the enemy's leadership.

The UN Security Council adopted Resolution 598 nearly one year earlier, on July 20, 1987. The unanimous resolution called on both countries to retreat to the international border between them.[2] Iraq, at this stage, was supported by the United States and the Soviet Union. Iran could count Syria and North Korea among its supporters. The Iranian economy was in tatters, its oil revenues shrinking more than threefold during the war.[3]

Still, the Iranians kept coming. During the final months of 1986 and the beginning of 1987, the Iranians were hurling all they had at the Iraqi heartland. Iran's supreme leader, the Ayatollah Khomeini, had instructed

---

[1] See https://en.wikipedia.org/wiki/Iran_Air_Flight_655.
[2] See https://en.wikipedia.org/wiki/United_Nations_Security_Council_Resolution_598.
[3] See Efraim Karsh, *The Iran–Iraq War, 1980–1988* (Osprey Publishing, Kindle Edition). For technical reasons, I used the Kindle edition of the book. For this reason, the citations will be of the work in general.

his forces to win the war by the beginning of the Iranian new year on March 21, 1987. Two major offensives, directed at Basra, Iraq's second largest city, were launched at the end of December 1986 and during the early days of January 1987. The Iranians lost nearly 20,000 troops and did not manage to take Basra.[4] The Iraqis, emboldened by their international support, were securely dug in behind their impregnable defenses. Try as they might, the Iranians could not break the Iraqi lines.

During 1987, the Iraqi army began to change its demeanor. At first, the Iraqi generals used ferocious chemical weapons on Iraqi Kurds, killing them by the thousand. This rampage continued into 1988, including within it the horrific attack on the town of Halabjah in March 1988, in which 5,000 Kurds were killed and more than 10,000 wounded.[5] Between February and April of 1988, Saddam attacked Iranian cities with surface-to-surface missiles and bombing raids. This was the fifth such campaign, referred to by both sides as "The War of the Cities." Previous campaigns had been mutually inflicted. This time, Iran's air force was no longer equipped to retaliate against the Iraqi initiative. Iranian morale, stagnating for some time, was at an all-time low. Many government employees and civil servants fled bombarded Tehran, slowing the ship of state nearly to a standstill.

Iraq continued to press its advantage. In mid-April 1988, the Iraqis drove the Iranians out of the Faw Peninsula. This marshy region in the southeast of Iraq lies between Basra and the Iranian oil city of Abadan. It is home to Iraq's two main oil terminals. More importantly, it controls access to the Shatt al-Arab river, Iraq's channel to the Persian Gulf. Iraq's main naval base under Saddam Hussein was located in Umm Qasr, the largest town on the peninsula.

The Iranians had managed, after several casualty-laden attempts, to take the peninsula from the Iraqis in February 1986. This was a strategic triumph, disrupting Iraq's oil production and gaining a major foothold on the road to Basra. It was a major moral victory as well, as the operation was the first successful Iranian invasion and occupation of Iraqi territory during the war.

On April 17, 1988, The Iraqis launched operation "Ramadan Mubarak" in order to drive the Iranians out. More than 100,000 troops from Iraq's elite Republican Guard fought against 15,000 members of

---

[4] See ibid.

[5] See, for example, http://news.bbc.co.uk/onthisday/hi/dates/stories/march/16/newsid_4304000/4304853.stm (last accessed on October 18, 2016).

Iran's Basij militia. Basijis were known for their zeal, not for their military skills. The Republican Guards were assisted by massive air and artillery fire, as well as extensive use of Sarin gas. They managed to drive the Iranians out in 35 hours, after having attempted to do so for more than two years.[6] The event was proclaimed a national holiday by Saddam.

The Iraqis then embarked on a series of four offensives over the length of the Iranian front. Most of the attacks involved massive use of chemical weapons. All of them were successful, and resulted in thousands of Iranian casualties and the expulsion of Iranian forces.[7] Iranian morale reached new lows while the leadership in Tehran debated the possibility of throwing in the towel. The military defeats, however, did not provide sufficient impetus, in and of themselves, for a public declaration of effective surrender. This sea change required the downing of Iran Air 655.

The United States had initially asserted neutrality in the war. The Reagan administration had even allowed Israel to ship several billion dollars' worth of American weapons and spare parts to Iran in 1981. Still, when the Iranians gained momentum during the first months of 1982, American authorities became concerned that Iraq might be "run over" by the revolutionary Shi'i regime. According to the *New York Times*, they began to provide Saddam's military with intelligence during that year.[8]

In 1987, the United States became officially involved in the War of the Tankers between Iran and Iraq. This aspect of the war had both countries targeting each other's oil tanker fleet and refining facilities, attempting to hinder each's ability to transport and export their oil. Neither country succeeded in shutting down the other's commercial oil traffic, but both did massive damage to each other's ships and equipment.[9]

During the seventh year of the war, Iran and Iraq conducted their Tanker War differently. Iraq used its air force, with its well-maintained fighter jets, in order to bomb Iranian oil traffic. The Iranians used the naval branch of the Revolutionary Guard Corps (IRGC), deploying small swarms of speedboats staffed by zealous volunteers meaning to wreak

---

[6] See Kenneth Pollack, *Arabs at War: Military Effectiveness, 1948–1991* (University of Nebraska Press, 2004), pp. 224–225.

[7] Ibid., pp. 226–228.

[8] See www.nytimes.com/1992/01/26/world/us-secretly-gave-aid-to-iraq-early-in-its-war-against-iran.html (last accessed on October 18, 2016).

[9] For an analysis of the Tanker War, see http://csis.org/files/media/csis/pubs/9005lessonsiraniraqii-chap14.pdf. Information presented on the Tanker War and the US *Vincennes* incident is based mostly on this document (last accessed on October 18, 2016).

as much havoc as possible.[10] At the request of its Gulf allies (Kuwait, the UAE), the United States augmented its forces in the Persian Gulf over three months, from June to September of 1987. The American presence was seemingly meant to ensure safe commercial traffic in the Gulf. Nonetheless, it was clear to the Iranian leadership that American vessels and troops were also there to keep a close eye on Iran, and perhaps even to assist in securing an Iraqi victory.

The American ships did not refrain from action. They ventured into Iranian territorial waters and fired on Iranian boats and toward the Iranian coast. The Iranians were afraid that these American actions were simply a prelude for the war's escalation beyond the seemingly permanent loop encircling themselves and Iraq. Come July 1988, as the war with Iraq appeared to spiral out of Iranian control, Iran's leadership and its general population could not but feel that the world was closing in on the Islamic Republic. Iranian troops were dying by the thousands. Iranian occupation of Iraqi territory, meager as it was, had dissipated. Now it was no longer a war with a known, if vicious enemy, a war decreed to end victoriously. Now it was a full-fledged disaster in mid-occurrence.

Iran's leadership had been spurning Iraqi (and international) attempts at peacemaking for more than a year. In July 1988, there can be no doubt that Iranian leaders knew they had no chance of altering the war's outcome. There were intense debates in Tehran regarding when and how to climb off the high horse of never-ending war. The tragedy of Iran Air 655 provided the necessary ladder. A mere two weeks after the tragedy, Khomeini executed a full reverse turn. In an open letter to the members of the Iranian parliament he confirmed his decision to sign the ceasefire.[11]

### God Turns Away: Sacrifice and the Necessity of Politics

Khomeini's letter is an exercise in the theology of the real. This political theology is an understanding and a performance of the political in the key of active faith. Such understanding and performance are anchored in a reality drawing coherence from its origins in the creative will of a unitary, all-powerful God. We will read the letter closely. We will consider

---

[10] We will discuss the nature of the IRGC and the differences between the Guards and the regular Iranian army later on.
[11] See www.nytimes.com/1988/07/21/world/khomeini-accepts-poison-of-ending-the-war-with-iraq-bitter-defeat-for-ayatollah.html (last accessed on October 18, 2016).

its text in some detail, reading it in the particular context of the war with Iraq and in the broader frame of Iran's 1979 Islamic revolution, as well as through the broadest frame – that of Shi'i faith and myth. The letter's theological realness, however, is not exclusively related to the veracity of its historical context.

The letter's resonance is a product of its simultaneity. It is a manifestation of faith within a cascade of political necessities. It is also an affirmation of the inherently political nature of true faith. Khomeini's most famous and effective work, *Velayat-e faqih*,[12] begins with what he understands to be the ultimate subversion perpetrated by the "imperialist" West: making Muslims believe that Islam is a benign, private religion when it is actually both militant and public.[13]

The basic Islamic political paradigm, according to Khomeini, is one of difference and convergence. There is a difference between the private and the public, one that should be acknowledged and respected. Still, they are both complementary branches of the same religious life, converging in the primary Islamic commandment/virtue of *Tawhid*, the celebration of God's oneness and unity. Faith is the cornerstone of *Tawhid*.

## The Shi'i Tradition of Sacrifice

After the death of the prophet Muhammad, the Islamic community struggled to find its way in a world devoid of prophetic leadership. Muhammad, after all, was the last prophet. The majority of the Muslim community believed that the prophet had brought with him stability and political order which led to unprecedented prosperity. A small minority believed that the prophet's revolution lay in his semi-divine nature, in his more-than-simply-human ability to commune with God.[14] The presence of such a leader sanctified the community which he led.

This ability was the result of a divine spark, a *nass*, carried by the prophet. The spark, the original *charisma*, was a tangible presence. The

---

[12] Literally translated as "Government of the Jurist," the technical term for a Shi'i cleric authorized to make legal decisions. The book is more popularly known as "Islamic Government," laying out the revolutionary notion of religious-legal scholars assuming political authority over the Iranian state.

[13] See www.al-islam.org/islamic-government-governance-of-jurist-imam-khomeini/necessity-islamic-government (last accessed on October 18, 2016).

[14] For an authoritative introduction to Shi'i history and spirituality, see Moojan Momen, *An Introduction to Shi'i Islam: The History and Doctrines of Shi'i Islam* (Yale University Press, 1987).

prophet's heir could only be someone related to him by blood, the preferable medium for acquiring (and symbolically passing on) the spark. As the prophet had no sons, the only reasonable choice for heir was Ali, the son of Abi Talib. Ali was the prophet's cousin and son-in-law, having married Fatima, the prophet's daughter, following a direct instruction from God (to Muhammad). Abu Taleb, the prophet's uncle, had been the one to raise Muhammad after the death of his parents.

Ali's supporters, known as his *Shi'a* (faction), believed that he should rule the Muslim community after the prophet's death. Still, they were forced to accept three rulers before seeing Ali take the throne as the fourth *khalifa* (substitute) of the prophet. These first four caliphs – Abu Bakr, Umar ibn al Khattab, Uthman ibn Affan and Ali – are known as the *Rashidun*, the rightly guided caliphs. Ali, who needed to wait 24 years before assuming the throne, personifies an end and a beginning within Islamic history.

He ended the era of leadership sustained by a direct link to the prophet. Ali was a master politician, and his works on political ethics and practice are considered some of the most inspiring and authoritative within the entire Muslim canon.[15] Following his brief reign, the Islamic empire-in-the-making was led by dynasties of warriors and noblemen, severing the immediate link between Muslim communal life and divine presence.

Ali also began a new Islamic tradition of authority. He was considered by his adherents to be the first *Imam*, a leader whose very presence manifested the divine in the midst of the community's daily life. Imams were infallible. As leaders, they drew their authority from their ability to perform two-way mediation. The Imam could translate divine will into realizable instructions for the believers. He could also project the routines of their daily lives onto a larger screen, providing them with context and direction.[16]

From its inception during the second half of the seventh century AD, the coherence of the Shi'i community was based on the Imam's presence. The Shi'a[17] were persecuted by the majority of the Islamic world, who referred to themselves as *Sunni*, those who follow the *Sunnah* (traditions of the prophet) rather than a specific human heir. The Sunni majority denied the Shi'i Imams the leadership of the Muslim community, beginning with the

---

[15] See www.al-islam.org/nahjul-balagha-part-1-sermons (last accessed on October 18, 2016).

[16] See Mohammad Ali Amir-Moezzi, *The Divine Guide in Early Shi'ism: The Sources of Esotericism in Islam* (SUNY Press, 1994).

[17] When discussed collectively, I refer to both "the Shi'i community" and "the Shi'a."

rejection of Ali's son Hassan (the second Imam) as his heir on the caliph's throne, following Ali's assassination in AD 661. In 680, the split between Sunnis and Shi'a became unbridgeable. Hossein, Ali's younger son and the third Imam, was killed by a vastly superior Sunni force, which lay in ambush for him on the plain near the town of Karbalah, located today in southern Iraq. The events of his death are still acted out as a passion play by Shi'a all over the world during the holiday of Ashura, commemorating his death on the tenth day of the month of Muharram.

The events of Karbalah became the cornerstone of Shi'i myth.[18] Traditionally, Imam Hossein's readiness to die was perceived as a supreme act of devotion. His acknowledgment and willing embrace of fate were understood to be among the ultimate Shi'i virtues. During the second half of the twentieth century, the myth of Karbalah was reread as the perfect demonstration of the Shi'i revolutionary spirit, fighting for justice even against insurmountable odds. In both cases, sacrifice was seen as the ultimate gesture of faith.

Nine of Hossein's descendants succeeded him as Imams. While there are various Shi'i sects,[19] the largest and dominant one is known as "Twelver" for its belief in the dynasty of 12 Imams. The twelfth Imam was born, according to the sacred history, in AD 869. He assumed the throne (such as it was) as a child after the death of his father. During most of his years as Imam, he communicated with his followers through four deputies. In AD 941, after 72 years of what is known as the "minor occultation," he is believed to have sent his followers a letter stating that he will go into a "major occultation," reappearing only when God decides that he may do so. Twelver Shi'a believe that the twelfth Imam will return as a messiah, restoring the persecuted Shi'a to their rightful place and bringing order and peace to the world.

The death of Imam Hossein was the epitome of individual sacrifice, providing a continuous reference for Shi'i behavior through its proscriptive evocation of suffering as well as its (evolving) prescription of moral and political propriety. The occultation of the Twelfth Imam was a communal sacrifice. The presence of the Imam was the cornerstone of Shi'i communal life. In his very person, he provided both spiritual and political leadership, a constant mediation of the divine and the human. His

---

[18] Michael Fischer coined the term "Karbalah paradigm" in Michael Fischer, *Iran: From Religious Dispute to Revolution* (University of Wisconsin Press, 2003).

[19] For a broad introductory discussion on various Shi'i sects, see Momen, *Introduction to Shi'i Islam*, pp. 220–232.

absence created a void at the very heart of Twelver religious experience. It may even be more accurate to say that experience of an unbridgeable void became the origin of Shi'i faith. The belief in his messianic return, says Abdulaziz Sachedina, helped the Shi'a survive a history of continuous oppression and persecution.[20] The inverse is immediately apparent: the absence of the Imam was the common thread linking these centuries of suffering.

Anthropologically speaking, sacrifice is often an execution of ritualized and controlled violence meant to stop or mitigate the uncontrollable violence of life.[21] This violence need not be a willful violence perpetrated by humans. Death by "natural causes" is also part of the uncontrollable violence of life. In religious contexts,[22] sacrifice can serve to regulate and maintain a human relationship with an all-powerful, often violent God who is the source of all life. The fullest sacrifice (that of a martyr) and even a sacrifice averted (the angel's voice forbidding Abraham from killing his son, Isaac) reinforce man's standing in relation to God.

But what if the sacrifice does not achieve its desired goal? What if, once made, the sacrifice leaves God indifferent? Shi'i tradition deferred its reply to this challenge by embracing messianic belief. The sacrifice of the Imams regulated a relationship which persevered in the present in order to reap in the future. This answer, which had sustained Shi'i faith for centuries, was no longer sufficient for Khomeini after the downing of Iran Air 655, at the end of an eight-year-long war which had killed Iranians in their hundreds of thousands.

## Tragedy: Pitfalls and Potential

The narrative of the war from Tehran remained upbeat up until the very last days of the war. About two years into the war, the pattern established itself. Iranian offensives, consisting of tens of thousands of infantrymen, were hurled at the impregnable Iraqi lines. Despite their ultimate futility, these offensives allowed the Iranian leadership to tell a story of valor and strength exhibited against Iraq. The fact that Iraq was supported by

---

[20] See Abdulaziz Sachedina, *Islamic Messianism: The Idea of the Mahdi in Twelver Shi'ism* (SUNY Press, 1981), pp. 181–183.

[21] For a broad overview on the issue of religious sacrifice, see Jeffrey Carter (ed.), *Understanding Religious Sacrifice: A Reader* (A&C Black, 2003).

[22] On the differences between the theological and anthropological understandings of sacrifice see, for example, Douglas Davies, "Sacrifice in Theology and Anthropology," *Scottish Journal of Theology* 35:4, 1982, pp. 351–358.

both the USA and the USSR expanded the Iranian story into a valiant fight against the entire world. Defeats were mounting, but the narrative, it least in its official recounting, remained firm. The tragedy of Flight 655 viscerally reconnected the political and military imperatives of the war with the faith tradition of Shi'a suffering.

Iranians were, suddenly, no longer a dynamic power on the move but once more the persecuted victims of a hostile world. The mixed blessing of a myth is that, once evoked, it appears though it has always been a viable frame of reference. The facts of Iran's dismal situation were integrated into a rhetoric of suffering and martyrdom that had been waiting constantly in the wings.

The key term is "integration." The sense of rupture and the mythical timing and dimensions of the civilian tragedy were such that the traditional discourse of pain and persecution could not but be sought. However, it did not replace the prevailing political and strategic demeanor. Both discourses needed to accommodate each other in order to provide succor and closure, both enhanced by each other's presence. Politics and faith required each in the wake of Flight 655.

Shi'a discourse had been present, of course, throughout the various stages of the war. Its prominent expressions were defiant and revolutionary, demanding victory for Iran and for Shi'a Islam. It was a logic of resistance intertwined with national and denominational glory. As Iranian attempts to break through Iraqi defenses were repeatedly foiled, these triumphal tales began to lose coherence. Flight 655, however, demonstrated that there was nothing new under the sun. The Shi'a were as alone as they had always been, facing insurmountable obstacles. Why fight if all is for naught? Left separate, the grand narrative of tradition and the grand narrative of political and military necessity would have negated each other. Khomeini, the supreme leader, faced the crucial ordeal of weaving both narrative strands into a tensile, sustainable dialectic.

There can be no historical certitude in claiming that the downing of Flight 655 served as the straw to break the Iranian camel's back. Countless explanations could properly be offered for Khomeini's decision to sign the ceasefire and end the war. The tragedy of Flight 655 does not necessarily provide an explanation, a fact-based resolution of the question at hand. It does, however, provide the impetus for reflecting simultaneously on the will of God and on Iran's defeat, political and military.

The loss of innocents placed Khomeini on well-trodden ground as the leader of a religious community. Mourning has always been a primary

Shi'i mode of performance.[23] The rituals of mourning affirm the bonds of the Shi'i collective and place it within a coherent holy history. Comfort, if not solace, comes from the knowledge that this holy history has and will run its course regardless of the history recounted by the "winners," the Sunni majority.

This coherence was not accessible to Khomeini as leader of the new Islamic Republic. The immediacy of mourning to the lay Shi'i believer could not be automatically translated into political reason, to say nothing of a political *raison d'être*. A reversion to a rhetoric of devotional purity would negate the Islamic Republic of Iran as a state, a political being. Talk of martyrdom and suffering would permanently hamper the clerical leadership's claim to sovereignty. Founding an Islamic Republic was feasible when it saw itself as resisting the tyranny of a forcibly Westernizing monarch. It was much more difficult when the republic was forced to differentiate itself from the timeless draw of the religious community, expressed most poignantly through the tradition and ritual of mourning.

Khomeini could not settle for mourning's greatest achievement, the seamless cleaving of eternity and immediacy. His decision to sign a ceasefire with Iraq can be presented as inevitable, a necessary outcome Iran's physical and cognitive condition in late 1988. Still, such expectations do not take into consideration Khomeini's unique predicament. As supreme leader, the threat he felt was not limited to the Iraqis or to American missiles. He needed a vision that would assert his authority while remaining under the broad mantle of faith. He needed to concretize a situation flirting perilously with ahistorical tradition. In stark contrast to this concretization, Khomeini needed to place before Iranians horizons to which they could aspire, a message that would get them and the new republic back on their feet. He could soar only by acknowledging the point at which he actually stood.

## Khomeini: A History – Triangulation

Attempting to consider that point, the point at which the real is zenith and nadir, is not an abstract exercise. For the point to mean anything, a real person must occupy it. Much of my effort will be devoted to exploring Khomeini's occupancy of the real. Tracing the contours of the man engaged in occupying is part of this effort.

---

[23] See Peter Chelkowski, *Ta'ziyeh: Ritual and Drama in Iran* (New York University Press, 1979).

It is difficult to construct a biography of Khomeini. Such endeavors are often hagiographies or debunkings of the Islamic Revolution and the ensuing Islamic Republic. Utilizing several prominent biographies,[24] I would like to approach Khomeini through triangulation. In mathematics, triangulation is a process for locating a point in space by measuring angles to that point from two points already known.[25] A more immediate way to locate a point is to measure its distance from another point. We are used to thinking in straight lines. Distance and direction offer us straight lines. How do we locate ourselves in space? By ascertaining how many kilometers we would have to travel from some point we already know and in what direction. We would always be able to draw a straight line from our location to another point when we measure distance.

Triangulation takes a different approach. The location of a point in space is most accurately determined when one is able to approach it relationally, through the angles in which it stands with regard to known points. One's location becomes a point on a triangle, part of an enclosed, defined space. A straight line can, theoretically, extend forever. A triangle is less absolute, because lines are drawn only after angles have been measured. Yet the triangle provides stability and accuracy in context, through relational anchoring rather than abstract exactitude.

The sad end of Flight 655 placed a challenge of triangulation on Khomeini's shoulders. He needed to provide a coherent story for Iranians, a story asserting divine providence and personal (as well as collective) resilience. The unique circumstances of his predicament prevented him from achieving this goal by drawing a straight line connecting him to the national narrative or to the religious one. The story he tells cannot be straight, because a straight story will end in crippling dismay: either God failed his believers, or they failed themselves. Initial closure, necessary for the well-being of the Islamic Republic, required the relational stability of triangulation.

Khomeini's authority and worldview were based on straight lines. He was a mainstay of the Shi'a establishment until the seventh decade of his life. Khomeini's religious authority grew in complex relation to

---

[24] These include Hamid Dabashi's biographical sketch (see Hamid Dabashi, *Theology of Discontent* (New York University Press, 1993), pp. 409–484), as well as Amir Taheri's highly controversial yet informative biography (see Amir Taheri, *The Spirit of Allah: Khomeini and the Islamic Revolution* (Hutchinson, 1987)). For the fullest, book-length biography available, see Baqer Moin, *Khomeini: Life of the Ayatollah* (Thomas Dunne Books, 1999).

[25] See https://en.wikipedia.org/wiki/Triangulation (last accessed on October 18, 2016).

the growing institution and sentiments of Iranian nationhood. While he adopted conservative positions against the Pahlavi Shahs' tangible and intangible Westernization, he saw himself as committed to the moral welfare of the Iranian state.[26] Against the absolutist monarchies of twentieth-century Iran, Khomeini's doctrine of *velayat-e faqih*, demanding unprecedented political authority for the Shi'i clerics, was based on the notion that the most able interpreters were the most capable political leaders.[27] The following history approaches Khomeini through triangulation, locating him through the angles formed between his personal life and the twin forces of faith and nationalism. This exercise will, I hope, bring into even sharper focus the ordeal Khomeini faced after the downing of Flight 655, at the end of the Iran–Iraq war.

## Lines and Angles

Khomeini was born as Ruhollah Musavi in the town of Khomein, about 300 kilometers southwest of Tehran. He was born on September 24, 1902, to Mostafah, the son of a land-owning family in the region and to his wife, Hajieh Khanum. His family was a family of Musavi Seyyeds, meaning that they claim descent from the prophet through the seventh Shi'i Imam, Musa al-Kazem. Religion was always a family profession. Originally, the family came from Northeastern Iran, but in the eighteenth century the family immigrated to India. Khomeini's grandfather, Sayid Ahmad left India around 1830 to make a pilgrimage to the Shi'i holy city, Najaf. He never returned to India. He struck up a friendship with a landowner from the Khomein area, returned there with him and settled in the town.

Khomeini's father, Mostafa, trained for the clergy as well. He married the daughter of a high-ranking cleric and went with her to Najaf in 1892. This was a heady time for a young cleric in training. In December of that year, the chief Shi'i cleric, Mirza Hassan Shirazi,

---

[26] See Fakhraddin Azimi, "Khomeini and the 'White revolution'," in Arshin Adib-Moghaddam (ed.), *A Critical Introduction to Khomeini* (Cambridge University Press, 2014).

[27] Making God's absolute truths into livable human truths while endowing human actions with meaning and context larger than their limited nature. For an enlightening analysis of *velayat-e faqih*'s historical evolution in the Islamic Republic, see Ali Rahnema, "Ayatollah Khomeini's Rule of the Guardian Jurist: From Theory to Practice," in Arshin Adib-Moghaddam (ed.), *A Critical Introduction to Khomeini* (Cambridge University Press, 2014).

directly challenged the Qajar Shah. The Qajars had engaged in selling off state services as concessions to foreign firms or governments. As part of that policy, they sold the concession for tobacco-related services, from growing the leaf to its processing into cigarettes. This was perceived as an imposition on the most private of Iranian private spheres. Shirazi ordered a boycott of all tobacco products on religious grounds of impurity, and an entire nation stopped smoking. The Shah was forced to cancel the concession. This challenge by the clerics served to increase their public reputation and marked the beginning of their direct involvement in politics.

However, Mostafa returned to his family's estate and settled down to live the quiet life of a local nobleman. He enjoyed the prestige his religious schooling gave him, but did not fulfill the duties of a country cleric. He was a recognized social presence in the area. When three local warlords began to extort money and produce from the people of the region (the central government was, at the time, not strong enough to collect its own taxes and farmed these services out to powerful local figures), Mostafa decided to ride and ask for help from the provincial governor. The two warlords ambushed him and shot him on the road to Arak, the provincial capital. Ruhollah was six months old.

Khomeini was raised by his mother and aunt. He received his early education at home and at the local religious school, studying with local teachers and even with his older brother, Mortaza (later Ayatollah Pasandideh). In 1919, he began to study at the seminary in Arak, led by the noted Shi'i cleric Ayatollah Abdolkarim Ha'eri Yazdi. One year later, in 1920, Ha'eri was asked to move his seminary to the city of Qom and to transform that city's seminary into a leading one. Ha'eri agreed, and Khomeini followed his teacher to Qom. Khomeini embarked on the traditional course of Shi'i higher education, immersing himself in the canons of Shi'i law and ethics. However, his initial interest was a rather unorthodox one for seminary students: philosophy and mysticism. Many seminary students studied privately with teachers of mysticism, as the subject was not usually a part of the official curriculum. Khomeini studied with some of the philosophical mystics and luminaries of the age. Khomeini began teaching mysticism and philosophy in 1928, long before he took up teaching advanced Shi'i law. While mysticism is a part of the religious curriculum, it is not a specialty adopted by many would-be sages. Khomeini's attraction to, and ultimate mastery of the field set him apart among most of his contemporaries and remained a major influence on his later work.

In 1925, Reza Khan, formerly an army office in Iran's Cossack Brigade, crowned himself Reza Shah Pahlavi. He enjoyed both British backing and the support of secular Iranians. He had taken charge of the country four years earlier, arranging a military coup that deposed the last Qajar Shah. In the following decades, Reza Shah and his son, Mohammad Reza Shah, embarked on a quest to transform Iranian society and polity. To varying degrees, they perceived the source of Iran's problems to be its fragmented public sphere. While the Qajar Shahs held nominal authority, no single actor held complete, effective central authority. Landed aristocracy and rich merchants dominated many of the country's economic interests. The Shahs treated the country as their own household. Iran was a molten mix of communal, class and foreign interests.

The Pahlavis attempted, in response, to coalesce and coerce the different elements in Iranian society into a single entity dominated by the monarchy. This desire was supported by countless Iranians belonging to all sectors of society. These Iranians grew disillusioned with the Qajar state; the extravagancies of the Qajar Shahs combined with their devotion to the interests of Western governments and business tycoons created a sweeping demand for change.

While Reza Shah did much to alter Iranian society, he was not an overt ideologue. He did not justify his endeavors through recourse to a clear ideational framework. His stage of Pahlavi rule amounted to creating Iran's first unified, monolithic state infrastructure. Reza Shah was enamored with the "Western State." He saw its main appeal in the successful imposition of a single, homogeneous space over all alternative spaces. Reza Shah believed that the state, under its rightful monarch, should retain sole authority over all aspects of its citizen-subjects' lives. The community of lay Shi'i believers, a focal point of identity for most Iranians, as well as its traditional, informal network structure, was to be replaced by the state, a community of individual citizens within a clear, administrative hierarchy. Every aspect of the material state created in his image was to proudly resound with a collective, Iranian identity. In fact, he saw collective identity as a result of this consolidation of interests and communities.

While Reza Shah maintained a working relationship with Iran's economic elites, he took on the scholarly establishment of the clerics in a sophisticated way. He stripped the scholars of their executive authorities in the fields of law and education. His state created ministries of education and law, broadly modeled on European examples. The scholars were relegated to civil servant status, service providers for the new citizens who could engage in religious activities in their spare time.

Reza Shah was effectively forced to refrain from creating a republic modeled on Ataturk's secularizing state building project in Turkey, despite professing admiration for Ataturk's reforms. He publicly announced that his decision was the result of consultation with top clerics. Thus, he identified himself firmly as Shi'i although he made it perfectly clear that the perception of Iran as a religious community had only minor relevance to his monarchy.

Reza Shah placed significant importance on the creation of an economic and logistical infrastructure for the development of a modern economy in Iran. He industrialized the country and built extensive roads and railroads. He opened Iran's first institution of higher education, Tehran University, in 1936. He created an adult education program, striving to bring all Iranian citizens to a minimal standard of skill and competence in reading, writing and mathematics. All these measures were aimed at creating a clearly defined Iranian public sphere. This stood in stark contrast to the informal and somewhat amorphous nature of traditional public spheres, mostly interlinked by the general fealty to Shi'i Islam. Reza Shah sought to create a unified national space, a single entity managing to provide for all the material needs of those occupying it. In addition to the material needs, the new state would endow its citizens with a sense of shared vision and values.

Additionally, Reza Shah also enacted several provocative measures such as outlawing the veil for women, enforcing a Westernized dress-code etc. When Ha'eri Yazdi, Khomeini's teacher, died in 1936, Khomeini was a fairly high-ranking part of the Qom establishment. Due to the Shah's anti-clerical policies, he was also politically conscious, if not overtly active.

Reza Shah's regime ended in 1941. The allies forced his abdication for fear that he would side with Nazi Germany and allow Hitler use of both Iranian oil and Iran's strategic location. The allies assured Reza Shah that his son would succeed him, and he agreed to leave the country. That year also witnessed the creation of Iran's communist party, the Tudeh, soon to become the country's most powerful political organization. The spread of communism among Iranian youth was significantly responsible for the fact that the leaders of the Shi'i clerical establishment after the death of Ha'eri were fairly cooperative toward the Pahlavi state. The supreme Shi'i cleric, Ayatollah Hossein Borujerdi, adopted a quietist stance toward

Reza Shah and his son. After the latter's abdication, his son, Mohammad Reza Shah, ruled as a semi-puppet of the allies. Khomeini remained a senior cleric, attaining the position of personal secretary to Borujerdi, but he took advantage of the relative freedom under Mohammad Reza Shah at the time to publish a book named *Kashf al-Asrar* (The Unveiling of Secrets) in 1944. This book was directed at an anti-clerical book named *Asrar-e Hezar Saleh* (Secrets of a Thousand Years), written by a supporter of Ahmad Kasravi, a fervently anti-clerical intellectual. However, Khomeini's book was not only a refutation but also a harsh critique of Reza Shah's regime and of the creeping secularization in Iran's public sphere.

In 1951, Muhammad Mossadeq became the prime minister of Iran. Mossadeq, a provincial landowner, had studied law in Switzerland and was a lonely voice of opposition in Reza Shah's parliament. When he became prime minister, he began steering an independent course for Iran, free from the constraints imposed by Britain and the United States, as well as the unofficial meddling on the part of the Soviet Union. The first and the last of these world powers were traditionally involved in influencing Iranian affairs over the nineteenth and twentieth centuries, because of Iran's geostrategic importance to their broad political agendas. After World War II, with the ascent of the USA as one of the two main world powers, Iran remained an important strategic point in the battle against communism. Mossadeq proclaimed an independent path for Iran, detaching it from foreign interests. The most important aspect of this new path was the nationalization of the oil industry, traditionally controlled by Britain.

Once Mossadeq nationalized the oil industry, he was perceived as a threat by both Britain and the USA. In 1953, the CIA helped sponsor a *coup d'état* which unseated Mossadeq and gave full executive power to Mohammad Reza Shah. The Shah continued his father's reform programs at low volume, but had grander plans for himself and the country. Reza Shah, his father, was interested mainly in creating the infrastructure for the erection of a strong, unified Iranian state. He was inspired by the Prussian state of Otto von Bismarck and by the statist projects of Ataturk in Turkey. Mohammad Reza Shah, however, saw himself as a different kind of reformer. He wanted not only the logistics of a functional state, but had in mind a full, authoritarian regime, completely subordinated and consolidated under his monarchy. While claiming full allegiance to Islam, he actively attempted to replace the Islamic component of Iranian collective identity with an identity focused on the pre-Islamic

Persian Empire. The Shah portrayed himself as a direct descendant of those ancient Persian kings.

In 1963, The Shah put forward his first, comprehensive reform program. Called "The White Revolution," or "The Revolution of the Shah and the People," the program was approved by a referendum in January 1963. It initially included six points:

1. A land reform including nationalization of great tracts of privately owned land.
2. The sale of some state-owned factories to finance the land reform.
3. The enfranchisement of women.
4. The nationalization of forests and pastures.
5. The formation of a literacy corps, a national movement sponsored by the Shah in which literate, urban youth would perform their army service teaching basic literacy skills to peasants living in the Iranian periphery. With the literacy skills came indoctrination classes in the Shah's new conception of Iranian history as well as lessons enshrining the new, monarchical state as the origin of law, legitimacy and culture.
6. The institution of profit-sharing (or cooperative) schemes for workers in industry.

The revolution ultimately included 13 more points, ranging from the nationalization of water resources to anti-racketeering reforms. Most points focused on concentrating power in the hands of the Pahlavi monarchy at the expense of other actors in the Iranian social arena. Iranian identity had been dually defined by kings and sages since the sixteenth century. The kings were in charge of the state (body) and the sages in charge of the faith (spirit). Mohammad Reza Shah wanted full custody of both body and spirit. Land and gender were integrated with learning and industry into a grand vision of a unipolar Iran.

These reforms were perceived as a challenge to the existing power-structure in Iran, alienating the economic elites and actively targeting clerical sensibilities. The enfranchisement of women was certainly perceived as pandering to the West. The higher echelons of the clerical establishment, however, were also economic elites and dedicated to the protection of private ownership. Khomeini's sudden embrace of militant activism in 1963 was partly due to his assessment that the Shah's reforms represented an existential threat to the clerically led community of Shi'i faithful in Iran. He understood the Shah's tactics. He saw the Shah's plan to portray the clergy as obsolete and the threat in the Shah's attempts to provide an alternative social, cultural and historical vision of Iranian identity. He saw that the greatest danger to the scholarly community lay exactly there, in becoming obsolete, incapable of addressing the needs of its lay adherents and society at large.

Khomeini brought several other ayatollahs to Qom, persuading them to boycott the Shah's referendum. He publicly denounced the Shah and his plans. The Shah, in retaliation, delivered a speech attacking the clerics as obsolete relics of a bygone age. Khomeini and the Shah continued to trade public insults, the first pointing out publicly how and in what ways the Shah violated the Iranian constitution, the latter sending troops to subdue public oppositional gatherings. On the eve of Ashura, the holiday commemorating the death of Imam Hossein in Karbalah, Khomeini delivered an especially fiery speech in the courtyard of a Qom seminary. He compared the Shah to Yazid, Hossein's Sunni killer and warned the Shah that if he did not change his ways, his days were numbered. He was detained after two days. Riots erupted across Iran, and hundreds were killed. Khomeini was kept under house arrest for eight months and was released in 1964. However, in November 1964, after continuing to denounce the Shah, he was arrested again and sent into exile. Khomeini spent 15 years in Turkey, mostly in Iraq and finally, a few months near Paris. He returned from this exile only in 1979, after the departure of the Shah, to become the leader of the nascent Islamic Republic.

During his time in exile, which was spent mostly in Najaf, Khomeini continued to oppose the Shah. He spoke as a defender of Iran's constitution, which was approved at the beginning of the twentieth century after massive public protests. His network of students in Iran spread his critical gospel on diverse media, from cassettes to magazine articles. In Iraq, Khomeini gave a series of lectures on the subject of Islamic government. Bucking centuries of precedent, Khomeini called for active political leadership by the clerics, claiming that they are the most able and suited for this purpose since they are the best interpreters of Islamic law. These lectures, collected in a volume entitled *Velayat-e faqih* (The Government of the Legal Scholar), were Khomeini's most famous political work, going against the grain of Shi'i clerical traditions and offering a prospective revolution in clerical self-perception. The notion of *velayat-e faqih* became perhaps the central tenet of the Islamic Republic.[28]

Khomeini returned to Iran in triumph on Thursday, February 1, 1979. The Shah had left Iran two weeks before that date and the last vestiges

---

[28] Ibid.

of his regime were crumbling. On February 11, Khomeini declared a provisional government. On March 30 and 31, the Iranian public ratified, by referendum, the replacement of the Pahlavi monarchy by an Islamic Republic. An Islamic constitution, ratifying Khomeini's status as the supreme leader of the Islamic Republic as well as an Islamic system of government, was ratified in December of 1979.

Khomeini became the supreme leader of the Islamic Republic of Iran. His unprecedented demand for clerical political power was realized during a bloody, hectic decade.[29] The scope of his political endeavors is not, however, the subject of this examination.[30] The war he fought for most of his tenure as supreme leader brought him as low as he had ever been in late 1988. He was, as I suggested earlier, caught in an existential bind reflected most urgently by the tragedy of Flight 655. Embracing the mourning and suffering of the Shi'i narrative, he could cripple his hard-won vision of a new Iranian state. Rejecting the rhetoric of faith, he faced the wrath of his citizenry, a generation brought to its knees by the depravation of war. Khomeini rose to the challenge in the letter to which we now turn. Rejecting the zero-sum game of straight lines, he took triangulation one step further and created a theology of the real.

## Khomeini's Theology: Sovereignty and Faith

Khomeini's mediations, and his rationalizations, are intimately linked to his understanding of sovereignty. The Islamic Republic was groundbreaking in its insistence on faith as the origin of human sovereignty. The constitution ratified in 1980 states that:

The Islamic Republic is a system based on belief in:

1. The One God (as stated in the phrase "There is no god except Allah"), His exclusive sovereignty and the right to legislate, and the necessity of submission to His commands;
2. Divine revelation and its fundamental role in setting forth the laws;
3. The return to God in the Hereafter, and the constructive role of this belief in the course of man's ascent towards God;
4. The justice of God in creation and legislation;

---

[29] See David Menashri, *Iran: A Decade of War and Revolution* (Homes and Meier, 1990).
[30] See Shaul Mishal and Ori Goldberg, *Understanding Shiite Leadership: The Art of the Middle Ground in Iran and Lebanon* (Cambridge University Press, 2013).

5. Continuous leadership (imamah) and perpetual guidance, and its fundamental role in ensuring the uninterrupted process of the revolution of Islam;

6. The exalted dignity and value of man, and his freedom coupled with responsibility before God; in which equity, justice, political, economic, social, and cultural independence, and national solidarity are secured by recourse to:

    1. Continuous ijtihad of the fuqaha' possessing necessary qualifications, exercised on the basis of the Qur'an and the Sunnah of the Ma'sumun, upon all of whom be peace;

    2. Sciences and arts and the most advanced results of human experience, together with the effort to advance them further;

    3. Negation of all forms of oppression, both the infliction of and the submission to it, and of dominance, both its imposition and its acceptance.

Faith is the thread connecting all these noble principles.[31] "Fundamentalism" is a label often employed for a politics of faith. It is frequently employed with regard to the Islamic Republic of Iran, even if it is used merely as a foil for more sophisticated analysis. For example, Ervand Abrahamian, a venerable scholar of Iranian social history, wanted to describe Khomeini as a populist.[32] In order to do so, he saw fit to first criticize Khomeini's seemingly obvious description as a fundamentalist.[33] Fundamentalism is where learned discussions of the Islamic Republic begin and very often end. Torkel Brekke provides a definition of fundamentalism closely linked to concepts of sovereignty and authority.[34] Brekke suggests that fundamentalism is, in essence, a modernization of prophecy. As a movement, fundamentalism develops when prophetic leaders challenge the authority of the modern state and the traditional wielders of religious authority, the priests. Prophetic leaders are the promoters of total truths, seeking to imbue all the spheres state and society (with an emphasis, says Brekke, on law, politics, education and science).

---

[31] The Persian word used in the original text is *Iman*, encompassing both "faith" as noun and the act of "belief." See http://parliran.ir/index.aspx?siteid=1&siteid=1&pageid=219.

[32] Which is to say, to detract from Khomeini's faith as an important generator of his thought and practice. Populism suggests an interest-based political and ideological demeanor.

[33] See Ervand Abrahamian, *Khomeinism: Essays on the Islamic Republic* (University of California Press, 1993), pp. 13–38.

[34] See Torkel Brekke, *Fundamentalism: Prophecy and Protest in the Age of Globalization* (Cambridge University Press, 2012).

Their religious authority is a product of charisma and preaching, a merging of the personal touch with a committed devotion toward realizing the absolute.

Priestly authority, the alternative logic of sovereignty, is entrenched in practical and hermeneutic traditions. Priests are agents and mediators of the divine, applying God's word to human lives and translating human actions into terms of divine value. According to Brekke's typology, Khomeini's Islamic Republic is not fundamentalist. Its clerical rulers build their sovereignty on law and tradition, two orders which can generate simultaneous competing practices and rationales.[35]

Khomeini's letter on the ceasefire with Iraq, his theology of the real, expands on the constitutional principles quoted above. In the Islamic constitution, it is easy to see such statements of faith as rejections of individual human sovereignty, the cornerstone of liberal politics. Khomeini could not be satisfied with rejection. His republic's crisis was real. His personal sovereignty merged with his political sovereignty, both under threat of annihilation. At the end of an eight-year war, nearly succumbing to the soteriological comfort offered by a massacre of innocents, Khomeini needed to embrace reality in order to proceed with real faith.

## The Triangle of Faith

Khomeini's faith in God is the guiding principle of his reasoning in general. This faith is not reducible to subordination, nor does it involve an understanding of and complicity in God's plans or actions. Faith, for Khomeini, is predominantly tension. He believes that humans have the ability to recognize and acknowledge God's presence in their lives. They perform this feat through their faculty of reason. However, most of a human life is not carried out in and through the grace of reason. Humans are flawed, dual or multiple where God is single. Their reason tells them one thing whereas most of their experience assures them of another.[36]

---

[35] For a scholarly analysis of different intellectual and political rationales within Khomeini's life, many of them simultaneous, see Mojtaba Mahdavi, "The Rise of Khomeinism: Problematizing the Politics of Resistance in Pre-Revolutionary Iran," in Arshin Adib-Moghaddam (ed.), *A Critical Introduction to Khomeini* (Cambridge University Press, 2014). Mahdavi comes to the conclusion that Khomeini's multiplicity of ideologies can be summed up as a commitment to his political survival. I think this plethora is regulated by Khomeini's faith.

[36] For an enlightening discussion on the duality of human reason, see Khomeini's thoughts on the fear of God in the 14th hadith of his *Chehel Hadith* (40 Hadiths),

The challenge laid at the believer's doorstep is to recognize and acknowledge the presence of God's truth in his or her life. God does not share human reason, but God's presence can be approached through human reason. This presence is, perhaps, the only aspect of divine existence that can indeed by pursued by human reason. This duty pertains to any and all aspects of the believer's life. In other words, the believer's main duty is to recognize and acknowledge those truths which he or she cannot change. Having acknowledged their inevitability, the believer can begin to live. Absolute truths are limits and catalysts. There is no doubt that they represent divine perfection, the only truly true truth. On the other hand, there is no doubt that they are closed. Only God knows God's whole truth. Its wholeness is based on the condition that it is the sole prerogative of God. The barrier erected by absolute truth cannot be breached, and for precisely this reason it opens up other options. After all, if one simply cannot progress in a chosen direction, no matter how hard one tries, what can one do but move in another direction? A believer wishes to lead a meaningful, good life. When perfection is denied the believer as a possible mode, imperfection needs to be shaped into a suitable alternative. The middle ground, defined by the real-yet-unachievable absolutes, is where the believer can get on with the business of actually living.

Understanding one's limits is not an easy task. Attempting to complete it may be the most difficult decision a person can make. True acceptance of one's inability to alter circumstances in one's life is a tall order, as most of us would like to think that nothing exceeds our abilities and desires. This acceptance is, indeed, a matter left to human decision. It is the ultimate test of human resolve, the ultimate expression of responsibility. It is also a test of faith. God's presence is not accessible to humans in its pristine form. Normally, in the course of an ordinary life, humans must mediate and interpret God's truth in order to make sense of it.

Once this leap of faith has been undertaken and the middle ground of human experience has opened up, a spectrum of potential decisions presents itself. None of these decisions is completely at odds with any of the others. They are all initiated and pursued within a continuum originating and culminating in faith. Divine presence is omnipresent, and engagement with it needs to be concentric rather than linear. The act of deciding reflects a subjectivity that defines its reason in concentric fashion while

a customary format for ethical works by senior Shi'a sages: www.al-islam.org/forty-hadith-an-exposition-second-edition-imam-khomeini/fourteenth-hadith-fear-god (last accessed on October 18, 2016).

demanding that it is, indeed, reason which guides its self-perception and its actions.

The ceasefire with Iraq was, and can be, often construed as a triumph of instrumental rationality. Iran had expended all its strength and resources on futile offensives until the balance of power had shifted. Iran's fervor (and military might), which had seemed unquenchable at the beginning of the war, faded to near-nothingness before Iraq's impregnable defenses. When one follows the orderly progression of events, Khomeini appears to have had no choice. He, however, considers the actual signing of the ceasefire to be justified by and through its location on a spectrum of possible actions and not because it realizes an ultimate agenda. Such action is both purpose and validation for a life lived in the presence but always short of perfect truth.

The logic and dynamic behind Khomeini's reflections are theological. Their axis is a relationship between a person, flawed and contextual, seeking a relationship with the divine, perfect and closed while constantly present in the person's imperfect life. The yearning of Khomeini's theology for totality cannot be answered by a project of globalization and is thus, according to the definition offered by Brekke, non-fundamentalist.

Khomeini's theology is personal precisely as it is promulgated. His personal faith places the sovereignty of leadership on his shoulders. It provides political guidance as it situates itself on an intimate, contextual continuum. This continuum stretches between two positions redolent of the modernist, enlightened spirit. At one pole stands the notion of "sovereign subjectivity." The subject is the primary agent of modernity, cohesive and rational. Subjectivity is unique in each subject while common to all of them. The world of the subject is made coherent through subjectivity, just as it is made personal and inviolable. From this inviolability springs sovereignty. Since the subject is unique, no external power can wholly dictate values or practices to the subject. There is a subjective part of being which cannot be relinquished. A sovereign polity, comprising sovereign subjects, focuses on allowing each of them as much sovereignty as possible over their lives without impeding the sovereignty of others. This is true even if one believes sovereignty was granted by God,[37] but

---

[37] As it was, for example, in the creation story offered by the book of Genesis: "God blessed them and said to them, 'Be fruitful and increase in number; fill the earth and subdue it. Rule over the fish in the sea and the birds in the sky and over every living creature that moves on the ground.'" (Genesis 1:28, at www.biblegateway.com/passage/?search=Genesis+1&version=NIV, last accessed on October 18, 2016) and by the Quran: "And We have certainly honored the children of Adam and carried them on the land and sea and provided for them of the good things and preferred them over much of

the sovereignty of a rational, individual subject is not dependent on the existence of God.

Modern subjectivity has, of course, been the focal point of broad, complex intellectual debates.[38] Scholars of subjectivity and modernity have developed much more nuanced definitions of subjectivity. Still, at the level of cultural tropes, individual subjectivity is often equated with an individual's sovereignty over his or her life. A sovereign subject is a person capable of making decisions that realize his or her own unique potential.

At the other pole of Khomeini's personal spectrum stands the notion of ontotheology. This neologism integrates the science of God (theology) with the science of being (ontology). Ontology is concerned with things "as they are," with their essence which is so basic that it just "is." This concern with essences spirals into "metaphysics," the attempt to understand being in the world in purely conceptual, abstract terms. Immanuel Kant criticized those medieval ontologists who incorporate God into their metaphysical project. Kant's difficulty was the implied proximity (and perhaps, similarity) between God and man when considered through metaphysics. Kant was the champion of human enlightenment, seeking the removal of human affairs from the sphere of divine influence in a way that would expand human sovereignty over human lives. In ontotheology, God and man share an abstract "being," and one could understand this sharing as the basis of further identity.[39]

Martin Heidegger, the famous twentieth-century German philosopher, expanded Kant's critique. Heidegger used ontotheology as a blanket term covering metaphysics in its entirety, decrying its destructive potential with regard to human being. In his *Identity and Difference*, Heidegger decries ontotheology as a blurring of differences between theology and philosophy, reducing the mystery at the heart of the first as well as the honest, straightforward analysis of the second. This leads to a weakened hybrid, the ontotheological subject believes she can do anything and everything, having reconciled mystery and analysis. However, the existence of such a subject is nearly devoid of effect, having forgone the powerful sources

---

what We have created, with [definite] preference." (Quran 17:70, at http://quran.com/17, last accessed on October 18, 2016).

[38] Charles Taylor's *Sources of the Self: The Making of the Modern Identity* (Harvard University Press, 1992) is a particularly sophisticated and engaging combination of history, ethics and intellectual inquiry.

[39] See http://genius.com/Immanuel-kant-the-critique-of-pure-reason-part-24-annotated (last accessed on October 18, 2016).

of meaning inherent in both mystery and analysis. Ontotheology, for Heidegger, represents the failings of Western metaphysics and its inability to tackle the question of being in a real way.[40]

These critiques demonstrate the force of the ontotheological position. I will discuss its origins later in this book, but its allure is clear even now. Persons of faith who see themselves as modern can be eager to eliminate mystery and uncertainty from their belief. Why should they be satisfied with open ends and suspended gratifications? They know God "is," and they know they themselves "are." This similarity links their subjective being with the general state of things. These modern believers are synchronized with God's plan. If they work hard enough, they will play a role in the fruition of this plan and will themselves be carried to glory with this fruition. This conviction is, for example, a hallmark of modern fundamentalism and its totalizing tendencies explored earlier. A person who believes in God has a competitive advantage over non-believers in the race to win, achieve and be a better human.

Khomeini's theology of the real approaches these two concepts, sovereign subjectivity and ontotheology, as defining between then a spectrum of relevance. At one end, a person's understanding of reality is relevant when this understanding is based upon his or her own facts and experiences. At the other end, an understanding of reality is relevant when it reflects deep similarity between human beings and God. Khomeini's decision to sign the ceasefire cannot be attributed simply to "fact" or to "God's will." He needs to provide a consistent account of his decisions as leader, from the beginning of the war to its bitter end. He needs also to reinforce the foundational role played by faith in the politics of the Islamic Republic. Khomeini, reflecting on his decision, must be both his own man and God's man. If he does not accept personal responsibility, he risks not just public discontent but a potentially fatal blow to authority. Instead of supreme leader, he will become simply another Shi'i cleric offering the traditional solace of mourning and a long wait for a messianic redeemer. If Khomeini does not reinforce his commitment to God, he will become a politician, defender of self-interest and particular agendas.

---

[40] For an interesting study of Heidegger on ontotheology in a different context, providing a concise explanation of Heidegger's approach (which is also much more accessible to the lay reader than Heidegger's own explanation), see Iain D. Thompson, *Heidegger on Ontotheology: Technology and the Politics of Education* (Cambridge University Press, 2005). See also Lee Braver (ed.), *Division III of Heidegger's Being and Time: The Unanswered Question of Being* (MIT Press, 2015).

These two outcomes seem paradoxically inevitable. Each one is a logical outcome of Khomeini's predicament. How can he reject his own traditional and clerical basis of authority, denying a history of suffering and a hope of salvation? How can he trivialize the institutional revolution he managed to perform, the singular achievement of a modern Islamic state? Khomeini accepts the challenge by making two decisions. He acknowledges that sovereign subjectivity and ontotheology are two absolute formulations of political faith. The first demands faith in an inviolable individual core. The second requires faith in an accessible, all-powerful God. Once one accepts the basic premise of either formulation, one must accept the entire system.

Khomeini decides, twice, to engage personally with both systems. He commits to neither, and he does not seek a synthesis. He initiates a process of triangulation, unwilling to accept the tyranny (and mutual exclusion) of straight lines. He cannot be a simple extension of either absolute. His particular place must be defined in relation to both. His letter on the ceasefire, the founding statement of his theology of the real, is the story of these two decisions.

## Khomeini's Letter

The following translation of Khomeini's letter was adapted from a translation made by the Council on Foreign Relations which appears on the CFR website.[41] The letter, written in 1988, was revealed to the West only in 2006 by Hashemi Rafsanjani, one of the Islamic Republic's most prominent leaders. It was covered by Western media as an indication of Iran's desire for nuclear weapons.[42]

### Part I

*In the name of God, the Merciful, the Compassionate.*

*With the grace of God and salutation to great prophets and infallible imams ... Now that the military officials, including the IRGC and the Military commanders who are (the) experts at war, openly confess that the Islamic military will not be victorious for some time, and considering the view of the ... officials of the Islamic Republic who consider a continued war effort to be inadvisable and state resolutely that they cannot, under any circumstance and at any price, obtain even*

[41] www.cfr.org/iran/letter-ayatollah-khomeini-regarding-weapons-during-iran-iraq-war/ p11745 (last accessed on October 18, 2016). The text does not appear on the new CFR website, but I have archived it in my personal records.

[42] See, for example, this BBC story: http://news.bbc.co.uk/2/hi/middle_east/5392584.stm (last accessed on October 18, 2016).

one-tenth of the weapons put at Saddam's disposal by the Eastern and Western arrogant [powers], and in view of the shocking letter of the IRGC commander, which is among tens of military and political reports that I have received after recent instances of defeat ... and in light of the enemy's extensive use of chemical weapons and our lack of equipment to neutralize them, I give my consent to the cease-fire, and in order to clarify the reasons for taking this bitter decision, I refer to some points of the IRGC commander's letter dated 2.4.1367 [June 23, 1988].

In his letter the IRGC commander has written that there will be no victory in the next five years and he may be able to embark on offensive operations or retaliate if he obtains the necessary equipment during the same period.

He said that, with the grace of God, he can embark on such offensive operations if after 1371 [1992] the Islamic republic is able to have 350 infantry brigades, 2,500 tanks, 300 fighter planes and 300 helicopters as well as having the means to manufacture a large number of laser and atomic weapons which would be necessary to ensure victory at that time.

He adds that the strength of the IRGC must be increased seven times and the Military by two-and-half times.

He also said that a condition of his success would be the expulsion of America from the Persian Gulf. He stated that the most important requirement for his success was the proper planning and allocation of resources, and that he believed the government and the military leadership could not meet their commitments.

In spite of stating this, he said the Islamic republic must continue fighting which is now no more than a slogan.

The prime minister ... said that the financial situation of the country stood at below zero and the military officials underlined that the value of the weapons lost during recent instances of defeat was equal to the entire budget allocated to the IRGC and the Military for the current year. Moreover, political leaders have pointed to the people's lack of desire to report to the front lines, as the people knew no victory would come.

You dear ones, more than anyone else, know that this decision is like drinking the poisoned chalice. I submit to the Almighty's will, and for the safeguarding of Islam and the protection of the Islamic republic, I do away with my honor.

## Part II

Oh God! We rose for your religion, we fought for your religion and we accept the cease-fire for the protection of your religion.

Oh God! You know that we did not collude even for a moment with America, the Soviet Union and other global powers, and that we consider collusion with superpowers and other powers as turning our back on Islamic principles.

Oh God! We are alone in a world of polytheism, blasphemy, multiplicity, money, power, deceit and double-dealing, and we seek your help.

*Oh God! Throughout history, whenever prophets and wise men decided to make peace by combining practice with knowledge, whenever they sought to organize societies free of corruption and decay, they faced resistance from the Abu Jahls and the Abu Sofyans [opponents of Prophet Muhammad] of their time.*

*Oh God! For your satisfaction, we sacrificed the offspring of Islam and the revolution. We have no one but you. Help us to realize your commands and laws.*

*Oh God! I beg you to grant me a quick martyrdom.*

## Part III

*I said that a session (of parliament) should be convened so that the people are informed about the cease-fire. Proceed with caution, because some extremists with their revolutionary slogans might divert your attention from what is best for Islam.*

*I say clearly that all your efforts should be directed at justifying this [the cease-fire]. I forbid [the word used is haram, a religious prohibition] actions meant to divert you (from this course). Such actions will lead to reactions.*

*You know that the leaders of the [Islamic] regime have made this decision with the utmost sadness, and with hearts overflowing with love for Islam and for our Islamic country. Be mindful of God. Whatever happens, it is His decision.*

*Peace be upon pious people*

*Ruhollah Al-Musavi al-Khomeyni*

## Khomeini's First Decision: Who Is He as a Sovereign Subject?

Khomeini's analysis of reality begins with a detailed, nuanced evaluation and understanding of the facts at hand. He speaks to all the professionals at his disposal: the prime minister, the commanders of the army (*artesh*) and the IRGC, ministers and others who remain unnamed. These senior leaders present Khomeini with truths difficult to stomach. In mid-1988, Iran has no money and no armaments. It is vastly outnumbered. It has suffered damage bordering on the irreparable. Things have gotten to the point where political leaders point to "the people's lack of desire to report to the front lines, as the people knew no victory would come."

These assorted officials expound on the subject in different fashions. There are those who do not pull their punches, simply telling Khomeini that the coffers are empty and even negatively balance. There are those, such as the commander of the IRGC (Mohsen Reza'i), who reveal the dearth of the situation while exhorting Khomeini to continue the fight. The IRGC commander specifies the logistical and personnel means required to reach the desirable end of winning the war in four years: "350 infantry brigades, 2,500 tanks, 300 fighter planes and 300 helicopters as well as having the means to manufacture a large number of laser and atomic weapons which would be necessary to ensure victory at that time." The commander's other requirements include increasing the strength of the IRGC sevenfold, and that of the army by two and a half times, as well as driving American forces out of the Persian Gulf. One does not need to be an expert on military affairs to understand that there is no way such numbers could actually be realized. Khomeini himself comes to this conclusion when he says: "In spite of stating this, he said the Islamic republic must continue fighting, which is now no more than a slogan."

Khomeini's account is an account any Western observer would immediately define as rational. God plays no part in this story. Khomeini takes all the responsibility upon himself, referring to his own actions, from receiving information to processing and deciding upon it, in an active voice. This grammatical choice is unusual. A convention of Persian culture is to draw attention away from oneself. For example, if a person is given a compliment, he or she would customarily demur and claim their unworthiness.[43] Additionally, the passive tense in the Persian language completely removes the explicit agency of the subject from a sentence. It is considered a signifier of objectivity, and is used to convey impartial information.[44] Such information is both a generator and a product of rational analysis. Khomeini's choice to place himself at the center of his letter in an active capacity demonstrates his commitment to engage meaningfully with sovereign subjectivity. His choice also indicates to his Iranian readers that he finds himself in unconventional distress. While his explanation seems coherent and plausible, something is not right.

The factual analysis ends with this somber proclamation: "You dear ones, more than anyone else, know that this decision is like drinking the poisoned chalice and I submit to the Almighty's will and for the safeguarding of Islam and the protection of the Islamic republic, I do away with my honor." This seems, once again, to round out a factual, objective explanation for Khomeini's decision. It is an explanation many readers would find sufficient. The facts are clear, and Khomeini himself seems able to tell politesse from professional opinion.

[43] See Akbar Afghari and Amin Karimnia, "A Contrastive Study of Four Cultural Differences in Everyday Conversation between English and Persian," *Intercultural Communication Studies* 16:1, 2007, pp. 243–250.

[44] See, for example, Bahram Hadian, "A Functional Analysis of the Passive Structure in Persian," *International Journal of Linguistics* 5:4, 2013, pp. 22–37.

This is obviously not the case, as the next sentence launches into a monologue directed at God. The factual, rational explanation is not meant to be sufficient or holistic. Following the seemingly inevitable process of deduction, Khomeini ultimately finds himself veering off the straight line of sovereign subjectivity. Once he has taken the facts in and analyzed them himself, he comes to a very disturbing conclusion. The facts indicate that Iran's loss and the disgrace of the ceasefire are God's will. The physical facts are not neutral. They do not reflect a "natural" state of affairs. Facts reflect God's presence just as miracles and visions do.

This point requires some more thought. Western rationality[45] considers facts to be verified simply through their existence. The difficulty lies in establishing their factuality. This is achieved through diverse means, all striving for impartiality and objectivity. Once facts are certified as facts, Western rationality treats them as axiomatic constants. They are what they are. At this point, Khomeini locates himself at an angle to the straight, rational line. His leap of faith comes when he decides to accept facts as revelations of God's will.

This is a difficult decision. Its immediate implication is that God wanted the Islamic Republic to lose the war. It is a decision that must be consciously made by a believer. Only an actual believer, a person, can willingly accept facts as reflections or realizations of some unknowable plan. Woody Allen wrote that "in perpetrating a revolution, there are two requirements: someone or something to revolt against and someone to actually show up and do the revolting."[46] This is true for faith as well. Khomeini makes a real effort to show up. He strays from cultural convention when he takes full responsibility for his actions. His final statement, which could initially be read as a rejection of responsibility, is an expansion of his own responsibility. His sovereignty is validated by his recognition that the facts are not simply what they are. Khomeini could have stayed on the straight and narrow of sovereign subjectivity, assuming that the facts are value free and do not indicate any divine preference. Khomeini begins to become a real believer, a singular point in space, when he allows that the facts represent God's having rejected Khomeini's actions and intentions.

Perhaps this point is illustrated more effectively in a seemingly marginal remark made in the letter's first part. Khomeini ends his reference

---

[45] I use "Western" but could be using "liberal," "instrumental" or various other terms describing the prevalent strain of thought originating in the European Enlightenment.

[46] See www.goodreads.com/quotes/645622-in-perpetrating-a-revolution-there-are-two-requirements-someone-or (last accessed on October 18, 2016).

to the IRGC commander's statement with the words "In spite of stating this, he said the Islamic republic must continue fighting which is now no more than a slogan." Respect for one's elders is a basic convention of Iranian culture.[47] One expression of such respect would be an inability to answer in a clear negative when asked a direct question by the supreme leader, "the old man." If the "old man" faces you across his desk and asks if you think the war can be won, you do precisely what the IRGC commander did. That is, you answer affirmatively but provide such a comprehensive list of stipulations and disclaimers that your answer becomes, in effect, completely negative. Social convention, the foundation of social and communal coherence, demands this course of action.

Khomeini exposes this as fiction when he describes the words as "no more than a slogan." Khomeini accepts full responsibility for gathering and processing the facts, as well as for deciding upon them. Willingly exposing social convention as fiction is, perhaps, even more radical than an embrace of executive responsibility. This exposure demonstrates Khomeini's commitment to sovereign subjectivity. He is willing to do this in order to achieve high factuality. Yet this exposure also shows Khomeini's self-location at an angle to sovereign subjectivity, rather than as an extension of it. Only a real person, a known point in space, can subvert a broad, social construction. Khomeini ends the first part of the letter by sovereignly doing away with his honor. He acquires the authority to do so by pitting himself not just against facts, but also against the "common sense" of social protocol.

Why is this subversion? Once reality is understood as something other than Khomeini's immediate impression of it, his immediate sovereignty over it falters. His authority with regard to this reality is less than absolute. This authority becomes a license to interpret and adapt, rather than the power to shape and create. The decisions of a sovereign subject reflect this subject's ultimate achievement: having reality conform to his or her thoughts and actions. What the subject rationalizes is concretized through his or her decision and its application. Khomeini's decision can only be penultimate. His decision underscores his realization that this ultimate fusion is beyond him.

Khomeini's engagement with the facts begins with the overt defeats on the battlefield and ends with the hard numbers, those accessible only

[47] See, for example, this code of cultural behavior presented by the Iran Chamber Society: www.iranchamber.com/culture/articles/codes_behavior.php (last accessed on October 18, 2016).

to high-ranking ministers. He could have settled for either, or none. In any case, both pass through his personal filters, either in conversation or reflection. The worst fact, mentioned last, is that the politicians have informed him that popular resilience has eroded, since everyone knows an Iranian victory will not materialize. Khomeini decides to accept that he is not aligned with God's plan. Khomeini, fervent believer that he is, obviously thought that he remained on God's good side for the duration of the war. The most difficult part of his decision is not to relinquish his honor, but to maintain his authority and integrity while doing so. This is Khomeini's relation to subjective sovereignty. He is not wholly removed from subjective sovereignty and he is not completely subsumed by it. He asserts himself by establishing his angle.

This understanding cannot come naturally to a fervent believer, instinctively identifying his welfare with God's intentions. He must decide that this is the case, that physical reality is not an obstacle to transcend. The decision having been made transforms the physical world into an arena in which Khomeini can act. Such actions are not the simple execution of a sovereign will. They are always experiments which take part within borders that are not to be crossed. God's power is absolute. Subjectivity, on the other hand, can never stabilize itself enough to assume complete sovereignty. Once the borders of the arena have been established, nothing is out of bounds within the arena. Having set out the limits of his own actions, Khomeini places himself in a zone composed fully of possibilities for action. These possibilities are less than extreme. The extremities are God's domain.

Using the terms proposed above, Khomeini has understood who he can be in relation to sovereign subjectivity. Now he must consider the question of ontotheology. Reality is a reflection of God. But who and what is God? Perhaps more importantly, who and what is Khomeini with regard to this God? Having properly addressed the facts, he must now take on intentions, the motivation and explanation achieved through faith. He knows how things are, but he has not yet established why things are not as they should be.

## Second Decision (Ontotheology): Why Is God so Unlike Khomeini?

The second part of Khomeini's ceasefire letter is devoted to a monologue directed at an absent partner. That partner is God. Khomeini needs a system of rules to regulate his interaction with God. He hopes, by recourse to such rules, to change the unlucky ending. He has found himself by deciding to accept reality as God's will. His next challenge is finding himself in relation to God. If he reestablishes his rapport with God, could he perhaps get God to change his mind? We cannot rule out this possible motivation. When the facts fail us, we often get personal. Khomeini, knows, of course, that God has made his desire clear, and that desire was that the righteous lose. Still, he hopes that having lost the straight line of subjective sovereignty, he can still rely on his straight line to God.

When considering reality, Khomeini took full responsibility for its processing (although not for the war itself). His responsibility culminated in the decision to refrain from claiming the fullest responsibility. Such a claim would have been tantamount to claiming that he was God, or that he understood God's plan completely (both amount to the same end). Now, Khomeini presents himself as a supplicant whose wishes are made from a position of kinship with God. God is, no doubt, stronger and more powerful. Still, Khomeini begins the second part of the letter as someone who can speak directly to God and be heard. He wishes for help which should be delivered because he, Khomeini, has done his part. It is as though he and God agreed on a division of labor, and now Khomeini has come to claim what is rightfully his. He might be saved from the need to triangulate in order to assert himself, because God will simply come through. Triangulation, after all, is more cumbersome and less immediately satisfying than the stability of a straight line.

When examining the facts, Khomeini processed them through his own discernment and conviction. In order to decide that God spoke through facts, he himself needed to be God's partner in conversation. Having considered reality through numerous facets, Khomeini could then decide that his dismal situation was of God's choosing. This allowed him to locate himself within reality, to shed any pretense that his predicament was any better than it actually is. Following this location, he is able to truly consider his options and make his choices. None of his actions can be considered radical or illogical once he is inside that spectrum. Thus, his final statement about bowing his head and drinking from the poisoned chalice is sad and disturbing, but quite real in the less than absolute sense of the word.

That is not enough. As a believer, Khomeini decided to accept that the reality he saw through his own eyes was God's will. That reality failed him and did so despite his heartfelt conviction and intent to do God's will. Pursuing the facts, Khomeini has located himself in relation to them.

He is not well off. Yet he did not mean for things to end up this way. In fact, as he was going about the business of fighting the war with Iraq, Khomeini believed not only in God's realness but in the realness of his own intentions.

What are Khomeini's intentions? His first intention is to recognize in all he does the unity and perfection of God. In his own words: "We rose for the sake of your religion, we fought for your religion and we accept the cease-fire for the protection of your religion." These three actions can be harmonized only if they all originate in God's wholeness and fullness. Khomeini doesn't want to tell a factual story. He wants, through the facts, to state that all he does begins and ends with God. Whether this is a straight line or a circle, Khomeini commits to ontotheology by presenting himself as an extension of God.

Khomeini's second intention is intimately related to the first: "we did not collude even for a moment with America, the Soviet Union and other global powers, and we consider collusion with superpowers and other powers as turning our back on Islamic principles." Why would the collusion with other countries be considered a grave sin? In Persian, just as in English, "Power" is used to describe a remarkably strong country as well as the quality of potency or strength. Khomeini's letter was written in a world still divided between the United States and the USSR. Khomeini suggests that any nation referring to itself (or being referred to) as a power is playing God.

The misguided appropriation of power by humans is a grave sin. Divine power is linked to God's quality of wholeness. Humans are not whole. They do contradictory things, often undermining their own efforts. They sign a ceasefire agreement after having demonstrated their readiness to fight a war to the death. It is God's power which provides a common underpinning for human contradictions. Human aspirations to such power, the claim that human vision and understanding can explain the world in its entirety (through capitalism or communism; it doesn't matter), are sinful by definition.

Khomeini, leader of the true believers, sees no place for himself with these extremists. Moreover, as his reality emerges to his detriment, he hopes for salvation from the ultra-real, directly from God. He already knows that physical reality reflects God's will, and that he cannot deny this reality. Still, God did more than drive Iranian troops back and Iraqi missiles forward. God ignored the purity of heart displayed by Khomeini and his people. Why did this happen? What does it say about Khomeini's understanding of himself, and his people, as believers? How does Khomeini's faith shape his ontological awareness, his knowledge of who he is?

Khomeini looks for answers. He reminds God of all that was done in his, God's, name. He calls out to God: "We have no one, but you. Help us to implement your commands and laws." God does not answer. The silence seems persistent. An answer will not present itself. Khomeini cannot ignore the silence, just as he cannot ignore the facts about Iran's military and financial situation. However, he cannot simply accept this silence. Can he still claim to have a straight line to God if God remains silent? In his historical review, he grants once again that sovereign subjectivity cannot provide him with a straight line. This is evident when he makes it clear that no wise man has ever succeeded in making peace through the unification of thought and practice. When thought and practice are unified the sovereign subject is equal to God. This cannot happen. Khomeini and his people have made so many sacrifices. They have paid too much. Khomeini began his monologue by flaunting his rootedness in God. He ends it with what can be read as professions of weakness. Iranians are alone. They have nothing but God, while the rest of the world has each other. Flight 655 resonates here as well. The entire world is up at arms against Iran, not just through Iraq as proxy, but in the open sky as well. Can God explain why it has come to this?

The answer, and Khomeini's decision, are both in his final request from God. Khomeini's final request from God: "Oh God! I beg you to grant me a quick martyrdom." At a first glance, Khomeini seems to be committing to the straight line to God. If that God cannot provide a justification for his rejection of Khomeini, Khomeini can still reaffirm his faith by dying as a martyr. This death will increase God's glory and reaffirm Khomeini as God's ultimate subject. Dying becomes the only measure of sovereign subjectivity. The martyr leaves behind all authority and integrity in the moment of death. He has forsaken life and with it any and all opportunities to explore or assert such authority. By giving up his own presence, the martyr affirms God's exclusive presence. In spite of this undeniable reading, I think Khomeini's request represents the point where he rejects the straight line and angles himself in relation to the ontotheological axiom. Khomeini decides that he is not one with God. He decides to continue living.

Khomeini has decided that he does not know why God does what he does. Speaking "rationally," Khomeini cannot expect to be affirmed in his faith until he is united with God in death. Death, however, can only be granted by God. Khomeini now knows that God will not change his

plan or even explain his actions or listen to Khomeini's reason. God will
remain silent. Until this final sentence, Khomeini remains grounded in a
notion of similarity. "We did our part, why didn't you do yours?" he asks,
an instrumentally rational plea if ever one was made. When he asks God
for death he already knows God will not answer. How can we tell? Most
immediately, because the letter does not at this point. Had it ended, had
the ultimate sacrifice remained open-ended, we could have surmised that
Khomeini was willing to wait as long as it took for his martyr's death.
After all, he was already an old man. No one can clearly define God's
concept of quickness. But this is not the case. The first sentence of Part III
immediately embarks on a working plan to regulate Khomeini's current
reality. Khomeini does not expect God to offer him real salvation. He
locates himself at an angle to the divine, rejecting the ontotheological premise but not his faith in God. He rejects this similarity. He understands
that the notion of ontotheology cannot provide him with the explanation
which he first sought through the notion of sovereign subjectivity.

Returning to Torkel Brekke's definition of fundamentalism as the
globalization of prophecy, we can say that Khomeini has rejected fundamentalism. He has forgone the universal comfort of straight lines
stretching from himself to two fundamental principles. Khomeini found
himself by discovering that he was less than a sovereign subject in the
rational sense. He was also less than a perfect, self-negating believer. He
could not be satisfied by being an ultimately redundant copy of God.
Khomeini has relinquished any power he may have had to shape reality
in his image. He has, in fact, refused to have anything to do with those
who would claim such power. Most immediately, he has forgone the
solace of prophecy. What was said, what was meant, what was to come –
all pales before what is. Brekke describes the propagation of prophecy as
dependent on continuous charisma and flourish, meant to bridge the gap
between the lackluster present and the assured salvation of the redeeming future. Khomeini's attempt at charisma failed miserably. He was not
redeemed.

## Signing the Ceasefire

The final part of Khomeini's letter, the only one dealing directly with the
ceasefire and its implications, is almost an anti-climax. He has created
a theology grounded in his present reality. Khomeini does not bask or
reflect. He goes directly to work. Addressing the members of the *majles*,
he tells them:

I said that a session (of parliament) should be convened so that the people are informed about the cease-fire. Proceed with caution, because some extremists with their revolutionary slogans might divert your attention from what is best for Islam.

Extremists are those who cannot decide to let go of straight lines. They can be those who advocate faith to the death. They can also be those who cling to "neutral" facts and numbers, explaining their decisions as rationally inevitable. Khomeini does not (and cannot) say the extremists are wrong. I would go as far as saying that he acknowledges the justice in their claims, at least when considering the problem from the perspective of "correctness." The straight lines are correct. As a believer, Khomeini knows that absolutes are true enough. Nonetheless, they cannot help him locate himself.

Khomeini does not have correctness in mind. That is a project better left for the "powers" and "powerbrokers" of the world. Khomeini has reality in mind. He cannot alter physical reality, which is a reflection of God's will. He cannot wear the mantle of ontotheology, equating ontology with theology, because he has affirmed that the basic relationship between God and man is difference. Following the tragedy of Flight 655 and the eight-year war, Khomeini needs a political theology that integrates faith in God with an embrace of the real. He cannot settle for one over the other. His theology of the real makes sense only if it begins and ends with his reality.

Those who accept this reality, Khomeini says, are the ones who have Islam's best interest at heart. The work involved in a theology of the real is negotiation, adaptation, approximation. It is a personal theology, because only persons can both affirm and subvert timeless principles. When such principles do battle at an abstract level, it is a zero-sum game. A human consciousness mediates their tensions and contradiction because a human consciousness must make do with its limitations. The mediation of such principles must be focused on work. It needs to be situated in a functional view of reality and to strive toward enabling a meaningful life within this reality. A person, Khomeini, can assert his realness only as a third point in a triangle, ascertained at an angle from the preordained points of absolute truths. The sovereign subject is an abstract entity, as is similarity to God. A person can truly exist in relation to these two fixed points, but not simply occupying or extending from either one of them.

Realness becomes the source of Khomeini's authority. His two decisions mark two initial tests for a leader, which are not far removed from the tests of faith described above. First, Khomeini must resist the temptation of relying solely on himself. Second, he cannot justify his understanding through recourse to the external, absolute truth of God. The third test is the most difficult. Khomeini must move on. He will lose if he remains mired in the real. Realness is a medium for motion, even if such motion is at times circular or repetitious. This is a leader's task, a formidable responsibility.

Khomeini ends his letter with the following words:

You know that the leaders of the (Islamic) regime have made this decision with the utmost sadness, and with hearts overflowing with love for Islam and for our Islamic country. Be mindful of God. Whatever happens, it is His decision.

All decisions originate with God, because our first decision is to discover God in our lives. Our sense of reality is defined by God's expression (in reality) and by God's silence. Both mark the borders we cannot cross. Within them, we are able to attempt meaning. God lies at the root and crown of every decision, yet we make them all. God's perfection allows us to make the decisions we want least. Our imperfection places those decisions in relation to other decisions, other contexts. This is what allows us, ultimately, to move on.

Khomeini believes that God gives us first, painfully, almost fatally, our limitations. Once we exercise our will (our humanity) and accept them, we can act. Such action is not a compromise, even if it is always less than absolutely true, or justified, or representational. We are not meant to be perfect. We are meant, in God's presence, to act. We are not, however, forced to act. Action is a struggle. We choose to act, even though we can do nothing but act, and we are free to choose. Such freedom comes at a great price. It is not a reward, nor is it fulfillment. The decisions made through it are not necessarily cause for celebration. Being less than perfect, our decisions and our selves do not stand alone. We act and think in scale, on a spectrum. Our actions and thoughts are legitimate if they are part of this imperfect spectrum, related to other actions taken and considered. Nothing is erased, nothing left behind. Khomeini's theology of the real boils down to this; we compose ourselves through moments of awareness, rising from the ashes and moving on.

## Interlude I

Khomeini's theology of the real is driven by a desire for the realization that is performed by understanding. A believer must understand that God is actually speaking through reality, rather than through miracles and exceptions. This is the basis of sound sovereignty and of a sound polity, but also the essence of faith.

Khomeini's politics are regulatory politics. He wants to live in the world in synchronicity with the world, to avoid the necessary downfall that follows the peaks of the extraordinary. In his quest for meaningful survival, Khomeini does not care for intensity. He does not wish to change the world or to ignore the world but to be, properly and truthfully, within the world.

## II

# THE SUBVERTING REAL

## *Mediating Absolute Perfections*

### Introduction: Shaping Israeli Space

On December 18, 2003, Ariel Sharon, the prime minister of Israel, delivered a speech at the Herzliya conference. In his speech, which we will read closely in just a bit, Sharon presented a plan for what he called "unilateral disengagement"[1] from "the Palestinians."[2] The plan called, in very vague terms, for Israeli withdrawal from some of the Palestinian territories it has occupied since 1967.

Sharon's plan shocked the Israeli political scene. In fact, the shock was so great that a prominent journalist, Ben Caspit, wrote on the following day that, "with all due respect, Sharon has not yet passed the action test."[3] Israel was in the midst of the "Second *Intifadah*," a popular Palestinian uprising that had begun in 2000 and included frequent terror attacks in Israeli cities. Sharon had first been elected prime minister in 2001. His extensive defense credentials (he had been one of the most successful generals in the history of the Israeli military) were crucial to his election. He had vowed to fight terrorism firmly and effectively.

---

[1] In Hebrew, the term used was *hitnatkut*, a word that can also be translated as "detachment" or even "cleaving." The English term, "disengagement," sounds almost trivial in terms of consequences. Disengaging can simply refer to the act of breaking existing contact. *Hitnatkut* carries undertones of permanent separation. It is a term that sounds almost clinical to the Hebrew-speaking ear.

[2] Who were intentionally defined with such a loose term, giving them coherence as an "other" but denying them any clear mark of sovereignty. One who wishes to unilaterally disengage from another has no interest in bolstering the other's distinctiveness or jurisdiction over that other's fate.

[3] Quoted in Haim Misgav and Udi Lebel (eds.), *In the Shadow of Disengagement: Strategic Dialogue in Crisis* (Carmel Publishing, 2008), p. 313.

Sharon had also been one of the champions of Jewish settlement in the territories throughout his political career. In January 2003, he had been elected prime minister for the second time with a resounding victory, doubling his Likud Party's number of Knesset seats from 19 to 38. The settler lobby, perhaps the most influential on the Israeli political right, was certain of Sharon's active support. The Israeli left had abhorred Sharon since his ruthless leadership of Israel's First Lebanon War (1982). Sharon's embrace of territorial withdrawal, no matter how limited in scope, was so out of character that, indeed, both sides of the political spectrum were profoundly rattled.

Sharon's plan, which later focused on the evacuation of Jewish settlers from the Gaza Strip, pushed the Israeli state into an existential debate. The existential prize at the heart of the debate was narrative rather than territory.[4] The following chapter will consider the disengagement debate from this perspective. We will read Sharon's speech first, his call for a new narrative. Then we will explore one of the founding texts of the national-religious settler movement. In both narrative visions, we will trace themes of sovereignty and faith and the ways in which they shape, and are shaped, by the real.

The dissonance of disengagement – the sovereign state of Israel relinquishing territory; the champion of the settlements opting for evacuation – will provide a setting for an Israeli theology of the real. As in the Iranian case, this theology rose with the necessity of action. Sharon's vision did battle with the vision of the settlers for nearly two years in the Israeli public arena. Numerous acts of protest were planned and carried out, some of which we shall discuss later on. Various legislative and executive maneuvers were undertaken by Sharon and supporters until the beginning of the evacuation on August 15, 2005. Those conducting the debate assumed the evacuation itself would require, at the very least, six weeks.[5]

The evacuation was completed in nine days. Each side explained this unexpected rapidity in different ways. I am interested in the analysis, the

---

[4] Obviously, there are many who would disagree with me. The question of the Palestinian territories and of Palestinian and Jewish territorial self-definition has been the single, most prominent and most constitutive divide of Israeli politics over the past half-century. Still, for the purposes of our discussion, I chose to consider the debate initiated by Sharon's speech as the opening salvo of a battle for the control of Israel's evolving national narrative.

[5] Estimate made by Major General Giora Eiland (retired), head of the steering committee established by Sharon. Others estimated the required time at anywhere between three and six months.

theology of the real, offered by Brigadier General Hacohen. Hacohen, an unconventional senior military officer, commanded the "evacuation division." This special taskforce consisted of an IDF division complemented by various national police units. Before carrying out his mission and particularly after the mission was over, Hacohen, the man in charge of deciding the narrative battle in actuality, spoke about his dilemmas and decisions. I will present these deliberations, revealed significantly in a published conversation.

Hacohen's theology of the real connects sovereignty and faith in ways which simultaneously incorporate and disentangle Sharon's secular message of faith from the settlers' theology of redemption. Like Khomeini, he formulated his theology when faced with a no-win situation. Hacohen's family played a dominant role in the creation of the settler movement. Several of his siblings and their families are, in fact, settlers. He expressed his objection to the evacuation of Jews even as he was preparing to carry out his mission. Still, he remained a senior military officer, wholly committed to the sovereignty of the Israeli state and to his duties as a soldier. His theology emerges from this inevitable clash.

The "default" national narrative of the Israeli state, the narrative of Israeli sovereignty, defined Israel as a "Jewish and Democratic state." This formulation appeared in Israeli legislation for the first time in 1958, in the Basic Law regulating the status of the Knesset, Israel's parliament.[6] Israel's declaration of independence, in 1948, proclaimed it to be a "Jewish" state without directly mentioning its "democratic" nature. Still, the declaration expressed a commitment to democratic values. While the reconciliation between the two concepts is not trivial,[7] the Israeli Democracy Index of 2013 states that 74.8 percent of Israeli Jews believe that Israel can be both Jewish and democratic.[8]

Despite this collective act of sovereign imagination, both "Jewish" and "democratic" supported their own national narratives of sovereignty. Both attempted to provide comprehensive justifications for the Jewish national project in Israel by offering conceptions of Israeli space. The

---

[6] See www.mfa.gov.il/mfa/mfa-archive/1950-1959/pages/basic%20law-%20the%20knesset %20-1958-%20-%20updated%20translatio.aspx (last accessed on October 18, 2016).

[7] The clear preference of Jews, expressed (for example) by the "Law of Return" ensuring every Jew who immigrates to Israel an Israeli citizenship, can be seen as favoring ethnocracy over democracy.

[8] See http://en.idi.org.il/media/2726731/2013-Democracy-Index-Main-Findings.pdf (last accessed on October 18, 2016).

question of Israeli space is, perhaps, the most hotly debated public issue in Israel. The creation of a Jewish polity in the biblical *Eretz Israel* (land of Israel) has been the stated object of Jewish prayers for many centuries. Still, Jews living in the diaspora (very few remained in Israel after the destruction of the first temple in 586 BC and the second in AD 70) did not actively attempt to create such a polity. This was generally seen as a sign of redemption, a challenge to be addressed with the coming of the messiah.

The creation of the Israeli state, and particularly Israel's victory in the 1967 Six-Day War, thrust Israelis into the tumultuous reality of a prophecy fulfilled. The question of Israeli space, the borders defining that space, became the defining debate regarding Israeli sovereignty. Was this sovereignty legitimate because of divine origins? Was it the sovereignty of a modern nation-state, that of a people recognized and practicing as a legitimate polity? What sort of relationship would the new Jewish state have with the Palestinians and their national aspirations? How would Israel locate itself physically in the Arab Middle East? Would it strive for isolation? Friction? Integration? Framed in terms of the flexible bond between "democratic" and "Jewish" narratives, the specter of permanent borders and the Israeli space to be created within them hovered continuously.

The first narrative, epitomized by Sharon's disengagement plan and rhetoric, saw the redeeming value of a Jewish state in its functionality and minimalism. Such a state would keep its citizens safe and sound. It would have secure borders, enabling its leadership to manage collective resources effectively and ensure a life of prosperity. The second narrative, relatively marginalized throughout Zionist history, erupted after the Six-Day War. This was a religious narrative, grounded in maximalism, seeing the value of Jewish nationalism as its central role in a process of redemption initiated by God. The state of Israel, according to this narrative, is "the foundation of God's seat on earth."

The mutually exclusive natures of these two approaches had lain dormant, ensconced in the warm embrace of "Jewish and Democratic," until Sharon unveiled his disengagement plan. Between the 1967 war and the building of the first Jewish settlements in the contested Palestinian territories (1976), the ideology of the settler movement was forged with fiery passion. At the beginning of the twenty-first century, the settler movement had been transformed into a sectorial lobby. Its success was measured in structures built rather than souls won. On the other side, the 1993 Oslo Accords, which were meant to be interim stepping stones toward a comprehensive peace, did not deliver stable negotiations. The "democratic" narrative depended on the normalizing effect of Israeli–Palestinian peace. Its failure to arrive alienated many potential supporters. The ineffective-yet-comforting notion of "Jewish and Democratic" thus remained ascendant.

Sharon's plan revealed the unbridgeable gaps between the two narratives. He claimed Israeli withdrawal from the territories to be imminent and necessary, not just as an appeasement of the world but for Israel's very soul. Grown accustomed to the gradual advancement of settler agenda, supporters of the redemption narrative attempted to rekindle their ideological fire. While their leaders did not succeed in capturing popular support, they drew strength from revisiting the theological and political pillars of their movement. The clash seemed inevitable.

Gershon Hacohen created his theology of the real in direct contact with these two narratives while remaining distinct from their absolutist tendencies. Unlike Khomeini, he was not the leader of a state but its soldier. Israel of 2003–2005, as opposed to Iran of 1988, was a solid, stable country. During this two-year period, both sides of the Israeli struggle claimed a strong commitment to this national stability. Hacohen's challenge was not the validation of the state as a whole but the realization (through action) of a viable third way. Khomeini stood to lose his authority and the sovereignty of his unique Shi'a state. Israel between 2003 and 2005 was on the verge of losing its compatibility with its own internal and surrounding reality. Tension between the competing narratives was high. The proponents of each were busy circling their wagons, readying themselves for the outcome of a zero-sum game. They could win only if the other lost. Hacohen's third point allowed for thoughts of a triangle, a real Israeli space, integrating sovereignty and faith, redemption and *realpolitik*.

I begin by approaching and reading Ariel Sharon's first, broadest framing of his Israeli narrative. The speech was carefully written and carefully delivered, its timing and context pertinent to its content and reception.

# 2

## Sharon's Speech

### *The First Israeli Narrative – The Straight Lines of Leadership and Time*

In his Herzliya conference speech, Sharon does not mention the Gaza Strip and provides very little detail regarding his plan. This generality is what makes the speech important for our purposes. Sharon knew, at the time, that Israeli security forces were beginning to effectively limit Palestinian terror capabilities. Still, in early October of 2003, 21 Israelis were killed by a suicide bomber at "Maxim," a Haifa beach restaurant. Israeli public opinion was still dominated by the potential for civilian casualties.[1]

Sharon was, at the time, less concerned with the specific details of Israeli withdrawals. He and his staff were concerned by Israel's deteriorating status in the world, as well as by the escalating demoralization of Israel's population. Sharon was eager to break the stagnation, convinced that something needed to be "done."[2] Later on, there were speculations regarding Sharon's motives in breaking sharply with his long-held convictions. Sharon and his sons had been investigated by authorities on suspicions of bribery and corruption. An indictment was expected to be announced by Israel's attorney general. There were many who assumed that Sharon's plan originated in his desire to deflect media attention while

---

[1] See (in Hebrew) the detailed Wikipedia entry for the "second intifadah": https:// he.wikisource.org/wiki/%D7%90%D7%95%D7%A8%D7%95%D7%95%D7%AA_ %D7%99%D7%A9%D7%A8%D7%90%D7%9C_%D7%A4%D7%A8%D7%A7_ %D7%95.

[2] Dov Weisglass, head of Sharon's private office during Sharon's tenure as PM, made these statements at a symposium entitled "Israeli Society a Decade after Disengagement." The symposium was convened by the IDC Herzliya on August 13, 2015 (attended by the author).

harnessing the support of Israel's legal and political elites.[3] The Israeli right, and particularly the settlers, believed that these legal and political elites were manned predominantly by leftists who were, by definition, supportive of Israeli territorial withdrawal.

All these battles, however, were fought as the scope of Sharon's plan grew clearer. At this initial stage, in December 2003, Sharon staked his claim to decisive leadership by offering a vision of Israel's national narrative generated by and linked to his leadership. His speech and the circumstances surrounding its delivery amounted to the promulgation of an ethos.

## Location, Location, Location

IDC (Interdisciplinary Center) Herzliya is a private college established in 1994. It was one of the first private colleges in Israel, where higher education had been limited to research universities based on the European/German model. In the 1990s, colleges were created so as to make higher education more accessible to the general population. While the majority of them chose to accept state funding and some were affiliated with existing universities, several colleges chose to remain "unbudgeted."[4] The IDC describes itself in the following words:

IDC Herzliya's founders sought to create an Israeli university in which personal achievements go hand in hand with social responsibility. Our outlook is rooted in

---

[3] See, for example (in Hebrew), www.inn.co.il/Besheva/Article.aspx/3717. This piece, which appeared on the "Arutz 7" website (a website and radio station closely identified with the settler agenda), includes an interview with Tzvi Hendel, a Knesset member and a Jewish settler in the Gaza Strip, who was ultimately evicted from his home with disengagement. Hendel asserts that he has it from "an impeccable source in Sharon's office" that disengagement was planned in order to deflect attention from Sharon's wrongdoings. On the other side of the Israeli political spectrum, Amnon Abramovitch, a respected commentator and pundit, said at a conference held on February 18, 2005, at the Van Leer Institute in Jerusalem, that Sharon should be protected and guarded by the Israeli press as though he was an "Etrog" (citron) until the completion of disengagement. The Etrog is one of the four species of Israeli flora celebrated on the Jewish holiday of Sukkot. Its main quality is lack of blemish, a perfect combination of odor and flavor. It is thus preserved with great care, often in ornate jewelry boxes inlaid with plush velvet. Abramovitch's comment caused a tremendous uproar in Israel, winning condemnations from both the right and the left. It was generally seen as an acknowledgment of Sharon's dubious circumstances, if not his actual motives.

[4] This is the official Israeli term. The classification differentiates between "budgeted" colleges and "unbudgeted" colleges. See http://che.org.il/wp-content/uploads/2012/05/HIGHER-EDUCATION-BOOKLET.pdf (last accessed on October 18, 2016).

the concepts of "freedom and responsibility" and emphasizes initiative and leadership alongside community service.

IDC Herzliya is dedicated to the pursuit of excellence in education and research and the training of future leaders by providing educational programs which combine academic study with practical, hands-on training and encourage innovative thinking. Our faculty is dedicated to IDC Herzliya's primary goal: giving our students the tools they need to become leaders both in Israel and abroad.

In addition to the aforementioned goals, we are committed to dealing with issues of: Israel's social & moral agenda; constitutional & governmental reconstruction; economic growth based on a free enterprise system; reevaluation of Israel's diplomatic strategies and policies and more.[5]

The IDC's mission statement reflects a unique voice in the Israeli context. It is, first and foremost, liberal and individualistic. The values elaborated in the text stand in immediate contrast with Israel's foundational narrative, which was strongly communal. The sense of community came from two competing sources. Israel was founded as a Jewish state, a realization of Jewish hopes, considering itself the homeland of Jews all over the world. The Israeli state was also founded as a social-democratic state, remaining socialist for the first three decades of its existence. This social-democratic vision remained, of course, in constant tension with Israel's Jewish ethnocentrism. Still, both founding rationales were based on the resources of an Israeli community. The IDC's vision, while emphasizing social responsibility, places the individual in the forefront as both leader and generator of progress.

Education and the production of knowledge are, in the IDC vision, realized by leadership. Israeli leaders have traditionally drawn their authority from two sources: ideology and military experience. The founding fathers were ideologues, resurrecting Jewish nationhood with their foresight and their words. The next generation of leaders was drawn from the military. Having made the ideological breakthrough, the young nation needed experienced figures of authority who could see it through constant threats to its physical existence. Military service was the great equalizer of Israeli society, with all Jewish citizens obliged to serve. Those who rose through the ranks were considered Israel's best, bravest and most capable of leadership.

The IDC's notion of leadership is different. If there is an ideology, it is one that originates in the individual's talents and obligations. This

---

[5] See http://portal.idc.ac.il/en/main/homepage/pages/about-idc-herzliya.aspx (last accessed on October 18, 2016).

is an ideology fulfilled in balance (freedom comes with responsibility) rather than in the absolute conviction of a military charge or a fiery speech. A leader is a person capable of innovation. Innovation is possible when one combines study and action. The worldview expressed in this text eschews purity in favor of effectiveness. A leader is as a leader does and a leader does as a leader thinks. The three are distinct, but not separate.

Traditionally, the Israeli narrative has combined preservation and progress. Israel considers itself a safe haven for all Jews should they seek it. Israel also sees itself as the "Start-Up Nation," a hothouse of hip, innovative talent.[6] In both senses, Israel considers itself somewhat of a singularity. Jewish Israeli conventional wisdom suggests that Jews have been singled out by "the world," for better and for worse. Better, because Jews have always been successful and smart wherever they've lived ("look at the number of Nobel laureates" would be a typical refrain). Worse, because Jews have always been different, less than wholly local (when they've lived outside Israel), susceptible to double loyalties. The state of Israel is the setting for the normalization of Jewish existence, but not for its pluralization.

IDC sees itself as an "Israeli University," but it remains committed to providing its students with tools that will make them leaders "in Israel and abroad." IDC's commitment to Israel is an addendum to the main body of the vision. Commitment to one's community is the virtue of any leader worth her salt, anywhere in the world. This commitment is one of critical innovation and liberation. A leader strives for better government and more effective policies, as well as for clear moral and strategic agendas. A successful nation is known by its leaders, and these leaders possess skills that are recognizable in any context and applicable in all contexts. The normalcy IDC envisions for Israel is linked to effective leadership. Such leadership will, in turn, make Israel more open and attuned to its environment and to the world at large. A good leader makes the local global.

The Herzliya conference, the specific event at which the speech was given, is described by its conveners in the following words:

The Conference, held under academic auspices, in a non-partisan, informal atmosphere, facilitates and encourages an informed debate on the most pressing issues on the national and international agendas. The Conference covers the military and diplomatic domains, as well as increasingly important matters as economic

---

[6] See Dan Senor, *Start-up Nation: The Story of Israel's Economic Miracle* (Twelve, 2011).

viability, social cohesion, government performance, education and world Jewish affairs. Undertaking a policy-driven and action-oriented approach, the Herzliya Conference supports the formation of a "grand strategy" for Israel and the region by shaping decisions and influencing policy outcomes.[7]

The focus on "grand strategy," as well as on a "policy-driven and action-oriented approach," enhances the distinction between the IDC vision and the conventional Israeli narrative. Israel's strategic reality throughout most of its existence has been one of strategic isolation. Israeli policy has usually focused on maintaining the physical security of Israeli citizens, both offensively and defensively. At the offensive end, the IDF was ranked the strongest military in the Middle East.[8] At the defensive end, Benjamin Netanyahu, Israeli prime minister in 2016, said in February of that year that Israel must surround itself with walls and fences, in order to defend itself from the "wild beasts" around it.[9] The combination of might and willful insularity has encouraged Israeli leadership to refrain from policy-driven grand strategizing.

The Herzliya conference firmly places Israel within the larger contexts of the Middle East and the world. It brings together Israel's various elites – political, defense, diplomatic, economic and social. In fact, the conference strives for a Davos-like effect,[10] making one's participation a mark of national (and international) leadership. The conference vision integrates domestic Israeli affairs with those of world Jewry and with the "most pressing issues on the ... international agenda(s)." This is an attempt to reshape Israeli leadership, and not simply an expansion of scope or the introduction of a backwater to the mainstream. An Israeli leader, according to the conference vision, prizes integrative, dynamic action. Such action should not be limited by static convention, be it ideological or territorial. Israeli integrity should be preserved by and through the guarantee of Israel's place in the broader world.

---

[7] See www.herzliyaconference.org/eng/?CategoryID=436.

[8] See www.businessinsider.com/most-powerful-militaries-in-the-middle-east-2014-8?op=1 (last accessed on October 18, 2016).

[9] See www.haaretz.com/israel-news/.premium-1.702318 (last accessed on October 18, 2016).

[10] The World Economic Forum annual meeting at Davos brings together global political and economic elites. An invitation to Davos is a much sought-after status symbol and marks a politician or CEO as a member of these elites. See, for example, www.weforum.org/events/world-economic-forum-annual-meeting-2017 (last accessed on October 18, 2016).

## Sharon's Speech and New Narrative: Israeli Sovereignty as the Containment of the Real

As I described above, Israel at the end of 2003 was a shaken nation. The second *intifadah* (popular Palestinian uprising) had begun in September 2000.[11] Nearly 3,000 Palestinians and 1,000 Israelis (civilians and soldiers) were killed during the period many believe to have ended in February 2005, with the Sharm Al-Sheikh (Egypt) summit between Ariel Sharon and Palestinian president, Mahmud Abbas. On March 29, 2002, Israel launched an offensive into cities controlled by the Palestinian Authority, following a wave of suicide attacks in Israel. Operation "Defensive Shield" (the official Israeli name) lasted until the beginning of May. Nearly 500 Palestinians and 30 Israelis were killed during the operation. While the number of suicide bombings dropped significantly, the violence did not cease.

The theme of the Herzliya conference in December 2003, was "An Inclusive View: Priorities, Decisions and Leadership." The conference's executive summary presented an assessment of life in Israel in 2003, based on an "index of national resilience":

The objective is to express, in quantitative form, the economic, social and governmental crisis which has beset Israel over the last several years.

Economics – during the final decade of the twentieth century, Israel moved forward, closed the gap with the world's advanced nations and increased the gap between it and countries in the region. Since 2000 a sharp downward turn is clearly discernible, characterized by a decrease in GNP and GDP alongside a rise in public debt and unemployment. Economic indexes continued their downward trend in 2003.

Society – Between 1990 and 1996, Israel moved forward, closed the gap with the world's advanced nations and increased the gap between it and countries in the region. A downward turn has been discernible since 1996, characterized by a rise in poverty and inequality alongside chronic unemployment, with a decrease in living standards and male rate of participation in the labor market.

Government – Israel's situation has been systematically deteriorating since 1996. This deterioration is characterized by a decrease in political stability, ranked by experts as the most important variable, as well as oversight of public ethics, lawful behavior, government efficacy, the quality of regulation, representability and responsibility. A sharp decline

---

[11] For an introductory survey of the second intifadah, see www.globalsecurity.org/military/world/war/intifada2.htm; https://en.wikipedia.org/wiki/Second_Intifada (last accessed on October 18, 2016).

in civil liberties has been apparent since 2001, at the beginning of the intifadah.[12]

Sharon's speech was written and delivered within this context. Sharon, who had always been a maverick, had won the 2003 elections handily. He was the most popular person in Israeli politics. Still, he could not seem to shake off the stagnation he had inherited in 2001. Military and security achievements notwithstanding, Sharon felt called upon to define a new agenda. His choice of setting was intentional. The Herzliya conference and the IDC were the most suitable background for a call to reconfigure the Israeli narrative. The speech is remembered for having been the first call to territorial withdrawal from the Palestinian territories by a right-wing prime minister. I would like to read it as an attempt to define an Israeli national narrative grounded in a notion of sovereignty as effective leadership.

The text of the speech is presented in italics, with my commentary in regular font.

## Sharon's Speech

*My congratulations to the organizers of the important and interesting meeting you've held here. Over the last three days, you have discussed the situation of Israel. I, as Prime Minister, am responsible for the planning and execution of efforts that will shape the nature of Israel in the years to come.*

The substantive point of the speech is made in the first paragraph. "You" discuss the situation of Israel. "You," the discussants, are in the present and you are capable of talk. "I," the prime minister, have sole responsibility over both planning and execution for the future. As the leader, "I" will shape Israel's development, while you discuss its current situation. Israel's future is a function of Israel's leadership, and "I" am that leadership.

*All of us share the task of shaping Israel as a Jewish and democratic state, a state in which the burden of both rights and obligations is equally shared by all sectors through community service of one type or another; a state with a fine, effective educational system which raises a young generation full of values and national pride, capable of dealing with the challenges of the modern world; a state whose economy is geared to the advanced global economy of the 21st century, where per capita production exceeds 20000 US$ and is equal to the most developed states*

[12] See (in Hebrew) www.herzliyaconference.org/_Uploads/1189SummeryHebrew.pdf (last accessed on October 18, 2016).

*of Europe; a state that welcomes aliya*[13] *and is a spiritual and national center to all world Jewry, drawing tens of thousands of olim*[14] *each year. Aliya is the central goal of the state of Israel. This is the country we would like to create. This is the country in which our kids would want to live.*

After having assigned himself full responsibility, Sharon turns to touching his political bases. He seems to agree to a measure of cooperation (between himself and everyone else) in shaping Israel's future. Nonetheless, I propose that he is concerned mainly with accentuating his own authority. "An equally shared burden" is code for integrating the Jewish ultra-orthodox population into the general Israeli populace by means of compulsory military service. The ultra-orthodox have been effectively exempted from military service since the early 1950s. The exemption was initially granted to a select group of elite yeshiva students, as a gesture of the new Israeli state's desire to perpetuate the traditions of Jewish religious scholarship which had been lost in the holocaust. It grew with time to include tens of thousands of young ultra-orthodox men.

The Israeli political scene is a fractious one. Governments are most often based on coalitions. Ultra-orthodox members of the Knesset are permanent fixtures of all coalitions, because they care mostly about their sectorial needs. A politician who sees himself or herself as a potential prime minister would willingly pay the price required for his coalition's stability. The most immediately forbidden issue for such a politician would be the notion of military service for ultra-orthodox men. This is seen as an immediate deal breaker by the rabbinic and political leadership. Military service being a mobilizing and equalizing force within Israeli society, the rabbis fear that military service would compromise the closely maintained and supervised values of their communities.

Sharon's choice to begin his description of an idealized Israel with an equal burden places his leadership outside the traditional model of backroom deal-making. Sharon's ideal vision appeals directly to the *vox populi* of middle, secular Israel. This demographic is the holy grail of Israeli politics, the silent center which does not fit cleanly into categories of ideology, faith or class. If "burden equality" is the initial defining trait of a better Israel, Sharon's Israeli listeners know immediately that it can only be achieved under proper (that is, Sharon's) leadership.

Sharon's description of Israel emphasizes its global appeal. Future Israel's citizens will be able to function effectively within the global

---

[13] The Hebrew word, literally "ascent," refers to the emigration of Jews to Israel.
[14] Jewish immigrants.

community. They will have the required knowledge as well as the required resources. Israelis will receive state support through education and give back to the state through their resulting enhanced productivity. Talk of *aliya* as the main goal of Jewish statehood is often an assertion of Jewish national existence as morally and politically superior to Jewish life in the diaspora. The emphasis seems different in Sharon's speech. His Israel will be so globally appealing that it would simply draw tens of thousands of Jews to it from all over the world.

*Seven months ago, my government approved the "Roadmap for Peace" plan, based on President Bush's speech from June 2002. This is a balanced plan calling for incremental progress towards peace. Both Israel and the Palestinians have committed to executing this plan. A full, honest realization of the plan constitutes the best path towards true peace. The Roadmap is the only plan accepted by Israel, the Palestinians, the Americans and most countries of the world. We are ready to move forward with its execution – two states, the state of Israel and a Palestinian state – existing side by side in peace and security. The Roadmap is a clear, sensible plan, and therefore can and must be realized. The concept behind it – only security will lead to peace, and in that order. Without achieving full security, including the dissolution of terrorist organizations, we cannot achieve real peace, a peace for generations. This is the essence of the Roadmap. The opposite perception, according to which the mere signing of a peace agreement will bring about security "ex nihilo", has been attempted before and has resulted in abject failure. This will be the fate of any other plan advocating for such an approach. These are plans that mislead the public, planting false hopes. There will be no peace before terrorism is vanquished.*

The Roadmap for Peace was an American proposal for a peace process between Israelis and Palestinians. The Roadmap was presented by President Bush in June 2002, after Israel's operation "Defensive Shield" brought IDF forces into the heart of Palestinian cities. The logic of the Roadmap was, indeed, incremental. The plan focused on the gradual creation of a mechanism for a peace process, beginning with steps to end the violence that had peaked in 2002. The plan did not resolve any of the outstanding issues in principle, such as the fate of Jerusalem or Palestinian refugees.[15] The Roadmap's incrementalism is its main attraction for Sharon's purposes. Navigating the potentialities of such a plan requires effective leadership. This leadership is the source and the measure of national sovereignty. Leadership, bringing about the execution of the Roadmap, will bring physical security to Israeli citizens by dismantling

---

[15] For a concise presentation and explanation of the Roadmap, see www.cfr.org/middle-east-and-north-africa/middle-east-road-map-peace/p7738 (last accessed on October 18, 2016).

Palestinian terrorism. Leadership will also bring the state of Israel much desired international goodwill and recognition when it enables the creation of a Palestinian state. The occupation of the Palestinian territories has tarnished Israel's international standing as a wholly legitimate state since 1967. At its end, full Israeli sovereignty will be asserted when outstanding claims against Israel are dismissed.

*My government will not compromise on the full execution of the Roadmap, including all its stages. The Palestinians must uproot the terrorist organization and create a law-abiding society that struggles against violence and incitement. Peace and terrorism do not go together. The world is united today in a clear demand from the Palestinians to stop terrorism and carry out reforms. Only the transformation of the Palestinian authority into a different authority will allow progress in the process of negotiations. The Palestinians must do what they are obliged to do. A full, complete execution will lead, at the end of the process, to peace and quiet. We began executing the Roadmap in Aqaba,*[16] *but the terrorist organizations who had joined with Yasser Arafat disrupted the process with a series of terrorist bombings, some of the cruelest bombings we have known.*

Leadership means knowing what is right and doing everything necessary in order to realize this knowledge. This is what he expects of Palestinian leaders, even if it includes completely transforming the fledgling Palestinian Authority. A good leader commits, plans and executes. Still, sometimes reality cannot be coerced even by the best rational planning. As Sharon begins to recount Israel's well-led efforts with regard to the Roadmap, Palestinian recalcitrance rears its ugly head.

*Israel has taken, and will continue to take, significant steps towards substantially improving the Palestinian population's living conditions, even as Israel demands from the Palestinians that they eliminate terrorist organizations. Israel will remove blockades and lower the number of roadblocks; we will improve the Palestinian population's*[17] *freedom of movement, including both persons and goods; we will extend opening times at the international crossing points; we will allow a large number of Palestinian merchants to lead an orderly, regular economic and commercial life with their partners in Israel, and so on; all of these measures are meant to allow the Palestinian population not involved in terrorism better and more free movement. Additionally, we will, after proper security coordination, hand the security responsibility over Palestinian towns to the Palestinian security authorities. Israel will make all efforts to help the*

---

[16] The Aqaba summit (June 4, 2003), hosted a meeting between Sharon, Palestinian president Abbas and US president George W. Bush. The meeting was meant to jumpstart the Roadmap process.

[17] Sharon does not refer to a Palestinian "people" or even to "Palestinians." Doing so would bestow upon the Palestinians a quality of independence or even sovereignty. As long as they are a "population," it remains clear that the territory they occupy is not "theirs."

*Palestinians jumpstart the process. Israel will meet the obligations it has under-taken to fulfill. I have made a commitment to the president of the United States that Israel will dismantle unauthorized settlements. I intend to fulfill this com-mitment. The state of Israel is run lawfully, and the issue of the settlements is no exception. I understand the sensitivity; we will try to do it in a less painful manner, but the unauthorized settlements will be dismantled. Period, full stop. Israel will meet all its obligations with regard to building in the (authorized) settlements as well. There will be no more construction past the existing con-struction line, no land appropriations for future construction, no special eco-nomic incentives and no building of new settlements.*

Doing its bit for the Roadmap, Israel will increase Palestinians' freedom of movement. Israel will also freeze construction in authorized settle-ments and dismantle unauthorized ones. Sharon's effective leadership will allow the Palestinians to inhabit their physical space more fully. Sharon's leadership will also begin to wean "his" Israel from its excessive bond to the physical space of the territories. The forceful words reveal the polit-ical volatility of the prospect and the potential resistance. A leader has the foresight to define agendas which defy conventional wisdom and the courage required to see these agendas through.

*I would like to take this opportunity to address the Palestinians and say again, as I said in Aqaba: We have no interest in ruling you. We would like you to run your own lives in your own state. (This would be) a democratic Palestinian state, enjoying territorial continuity in Judea and Samaria as well as a sound economic rationale, a state enjoying a normal relationship of peace, quiet and security with Israel. Forgo terrorism, and let us stop the bloodshed together. Let us move together towards peace. We wish to move forward quickly with the implementa-tion of the Roadmap towards real peace and quiet.*

Sharon's vision represented a radical break with his publicly expressed views. He reiterated it several times during the executive, legislative and public process leading to disengagement and culminating in the evac-uation of the Gaza Strip from its Jewish settlers. Still, during this very first speech, when Gaza was not even mentioned as a potential loca-tion, Sharon's statement was powerful enough to make many observers assume he could not be serious. Perhaps the most radical thing about this message is the way in which Sharon's Palestinian state is a reflection of Israel. It is not a gesture, nor is it an Israeli abdication to the demands of the world. Both states are defined by their normalcy: democracies, terri-torial continuity and sovereignty, economic prosperity. Normalcy is an end, but it is also the means to itself. If one begins to behave normally, full-blown normalcy can be the only possible outcome.

Leadership is measured by its ability to achieve and maintain normalcy. Sharon is saying that in him, Israel has a leader aware of his capabilities and responsibilities. As I suggested above, this was not typical of Sharon's positions in the past, particularly with regard to the land, the physical space of Israel in general and the occupied territories in particular. It was Sharon who led Israel to a war of expansion in the early 1980s, explicitly seeking to occupy Lebanese territory in order to maintain Israel's security. When it came to the land occupied in 1967, Sharon acted continuously in settler interests from the very beginning of the movement, in 1976. After Sharon's death, in January 2014, he was eulogized in the Knesset by Ze'ev Hever. Hever, known to all as "Zambish," was perhaps the most influential operator in the process that has settled more than 300,000 Israelis in the occupied territories since 1976. Zambish was not the ideologue, but the man who knew all the byways of occupation and Israeli bureaucracy, the man who finagled funding, land and infrastructure for settlements both authorized and unauthorized all over the territories. Despite Sharon's presiding over the largest evacuation of Jews in Israeli history, Zambish began his eulogy by referring to Sharon as: "the great teacher of the settlement effort, the practical leader, the father of the settlement endeavor." Zambish's final words about Sharon were: "Your disengagement from the path we walked together during your final two years in office was difficult and painful, the questions remained unanswered, the pain is great, and all shall be covered by a great love."[18] Zambish was referring to the biblical verse, Proverbs 10:12, which states that "Hatred stirs up strife, but love covers all transgressions."[19]

Anyone described in such glowing terms by the operational "father of the settlements" could not be mistaken for someone who had suddenly grown committed to the human rights of the Palestinians, or to the evils of occupation. Sharon may have described the ends sought by the Israeli left, but he did not tell a story of humanitarianism. His story was one of stable sovereignty upholding, and reached by, normalcy. Normalcy, in turn, could only be reached through leadership.

*We hope the Palestinian Authority will play its part. However, if in several months the Palestinians continue not to carry out their share of the Roadmap – Then Israel will initiate a unilateral security effort of disengagement from the Palestinians. The purpose of the "disengagement plan" is to limit terrorism as much as possible and provide Israeli citizens with maximal security. The process of disengagement will*

---

[18] Quoted in: www.sos-israel.com/index.asp?catID=73897&siteLang=3.

[19] See http://biblehub.com/proverbs/10-12.htm (last accessed on October 18, 2016).

*lead to an increase in the standard of living, and will help strengthen Israel's econ-*
*omy. The unilateral steps Israel will take as part of the "disengagement plan" will*
*be coordinated to the maximum with the United States. We cannot compromise*
*strategic coordination with the Unites States. These measures will enhance the*
*security of Israeli citizens, and make it easier for the IDF and the security forces*
*to fulfill the difficult tasks they face. The disengagement plan is meant to provide*
*maximal security and to minimize friction between Israelis and Palestinians. We*
*are interested in holding direct negotiations, but we do not intend to place Israeli*
*society as a hostage in Palestinian hands. As I have already said, we will not wait*
*forever.*

A good leader upholds the rule of law, plans and executes within the rules
of reality. For a good leader, the Roadmap is an opportunity because it
has harnessed all the players to a shared yoke. If every side does its share,
the common effort should be enough to generate normalcy. A great leader
knows that opportunity can simply occur, because reality is not just the
product of planning. Reality can happen to you as it emerges, rather than
be shaped by you in advance.

Normalcy is a desirable outcome, but it cannot serve as the axiom
of Sharon's Israeli narrative. A leader should strive for rational arrangements, for the maximization of benefits to both sides of the conflict.
A win–win situation is always optimal. But a leader cannot count on
mutual rationality. Leaders must act, and at times the option for meaningful action arises when the conventions of normalcy are discarded. The
emerging real is not always normal.

Despite the best of efforts of Sharon and the world, it is clearly possible (perhaps even probable) at the end of 2003 that the Palestinians will
not live up to their end of the bargain. Sharon has already hinted expectations to the contrary are unfounded when he blamed the Palestinians for
ignoring the agreements of the Aqaba summit. The new Israel as reflected
by its leader, Sharon, cannot ignore this reality by yearning for peace or
by pushing ahead with the effective annexation of the Palestinian territories. The new Israel, faced with an emerging, compromising reality, must
act within it.

*Disengagement will include a redeployment of IDF forces at new security lines, as*
*well as a change to the layout of settlements so as to reduce, as much as possible,*
*the number of Israelis living at the heart of the Palestinian population. We will*
*draw temporary security lines and the IDF will deploy along these lines. Security*
*will be ensured by IDF deployment, the security fence and additional physical*
*barriers. Disengagement will reduce the friction between us and them.*

*Reducing friction will necessitate a most difficult change in the layout of some of*
*the settlements. I would like to repeat something I have already said: In a future*

*agreement, Israel will not remain in all the places at which we are present today. The transference of settlements will take place, first and foremost, in order to draw the most efficient security line, a line that will create real disengagement between Israel and the Palestinians. The security line will not be Israel's permanent border but until the implementation of the Roadmap is renewed, the IDF will be deployed along this line. Settlements to be transferred are those that will not be a part of Israeli territory within any possible future and final agreement. Simultaneously, disengagement will allow Israel to strengthen its hold over those parts of the land of Israel which would be an inseparable part of the state of Israel under any future agreement.*

*I know you want to hear names, but it is better to leave something for later. Israel will speed up the erection of the security fence. You can see the fence becoming reality even today. Its speedy completion will allow the IDF to lift roadblocks and ease the daily life of the Palestinian population which is not tainted by terrorism.*

Sharon's ultimate act of leadership is the containment of the real. He sees, in his speech, an Israel threatened by two deterministic scenarios. The first has Israel's leadership sign a peace agreement before it has established adequate security arrangements. Why? Because a peace agreement is what the world wants from Israel, perhaps so it can put the Israeli–Palestinian conflict out of its global mind regardless of the consequences. The Israeli left also wants an agreement, because an agreement is the product of a meeting between two rational wills. Signing a peace agreement before everything else will indicate Israel's rationality. A rational Israel is a normal state, a state like all others and not an eternal singularity.

There is no need for leadership in this scenario. Anyone could simply latch on to the rational goodwill of the world and the left and sign a peace agreement. Sharon emphatically states that this would be wrong. He cites security concerns, but I propose that his objection is broader and deeper. An Israeli state that would sign on the dotted line would be relinquishing a significant part of its sovereignty by denying its environmental condition. Israel's security, according to Sharon, depends on an intricate mixture of constants and dynamic evaluations and configurations. Israel needs a leader who can engineer and maneuver safe passage around, over and under the existential threats the country faces.

The second threatening scenario, for Sharon, is the one in which Israel abandons the world. Convinced of its singular nature, this Israel would avoid any negotiations with the Palestinians. It would also neglect (perhaps to the point of nullification) its strategic relations with the United States. Sharon states that this cannot happen. Israel, of course, gains much from its alliance with the United States, as well as from the global perception of it as a legitimate actor on the world stage. A rejection of negotiations would bring with it a circling of the wagons, an Israeli culture of willful isolation and suspicion.

In this scenario, there is also no need for a leader. This Israel would be drawn into an ahistorical maelstrom, shaken every which away at the mercy of forces greater than the Israeli state itself. This Israel could seek its justification in religious faith or in a ruthless war against its enemies, denying the relevance of democracy or human rights for its domestic and international legitimacy. In the previous scenario, a leader would be redundant because the "rationality" of the process would be cerebral and obtuse. In this scenario, the "anti-rationality" of the process would negate the need for institutional leadership, for a state functioning as an impartial regulator of society. This Israel would have no need for stability inherent in leadership, because it would always seek the absolute truth of a greater authority.

Sharon realizes that both of these scenarios are potentially at hand if Israel's situation continues to deteriorate. International pressure may mount and force Israel's hand. Domestic zealotry may also escalate, creating an unbridgeable gap between the institutional state and the conflicting myths at the heart of Israeli collectivity. The situation requires a true leader to negotiate, through the power of his own presence and vision, a middle ground solution.

Sharon does this through a vision of containment. His disengagement plan is an attempt to address the real by keeping it between secure borders. A leader, says Sharon, is one who holds the authority to draw lines and build fences. Initially, it seems that these lines are drawn to separate "us" from "them"; to minimize friction. This is true for what Sharon calls "the security fence."[20] The purpose of a physical barrier is clear and static. Most of Sharon's other lines are intentionally fluid. Later on, he will name Gaza as the focal point of disengagement. Gaza was an obvious choice. It was small, isolated, more removed from Israel proper than the West Bank, and was also the location of fierce resistance to Israeli presence. Gaza was also the center of support for Hamas, the Islamic resistance movement inspired by the Muslim Brotherhood. The immediate implications of this resistance were a high number of terrorist attacks and Israeli casualties.

---

[20] This is still the popular name in Israel for the massive stone barrier erected between Israel proper and the Palestinian authority. The Palestinians, and the rest of the world, refer to it as the "separation wall" or, simply, "the wall."

Sharon knew there was public support for an Israeli departure from Gaza. Had he been focused on withdrawal, or had he been seeking a diversion from his pending criminal investigations, he could have named his goal clearly and begun the effort to implement his plan. He chose not to name names and to speak of temporary lines and adaptable evaluations. Sharon demonstrated his authority and demanded legitimacy for that authority by refraining from naming names.

I propose that this reticence on Sharon's part demonstrates that his concerns are broader than the implementation of the Roadmap. Sharon is articulating a principle. Israel must draw lines in order to survive. These lines cannot be superimposed, nor can they transcend Israel's immediate concerns and contexts. The reality emerging in and around Israel is threatening. Allowed to emerge unchecked, it will entice Israelis into one of two extreme options constantly at Israel's door: rational, willful weakness or irrational, willful isolation. It takes a leader to constantly draw the lines which are the mark of Israeli sovereignty.

*So that the Palestinians may develop their economic and commercial life, and so that they do not depend exclusively on Israel, we will consider, as part of the disengagement plan, allowing, coordination with Jordan and Egypt, the more free passage of people and goods through the international crossing points, all the while taking the necessary security precautions.*

*I would like to emphasize this: the disengagement plan is a security effort and not a political effort. The steps that will be taken will not alter the political reality between Israel and the Palestinians, and will not remove the possibility of returning to the implementation of the Roadmap and reaching a settlement by agreement. Disengagement is not meant to prevent the implementation of the Roadmap. It is a step that Israel will take, if it has no other options, in order to improve its security. Disengagement will be carried out only if the Palestinians continue to drag their feet and delay the implementation of the Roadmap. Obviously, disengagement will bring the Palestinians much less than they can receive through direct negotiations over the Roadmap. It is possible that parts of the disengagement plan, meant to supply Israel's citizens with maximal security, will be implemented throughout the attempt to carry out the Roadmap. This will be decided according to circumstances at the time.*

Even Sharon's "carrot," an economy improved by enhanced circulation of people and goods, is a vision of containment. If the Palestinians adhere to the Roadmap, they will have a state of their own. That state will exist peacefully alongside Israel because a state is known by its borders. Sharon may wish for this to happen. He suspects it most likely will not. If there is no direct negotiation, Israel will disengage. Sharon will draw a line. The line will only be crossed in coordination with other states and through internationally recognized crossings. These crossings are not borders, and Palestinian freedom of movement will not be negotiated with the Palestinians. If the Palestinians are not mature enough to willingly draw a line between Israel and themselves, they must be contained by the responsible adults. Those responsible are, by definition, those who have agreed to draw lines (international borders) separating them from each other – Egypt, Jordan and Israel.

Sharon's disclaimer, his statement that disengagement is about security rather than politics, is lip service to the two narratives he is challenging. According to both narratives – the one in which Israel embraces the world and the one in which Israel rejects the world and embraces itself – there is conflict between Israelis and Palestinians. Within the framework of the conflict, there is a similarity between the two sides. They are both sovereign parties, deciding to carry on fighting. According to the world-embracing narrative, the conflict can be resolved if both parties accept that the legitimacy of sovereignty is relational. A nation is sovereign if it does not impinge on the sovereignty of its neighbors. The world-rejecting narrative understands sovereignty as a zero-sum game. One grows when one's enemies shrink. And so, Sharon says that disengagement is merely a measure of optimization, an expression of Israeli frustration. Ultimately, he seems to suggest, we will return to the conflict that must be resolved.

Having said as much, he almost immediately refutes his suggestion. Disengagement becomes the emerging norm, the constant of Israel's deployment vis-à-vis the Palestinians. Even if negotiations resume, the logic of disengagement is the logic that will prevail because it is born out of evolving context rather than general principles. Sharon's new narrative is not based on general principles. The happy end – two states, peacefully existing side by side – is where Sharon begins his speech. In this idyllic state, sovereignty is defined by stability and separation. Prosperity is a product of lines and borders. The Palestinians, according to Sharon, are less than capable of understanding this basic principle. They seek constant contact, friction that is at worst fatal and at best constantly frustrating. Israel cannot simply accept or reject a Palestinian state. The risk of making a mistake down both paths is too great. The reality of the Palestinians is too volatile, but it is also the only real reality. The friction inspired by the Palestinians, the Palestinian real, is itself a risk to an Israeli state attempting to lead an orderly existence. Israel needs to contain this reality in order to thrive. Containment is a fluctuating effort. In order to succeed, it needs to adapt constantly. This feat can only be pulled off by a real leader.

*Ladies and gentlemen, my experience has taught me that peace, just like war, requires broad consensus. We must maintain our unity, even as we hold a fierce internal debate. Over the last three years, Palestinian terrorist organizations have put us to a difficult test. Their plan, to break the spirit of Israeli society, did not succeed. Israel's citizens held firm, supported each other, lent a hand, volunteered and contributed. I believe that we must continue down this path, united, today, whether we move forward with the Roadmap or we need to implement the disengagement plan. Experience teaches us that together, with a broad national consensus, we can do great things.*

*Let us make no mistake. Any road will be complicated, full of obstacles, and will require discretion and responsibility. I am sure that just as we have withstood challenges in the past we will stand together, and succeed, today. On our way, we will always be accompanied by the words of Prime Minister Ben Gurion, one day after the declaration of independence:*

*"At this time we must only build the state of Israel with love, faith and Jewish fraternity, and defend it with all or might as long as there is need. We are in the midst of heavy battle, a double battle, political and military. Let us not decorate our actions, certainly not our speech, with high-sounding names. Let us be modest. We have come where we are standing on the shoulders of the generations that preceded us, and we have achieved because we have accepted and kept a precious tradition, that of a small nation, versed in trials and suffering but great and eternal in spirit, vision, faith and qualities."*

*I am also a great believer in the resilience of this small, courageous nation, versed in trials and suffering. I am sure that united by the power of faith, we can succeed in any path we choose. Thank you and have a happy Hanukkah.*

Israelis must remain united. Their unity is grounded in a story of containment, rather than normalcy or singularity. The situation, Sharon says, has not changed essentially since the day after independence (1948). Reality as it unfolds around Israel is one of constant battle. The Israeli real is proximity to the Palestinians, and the Palestinians are trouble. They will stop being troublesome only if they transform themselves into something other than what they are. While this is theoretically possible, it is not likely to happen. Meanwhile, the Palestinians are constantly shaking the Israeli boat. The friction created by Israeli–Palestinian proximity brings too many repressed and contested issues to the surface.

These issues have been repressed for a reason, because they cannot necessarily be resolved. What is the right path for Israel? Is it normalcy in the eyes of the world, peace/quiet/stability/prosperity? Is it the path of prophecy fulfilled, a Jewish nation unlike any other nation on earth? The battle between the two narratives lurks beneath the fragile Israeli surface. These murky depths are also the Israeli real. The worse things are in Israel (and at the end of 2003 they are quite bad), the more likely the battle is to erupt. Leadership is required to keep these issues at bay, to suppress them effectively. This leadership needs to contain the Palestinians, because they are a threat to Israel's physical existence. Sharon, as leader, needs (perhaps even more) to contain the battle beneath. For Sharon, national unity requires containment. Successful containment, the continuous drawing of lines and erection of barriers, is a leader's job.

In the Israeli mind, Israeli unity is the derivative of larger forces shaping Israel's existence. It can be a unity forged by shed blood. "A nation that fights together unites together," if you will. It can be a unity drawn from divine promise or from an authentic national drive for self-determination. Sharon does not believe in any of these platforms. He has faith in Israeli resilience. That resilience is tested by its ability to overcome the dictates of the Israeli real by limiting the real's scope. No single real variable is all-important. Israel's existence does not revolve around the plight of the Palestinians, the will of the world or the mandate of religious history. Even Israeli security is defined in context. Israeli sovereignty is at its most effective when it is dynamic, and it cannot be dynamic in any manner but the containment of the real.

# 3

## The Settler Narrative

### *Sovereignty as Faith – Redemption and the Expansion of the Real*

#### A Jewish Nation

Sharon's disengagement plan, as well as its execution, have been coopted by various ulterior narratives. The question of the "territories" has been the most important dividing line in Israeli politics since the Six-Day War of 1967. Israel was seized by a collective sense of euphoria after its resounding victory over a coalition of Arab nations.[1] The small, courageous nation echoed in Sharon's speech added, overnight, more than 6,200 square kilometers to its territory.[2] Perhaps more importantly, Israel came face to face with some of its foundational fault lines.

The Zionist movement was a project of Jewish national revival. "Jewish nation" is a difficult concept. A "nation" is a modern concept. Nations are not religious communities, unified by a shared model and object of faith and, in some cases, a shared religious establishment. Nations, and particularly nation-states, have a defined territory. Life within this territory may be the most basic aspect of belonging to a nation. Those living in the national territory see themselves as sharing a concrete history, as well as a common language (or related languages).

A nation is also more than its physical attributes. A national community is one which instills in its members a sense of belonging to something greater than themselves. This framework of belonging is based on a mythical history, alongside the concrete history of everyday life. Belonging is

---

[1] For a broad, thorough history of the war and its consequences, see Michael B. Oren, *Six Days of War: June 1967 and the Making of the Modern Middle East* (Oxford University Press, 2002).

[2] See https://en.wikipedia.org/wiki/Palestinian_territories.

also inspired by what is thought of as shared values and worldviews. A member of a nation is a link in a chain, generated by what came before and obligated toward what will follow.

Shared religious faith is common in nations, but there is more ground for real tensions between national belonging and religious belonging.[3] While there are numerous reasons for this tension, I would like to focus on one. A national community claims sovereignty – political and cultural, tangible and symbolic – for the nation and its members. A nation is perceived as one of the basic (if not the most basic) sovereign social units. For a monotheistic religious community, God is the only true sovereign. Human politics reflect humanity's obedience to God. Human politics also reflect the imperfect arrangements humans must create in order to try and comply with perfect divine commands or truths. Human sovereignty, individual and collective, is at least in some way suborned by divine sovereignty.

In the Jewish case, the tensions between the national community and the religious community are remarkably strong. European nationalism developed within the territories that later gave birth to nation-states. The Austro-Hungarian Empire, for example, broke into its constituent parts after World War I, Austria and Hungary among them. This reconfiguration was possible in large part because those who had been living in the territory called "Austria" considered themselves to be "Austrians." This linkage was common (*mutatis mutandis*) to other peoples in territories that had been a part of the Austro-Hungarian Empire. The Jewish case was somewhat different.

While Jews had been living in the Holy Land[4] consecutively after the destruction of the second temple in Jerusalem (AD 70), there were very few them. The great majority of the Jewish world lived away from the territory they considered to be their ancestral homeland. Jewish life and thought grew in the diaspora for long centuries. The lack of Jewish political sovereignty shaped Jewish notions of political order and morality. Legal and hermeneutic thought were the main intellectual venues, with Jewish law pragmatically addressing the concerns of a minority community. The Babylonian Talmud, the greatest and most authoritative compendium of Jewish law and hermeneutics, commits Jews to three oaths:

---

[3] This book is firmly located within a monotheistic context. "Religion," for the purposes of our discussion, is monotheistic religion.

[4] The least loaded term available when attempting to respect history and current political desires on both sides of the Israeli–Palestinian conflict.

One, that Israel should not storm the wall[5] {RaShI interprets: forcefully}. Two, the Holy One adjured Israel not to rebel against the nations of the world. Three, the Holy One adjured the nations that they would not oppress Israel too much.[6]

These oaths are not Talmudic law, but a "midrash," an extended development and interpretation of another text. One of their biblical reference is a verse from Solomon's Song of Songs, adjuring the "daughters of Jerusalem" not to awaken "love" until love wishes to wake, or until the time is appropriate. Despite their extra-legal status, the oaths have been evoked many times. Famously, they were mentioned by Maimonides in an epistle to the Jewish community in Yemen (ca. 1172). Local Muslim rulers had decreed that Jews must convert to Islam. In response, a local Jew declared himself the messiah and spoke of rebellion. Jewish leaders in Yemen wrote to Maimonides for a legal decision on the veracity of the messiah and on their general plight.

In his reply, he evokes and considers the three oaths:

Solomon, of blessed memory, inspired by the holy spirit, foresaw that the prolonged duration of the exile would incite some of our people to seek to terminate it before the appointed time, and as a consequence they would perish or meet with disaster. Therefore he admonished and adjured them in metaphorical language to desist, as we read, "I adjure you, O daughters of Jerusalem, by the gazelles and by the hinds of the field, that ye awaken not, nor stir up love, until it please." (Song of Songs 2:7, 8:4). Now, brethren and friends, abide by the oath, and stir not up love until it please (Ketubot 111a).[7]

For Maimonides, Jewish life in the diaspora (rather than in the promised land of Israel) is a state of affairs that will last until the time has come for God to fulfill numerous scriptural promises and redeem his people. The oaths were made metaphorically, but in order to make a very clear point. Jews must not seek out territorial sovereignty before the appointed time. Sovereignty is a mark of redemption, an expression of God's decision to actively intervene within human reality by gathering his forsaken flock from all corners of the earth. An active attempt to seek sovereignty before God grants it can be sacrilegious.

---

[5] Commentators have traditionally understood the first oath to impose a prohibition on coming to the Holy Land and attempting to establish a sovereign state.

[6] Babylonian Talmud, Ketubot 111a, quoted in https://en.wikipedia.org/wiki/Three_Oaths#The_Midrash_and_the_text_upon_which_it_expounds.

[7] Maimonides, "Epistle to Yemen," chapter xx. See https://en.wikisource.org/wiki/Epistle_to_Yemen/Complete#20.

This theological approach matched the reality of Jewish life. The survival of most Jewish communities depended on their ability to balance religious requirements with an adaptability required of an insular minority. Such communities had little use for doctrinal discussions on the ethics of kingship or even on what they might expect with the coming of the messiah. The everyday was challenging enough without the disruptive allure of a prophesied future.

Still, the oaths and the need to invoke them demonstrated the desire for redemption and with that redemption, for sovereignty. Judaism has always struggled with religious justifications for human authority. The first book of Samuel provides this speech from God, upon hearing from the prophet Samuel that the Israelites wanted a king placed over them:

And the LORD told him: "Listen to all that the people are saying to you; it is not you they have rejected, but they have rejected me as their king. 8 As they have done from the day I brought them up out of Egypt until this day, forsaking me and serving other gods, so they are doing to you. 9 Now listen to them; but warn them solemnly and let them know what the king who will reign over them will claim as his rights."[8]

The king could claim, as his rights, anything from territory to the service of his subjects. Still, the king remained, theologically, a flawed alternative to the true sovereign of the people of Israel: God.[9] Maimonides, who was perhaps the greatest systematic theologian in the history of Judaism, compiled the laws pertaining to both king and messiah. This compilation appears in the 14th and final part of his "*Mishne Torah*" (a summary of the Torah, a work meant to provide a summary of all Jewish law in clear, succinct language). The final book addresses a future unforeseeable in the twelfth century, when Maimonides lived and wrote. In this future, Jews have achieved sovereignty and are on the verge of full redemption, the coming of the messiah.

According to Maimonides, the king enjoys almost unlimited authority. The king can execute, based on his command alone, anyone the king has accused of rebellion. Judaism frowns upon state executions, normally allowing them only by decision of a full court manned by the greatest sages of the day. Even then, executions are technically rare and effectively nonexistent. Still, the king will be able to execute anyone accused of rebellion based on his decision.

---

[8] See www.biblegateway.com/passage/?search=1+Samuel+8.
[9] For a fascinating development of this concept, see Martin Buber, *The Kingship of God* (Humanity Books, 1990).

But the king's authority is limited in several ways. The king cannot order a subject to violate one of the 613 divine commandments which are the foundation of Jewish law. And the king, set apart by power, is also socially set apart. He may pass on his authority to his sons, but a woman who had been married to him cannot marry anyone who is not a king. When a king mourns and his subjects come to console him, he sits on a bench while the consolers sit on the floor. Family and mourning are two of the great equalizers of Jewish law. The king, superior in power and authority, is removed (with his family) from these essential strands of the social fabric.[10]

The notion of Jewish political sovereignty is fraught with unresolved contradictions. First, political sovereignty remains in constant tension with the foundational relationship of Jewish communal existence, the relationship with God. Jews thought (and think) of themselves as a chosen people, consecrated by God to be a "kingdom of priests and a holy nation."[11] In doctrinal terms, this relationship was the primary form of self-definition for the Jewish community. The Jewish kingdoms of old were justified and regulated by this relationship. The Jewish communities of the diaspora, who could not foresee a sovereign future, drew sustenance from this relationship in their mundane struggles with non-Jewish authorities.

Modern Jewish statehood, a nation-state for the Jewish people, taxed both tradition and the collective imagination. Zionism rose alongside other similar national movements in Europe. "National" was the new black, the fashionable standard of rationality and legitimate self-definition. Nonetheless, the Jewish case presented particular difficulties. The return of Jews to Zion was synonymous with a divine intervention in human history. Numerous prophecies spoke of this return as a sign that God had overcome his anger at the Jews. This return would constitute a true "redemption," the deliverance of the Jews from their human troubles alongside the deliverance of the world with the coming of the messiah.

These redemptive over- and undertones are a difficult match for a national movement. Nationalism is very much a modern creation. The national community creates among its members a sense of belonging and shared destiny that are rooted in a temporal and territorial context, in

---

[10] For an English translation of Maimonides' compilation, "The Laws of Kings and Wars," see www.chabad.org/library/article_cdo/aid/1188343/jewish/Melachim-uMilchamot.htm.

[11] Exodus 19:6. See www.biblegateway.com/passage/?search=Exodus%2019.

history and space. This stands in contrast to the sense of belonging typical of religious communities, which is rooted in an abstract, unseen deity whose reach transcends both the physical and the historical.

Most of all, perhaps, the two communities differ on the origin of sovereignty. A religious community sees any legitimate human sovereignty originating in God, the real sovereign of creation. The sovereignty of a national community begins with a group of human beings. These humans are sovereign on an individual basis as well, capable of rational thought and decision-making. A nation-state is as sovereign as its members.

These two fault lines make the Jewish national project a difficult one. Is the establishment of a Jewish state a sign of divine redemption, a disturbance of human history? Or is it a demonstration of sobriety, a Jewish people coming to its sense and seeking a "normal existence"? Should a Jewish state draw its sovereignty from God's law or from secular notions like "rule of law"? The Zionist movement battled with these dilemmas from the earliest stages of its inception.

## Religious Zionism: The Challenge

Most of the world's Jews did not become fervent Zionists when the movement began to form in late nineteenth-century Europe. Most of the Jews who became Zionists preferred the vision of a national community to that of a religious community. The founding fathers of Zionism saw themselves very much as Jews in terms of identity, culture and faith. Their model of community, however, was predominantly secular and socialist. They were eager to incorporate Judaism into their national vision as culture, but not as a rationale for a legal or political order.

Only a small group of Zionists could not forego their faith when they joined the movement of national revival. These religious Zionists were caught in many of the binds I described earlier. For the purposes of our discussion, I would like to focus on their struggle to envision a concept of community. The new national community of the secular Zionists stood proudly at one end of a Jewish communal spectrum. This was a modern community, a vision of normalcy and order. It had functioning institutions and feasible political goals. The secular Zionists saw redemption for the Jews in normalization. A national movement culminating in statehood was the epitome of the normal.

At the other end of the spectrum stood the ultra-orthodox community, the community of the European diaspora. This was a community of believers. It followed a well-known maxim from *Pirkei Avot* (Ethics of the Fathers), a Talmudic text providing the Torah's views on ethics and interpersonal relations. The sages offered the following three rules for a virtuous life:

Love work. Hate the rabbinate. Do not become a familiar of the authorities. (Avot, 1:10)

A commentary on *Pirkei Avot* offers the following explanation:

Why should you not become a familiar of the authorities? If the authorities know your name, they will ultimately seek you out, kill you and take all your money. (Avot of Rabbi Natan, chapter 11)[12]

This sort of distrust extends beyond a response to anti-Jewish sentiment. It amounts to a suspicion of any institutional authority. This is how institutions work, the text seems to say. Once an individual is known to them, authorities will need to exercise their sovereignty and empty the individual of his own sovereignty. A community is united by faith. Faith affirms God's sovereignty, and those who share this faith are certain in their disdain for human power struggles. Redemption for this community would come directly from God.

The religious Zionists needed to create a community that would incorporate elements of both models. They were a part of the national revival, but they could not sever their bond with the religious community, the community of the faithful. The religious Zionists saw themselves as a bridge between the two communal models, an attempt to have the best of both worlds. The seculars considered them unable to hitch their wagon to the progress train, wallowing in obsolete superstitions. The ultra-orthodox considered them either weak or messianic. The former was insulting, while the latter was dangerous, because the ultra-orthodox community was committed to the spirit of the three oaths, living in the everyday and not pondering the end of days. The religious Zionists sought their own definition of the Jewish condition, being unable to accept both "normalcy" and "isolation."

Two approaches to this quest can be seen within the religious Zionist community of the late nineteenth and early twentieth century. Professor Dov Schwartz distinguishes between the approach identified with Rabbi Yitzchak Ya'akov Reines and the approach identified with Rabbi Avraham Yitchak Hacohen Kook. Rabbi Reines, writes Schwartz, thought:

... the uniqueness of the people of Israel could be defined through the conceptual array of modern nationalist theory. "The Chosen People" represent the

---

[12] Both translations are my own.

extreme manifestation of national uniqueness, an emotional bond accompanied by total loyalty to the unique national foundations anchoring the very
peoplehood of the Jews – people, land, Torah. This loyalty, claimed Rabbi
Reines, even while it may be explained and described in rational and psychological terms, is unparalleled among the nations. However, according to
Rabbi Kook and his circle, the full uniqueness of the people of Israel cannot be
understood using rational, national concepts. Rabbi Kook acknowledged the
conceptual array of nationalism, but he considered it a mere cover for the true,
divine essence of the people of Israel. The people of Israel is, first and foremost,
a divine, metaphysical entity whose expression in the material world is social
and political.[13]

Rabbi Reines' approach was adopted by many religious Zionists. Its quietist, pragmatic reconciliation of modernity and faith became the position
of the religious Zionist mainstream. Those within that mainstream considered themselves a bridge, incorporating religious faith with belief in
the progress and prosperity of a modern national community. For Rabbi
Reines, the ways of the world reflected patterns of creation. Jews stood
out as the most authentic and highly evolved products of that creation,
but their uniqueness was still apparent within a worldly context. History
was the story of progress, and as the world progressed Jews moved along
with it. In the age of nations, Jews were the most sophisticated and worthy nation one could imagine.

Rabbi Kook saw the world in different terms. Divine existence was
the heart of all things, the truth of them. While the surface of everyday
life was not a lie, it was a diminished truth. Jews were God's most perfect creation because their existence in the world was the closest of all to
the divine fountain of being. Rabbi Kook was a Kabbalist, a thinker and
scholar of a powerful Jewish mystical movement.[14] He saw the Jewish
people as a conduit for the channeling of the divine into the surface
world. Jews accomplished this through their innate capacity for faith.
This faith placed Jews closer than any other people to the beating divine
heart of being.[15]

The national revival of the Jews was a surface manifestation of a
redemptive dynamic unleashed at the divine heart. The defining Jewish
trait was not excellence (as in the Reines approach), but authenticity.

---

[13] See Dov Schwartz, *Challenge and Crisis in Rabbi Kook's Circle* (in Hebrew) (Am Oved,
    2001), pp. 216–217.
[14] Kabbalah is, of course, the subject of an immense scholarly literature. For a concise, illu-
    minating introduction see Joseph Dan, *Kabbalah: A Very Short Introduction* (Oxford
    University Press, 2007).
[15] See Schwartz, *Challenge and Crisis*, pp. 233–236.

Jews were not a bridge, reconciling the best of devotion with the best of national thought. Rather, Jews reflected the whole of being by being the most transcendent element of being. Jews conferred transcendence upon the rest of creation. Zionism, the rebirth of Jews as a nation, was (according to Rabbi Kook) a movement of tension and appropriation. Because so much of the Zionist movement was secular, Zionism heightened the tension between the surface of human events and the underlying divine presence and providence. This tension, however, would ultimately be resolved as the undeniable truth of divine redemption emerged and appropriated the seemingly complete practical approach toward Jewish nation-building.

Rabbi Kook (senior) died in 1935, 13 years before the establishment of an independent Israel. He left a body of work remarkable for its interdisciplinary intellectualism alongside its mystical piety. This work took on the form of a concrete political theology due to the lifelong efforts of his son, Rabbi Tzvi Yehuda Hacohen Kook. The son and his students were the ones who adapted Rabbi Kook senior's highly personal philosophy of collective and individual awakening into a narrative vision for an existing state.

Rabbi Tzvi Yehuda, as he was popularly known, honed his father's rapturous, poetic esotericism into a gospel of hyperrealism. Heading the (then) small yeshiva his father built in Jerusalem, he wrote the following words in an article published in 1950, addressing a question he had been asked regarding the nature and identity of the Jewish state (my translation):

As to the point and direction of the rebuilding of the house of Israel, its full renewal ... in holiness and in the mundane upon its real place, (it) comes from our interiority and towards it ... the balance of power within us and the actual structure of our public shape will themselves be determined solely by the internal calculus of the depths of our being, absolute in its holiness above and beyond the fluctuations of temporal, superficial struggles ...

The forces of faith and action, emerging from the font of everlasting Judaism, they will be the leaders, shapers and builders, with God's help and in his light ... The test of faith is its practical emergence in action, in building, and the test of action is its continuation from within the county of faith, filling the soul, energizing it and pushing it forward to fulfill its being.[16]

---

[16] Originally published in *Hatzofeh*, the religious Zionist daily, and published later in *Lentivot Israel* (In Israel's paths), an anthology of Rabbi Tzvi Yehuda's works. Available online at: www.meirtv.co.il/upload/images/2007_1_29_14_6_13.pdf (last accessed on October 18, 2016).

Rabbi Tzvi Yehuda's words draw an image of a national revival which is an enclosed, circular system. At its core lies divine truth, the only "really real" truth. The interiority of the Jews is the most accurate reflection of this divine truth. Motion within the system is generated by the mutual dependence of faith and action, each requiring the other in order to be fully realized. Motion, and with it structure, occurs from the core and toward the core, a penumbra for the divine truth which does not shift or change. This, however, is not an effective narrative. There is no story in essence, no progression in circular motion. These are the theological pillars of a political narrative, a legitimate and functional narrative for a legitimate and functional state.

Rabbi Tzvi Yehuda's students were the founding fathers of the settler movement, also known as *Gush Emunim* (Bloc of the Faithful). The *Gush* spearheaded the effort to establish Jewish long-term presence in the territories conquered by Israel during the Six-Day War (1967). Most of these territories have never been annexed by Israel. They are, and have been, subjected to the authority of the general in charge of the Israeli military's central command. Israeli sovereignty over these territories has been, for the past half-century, the sovereignty of an occupying force. The *Gush* was a religious Zionist movement which considered these territories to be the ancestral, and divinely promised, homeland of Jewish national existence. Settling them with Jews was the ultimate Jewish obligation, the mark of virtue and sovereignty for a Jewish state.[17]

The story told by Rabbi Tzvi Yehuda and his students was one in which distinct narrative logics were merged through active faith. The first narrative was one of return. Jews returned to their promised land, restoring creation to balance after having been dispersed throughout the world. The second narrative was one of expansion. The divine truth at the heart of creation, the truth from which Jews sprang and which they reflected, was expanding. The redemption of the Jews, historically expressed as their return and revival in their land, was in truth the expansion of divine reality at the expense of the superficial, human one.

---

[17] For a thorough, unapologetically critical history of the settler movement, see Idith Zartal and Akiva Eldar, *Lords of the Land: The War over Israel's Settlements in the Occupied Territories, 1967–2007* (Nation Books, 2009). For a challenging, personal analysis of the *Gush* formed in real time, see Gideon Aran, *Kookism: The Roots of Gush Emunim, Jewish Settlers' Sub-Culture, Zionist Theology, Contemporary Messianism* (Carmel Publishing, 2013) (in Hebrew).

## Onward and Upward: Faith Generating Statehood

According to Rabbi Tzvi Yehuda and his students, Faith was the sheer quality of a Jewish polity because only faith could integrate these two stories into a coherent "Jewish"[18] narrative for a Jewish state. Faith transformed the dynamics of interiority into tangible action, returning only to expand. Moreover, faith performed this theological feat as a demonstration of Jewish sovereignty. The Israeli narrative as told by *Gush Emunim* considered that the real power and presence of the Jewish state were dependent on this practice of faith. How did faith manage to perform this feat and lay the groundwork for a functional state, one possessing institutions and procedures alongside devotion and piety?

In an attempt to answer this question, we will now read a seminal text, the record of a talk given by Rabbi Tzvi Yehuda at his yeshiva in 1967, on the eve of Israel's Independence Day. Rabbi Tzvi Yehuda did not write much, certainly when compared to his father. He devoted his life to the systematization of his father's work. Still, he was and remains the public and rabbinical figure identified with the emergence of a radical religious Zionist narrative for the state of Israel.

The still new state celebrated its 19th year of independence in 1967. Clouds of war (which would break out three weeks later) were gathering on the horizon. The first 19 years of Israel's existence were lean and besieged. Jerusalem, the Israeli capital, was divided. The old city with its holy sites was controlled by Jordan. Palestinian raiders routinely penetrated Israel's borders, terrorizing and killing Israeli civilians. The Arab states, particularly Nasser's Egypt, vociferously threatened Israel's existence. Arab leaders vowed to uproot what they saw as both a tool of Western imperialism and an oppressor of the Palestinians. The Arab defeat at Israeli hands in 1948 continued to weigh heavy on the minds of Arab leaders.[19]

The religious Zionist community was dominated by voices who supported, in differing intensities, the national vision promoted by Rabbi Reines. That is, most religious Zionists saw themselves as a bridge between the beleaguered state and its Jewish heritage. They thought of this heritage as a common ground that offers comfort and belonging, and certainly not as a political narrative or even a theology. Faith was,

---

[18] That is, "Jewish" removed from "Jewish and Democratic" and providing exclusive legitimacy to the Zionist project.

[19] See, for example: Adeed Dawisha, *Arab Nationalism in the Twentieth Century: From Triumph to Despair* (Princeton University Press, 2003), Chapter 6.

for the mainstream of the religious Zionist community, an inspiration best drawn quietly and communally rather than in committed, national fashion.

Rabbi Tzvi Yehuda's insistence on the articulation of a new, faith-based national narrative was a radical event. It was radical in circumstantial fashion, because of the turn of events that followed his words. In his talk, which we shall read shortly, he spoke about the sad, divided state of the Promised Land. He asserted Jewish and Israeli sovereignty over the biblical haunts of the patriarchs, from Hebron to Nablus and the Old City of Jerusalem. These territories were "liberated" three weeks later as part of the Six-Day War, a victory so comprehensive it seemed to many a prophecy fulfilled.

Another aspect of radicalness in Rabbi Tzvi Yehuda's words lay in their overt, unapologizing combination of the devotional and the political. He understood action to be inherently political. Since action and faith sustained and expanded each other, faith was politics. Rabbi Tzvi Yehuda was not the first to make this claim, but his message carries a sense of indivisible urgency. His father had pursued a project of modernist mysticism, reconciling observable realities with a divine truth. Rabbi Tzvi Yehuda was concerned with applying his father's truths to the imperfect realities of a functioning state. He was a radical, in other words, because he dove headfirst into the relationship between faith and sovereignty. If God is the ultimate sovereign and his divine truth, the redemption God offers, if manifested in the creation of a Jewish state, in what ways is that state sovereign? Rabbi Tzvi Yehuda's narrative rationale for Israel is an attempt to address this question.

After the Six-Day War, particularly at the end of the 1970s, Rabbi Tzvi Yehuda's vision was concretized with ever-growing success. The settlements in the occupied territories were the executive arm of this movement. Their growth, in defiance of international law and through the coopted compliance of all Israeli governments, was presented as a reinstatement of true Jewish sovereignty over land as well as history. Nonetheless, those same Israeli governments refrained from annexing the territories to Israel proper. The Israeli state exercised effective sovereignty over the territories through martial law, enacted and enforced on the authority of the local military commander.

This irresolvable tension between sovereignties gradually turned the settlers' leadership into one of the most (if not the most) powerful political lobbies in Israel. On the one hand, the settlements became a complex enterprise. They were (and are) home to hundreds of thousands of people; bolster Israeli presence, military and civilian, in hotly contested territory; and are extensively budgeted by the state of Israel. Many would have much to lose if settler interests are not properly addressed. On the other hand, regardless of how the settlements grow, no amount of rhetoric has been sufficient for the physical Israeli presence in the occupied territories to "settle in the hearts"[20] of Israelis. The occupied territories and the settlements are still considered removed from Israel proper by most Israelis residing within the 1967 borders. The settler lobby's other main task, alongside the physical upkeep of the settlements, remains the rhetorical battle for intra-Israeli legitimacy.

The settler movement (as it is known today) has for some time, then, dedicated itself to its own perpetuation and justification, as large, elaborate systems are prone to do. During disengagement, in 2005, even during the largest settler protests (and some of them involved hundreds of thousands of Israelis), the settler leadership did not offer a new, oppositional national narrative. Disengagement caused great anguish, drove thousands of people from their homes and created real tension between the Israeli state and its religious Zionist citizens.[21] Still, the settlers in Gaza and the West Bank focused on attempting to prevent the upcoming evacuation through acts of civil disobedience. Their Israeli narrative, the narrative grounding their perseverance within the Israeli collective despite the evils visited upon them by the state, was the narrative formulated by Rabbi Tzvi Yehuda Kook and his students.

This state of affairs leads me to offer Rabbi Tzvi Yehuda's 1967 talk as a foundational counterweight to Ariel Sharon's 2003 speech. Despite the chronological incongruity, I believe the Rabbi's text lies at the second defining end of the Israeli spectrum. The conflict between the narratives, which came to a head in the execution of Sharon's disengagement plan, set the stage for the Israeli theology of the real, which we will consider at the end of the chapter.

---

[20] An expression coined by Rabbi Yoel Ben Nun, a prominent religious Zionist and settler thinker, in an article published in the settler journal *Nekudah* in 1992.

[21] See, for example, Smadar Ben Asher's chapter (in Hebrew) entitled "Depression among Gaza Evacuees as Social Representation with a Rehabilitative role," in Haim Misgav and Udi Lebel (eds.), *In the Shadow of the Disengagement* (Carmel Publishing, 2008), pp. 183–203.

## Psalm 19: Rabbi Tzvi Yehuda Kook on Israeli Independence Day, 1967[22]

### A. The righteous and the honest look upon God's works

*Nineteen years. From time to time, and we should do so more frequently, we have the privilege of realizing the last verses of Psalm 107, the psalm we say on the eve of our independence as our Rabbinate has instructed us: "They saw the works of God ... The honest will see and rejoice ... Who is wise will remember this and observe the grace of God." The honest look upon God's works ... May we be included among the honest, and perhaps even the "righteous and honest" ... If honesty is lacking in the righteous – the acknowledgment of God's works is also lacking. We must observe, as much as we can, the works of God, his teaching and providence both collective and individual, within the introspection and the life of the people of Israel. We must grow accustomed to open our eyes and discover endless wonders from God's words (Torah) and endless wonders from god's actions.*

*Nineteen years. Things should appear as new to us every day. One must grow accustomed to feeling it. It seems we have progressed and grown accustomed to celebrating our acceptance of the holy burden, the burden which appears with the establishment of the kingdom of Israel. Still, there were times, during the state's first years, when we did not celebrate in the yeshiva, when I would walk the streets of Jerusalem to take part in the celebration of our people and our land with the crowd, the boys and the girls, the common folk. Unfortunately, the nearly sacrilegious question arose: where were the elders, the Torah sages, when the people celebrated on the streets of Jerusalem?*

Awareness of God's presence, of divine truth which is constantly occurring around us, demands work on our part. We must be honest, and the main expression of this honesty is the expansion of our awareness. The time that has passed since the establishment of Israel carries the threat of imperviousness and indifference to divine truth. This truth is the object of our aspirations, but it is also at the root of our daily reality. God ultimately redeems and routinely sustains. The tension inherent in this double function can be reduced if we are constantly in motion, upward and outward. Striving to expand is the basic act of a believer because it constantly challenges reality. Faith is nothing if it is not directed at something that surpasses (from above and from below) the (limited) human perception of the real.

The establishment of the Israeli state is a showcase of divine works and divine truth. It is a rare occasion in which simple faith and the joy

---

[22] All translations are my own. I've omitted certain references to rabbinic literature at times, in order to facilitate the reading of the text.

such faith creates are directed at an overt example of divine presence. The believer believes and God delivers. Still, there is one fly in the ointment. The sages, the carriers of Jewish sovereignty, they were not celebrating. As divine truth seeps into human truth, the wise remain aloof. What is the reason for this dissonance?

**B. With the decision of the nations on the resurrection of the state of Israel – came the decision on partition of the land**

*Nineteen years ago, on that famous night, when news reached us of the positive decision made by world leaders regarding the resurrection of the state of Israel, as the entire people celebrated their joy together in the streets, I could not go outside and join the merriment. I sat alone, shouldering a heavy burden. During those first few hours I could not accept what was done, the terrible news that God's word in the prophecy had come true – "They divided my land"! Where is our Hebron – have we forgotten? Where is our Nablus – have we forgotten? Where is our Jericho – have we forgotten? Where is our Transjordan? Where is every single clod of land? Each and every part of God's country? Is it in our hands to forsake even a millimeter of this land? Heaven forfend.*

*In such a state, my entire body shaken and bruised – I could not then be happy. This is how it was 19 years ago, on that night and during those hours. Our great friend, Rabbi Ya'akov Moshe Harlap came to our home the next day – He needed to come and how could he not have come? We sat together for a few moments, silent and shaken in that small, holy room ... Finally we came to our senses and said as one: "This comes from God, It is beyond our grasp." The seal had been set.*

There is a difference between leading a state and leading a community of faith. A state comes into being in an orderly way, subject to rules and regulations as well as the applier of such rules. The sovereignty of a state is contextual, created in relation to that of other states. A state has no inherent wonders or grace. It does what it can do, no more and no less. The state can be a manifestation of providence, but it is not providential in nature. A community of faith, on the other hand, is never simply what it is. In private, in "small (,) holy rooms," faith requires acknowledgment. The finality of divine truth is best approached alone (or with a trusted friend). A person is born alone and dies alone, the two most final truths of every life.

In public, however, in the political mode, faith demands aspiration. Alongside its finality, divine truth is a living, occurring truth. The single believer can accept the prophecy's remaining unfulfilled. The community of believers must actively not forget or forsake. This active memory is providential. It demonstrates a link to a divine reality pulsating above and below the ordinary, visible, every day. The politically faithful strive to discern God's work in every aspect of their lives. Political faith manifests a dynamic totality.

**C. Thank God that we have come to this that we no longer consider the opinions of the gentiles so much**

*And now, with the holy chain continuing to coalesce, the divine campaign revealed in all its spiritual and practical levels through political and historical events, we have come to this elaborate wonder, to our holy day – and without our gentile "in-laws," thank God! All these years we ask the Lord of the world: "Break our yokes from about our necks and lead us forthright to our land." We have, to some extent, both practically and symbolically, achieved the breaking of the gentile yoke from our necks – may we be blessed!*

*We should also mention this: Near the end of Rabbi Meir Bar-Ilan's life ... He served as the host of an important gathering of religious Zionists. The chairman of the Jewish Agency, Mr. Berl Locker, also participated and spoke. A discussion was held in the United Nations at the time regarding the possibility of internationalizing Jerusalem, and Berl Locker mentioned the Jerusalem issue and described it as extremely delicate, requiring much tact and careful handling, and so on and so forth. Hearing him, Rabbi Meir burst into his speech, speaking Yiddish, and called loudly from behind him: "War Hart Sei?" Who listens to them? Who cares about their opinion? They will tell us what to do with Jerusalem? This was the reaction of Rabbi Bar-Ilan, who was full of virtue and holiness, a reaction of faith, Torah, holiness, fear of God, a reaction of certainty and not doubt.*

This is not a discussion about political philosophy, but about politics. Rabbi Tzvi Yehuda considers the role of faith in the practical context of redemption. Let's turn that sentence on its head for a second. For Rabbi Tzvi Yehuda, this discussion is pertinent because redemption is occurring all around us. Training ourselves to acknowledge God's works all around us is not an ethical commitment. This acknowledgment is a practical necessity if we are to play our roles in the unfolding divine drama.

Of course, "we" and "us" refer exclusively to Jews. Rabbi Tzvi Yehuda paid lip service to the goodwill of the world, but the dynamic of redemption asserts the tension and the mistrust between Jews and the world. The work described by Rabbi Tzvi Yehuda, the striving for extension and expansion, depends on the ability to draw the initial line between Jews and the world. This line originates in the depths of the Jewish soul, a sort of id where one of the paragons of holiness and moderation, Rabbi Meir Bar-Ilan, loudly flouts courtesy and does so in Yiddish. The truth of

Jewish uniqueness is a basic one, perhaps the most basic, when the political reality of redemption is acknowledged.

**D. The Chief Rabbinate did not decree that Hallel should be said with a blessing on Independence Day because a large part of our public does not believe in the scope of God's works**

*As for the day itself, we should ascertain a few things:*

*One Friday evening, before Independence Day, an important man asked me why our rabbis do not allow us to say the Hallel with a blessing on Independence Day. I told him that the Chief Rabbinate's instruction is just and proper. Its regulations are meant for the entire public, and as to our sorrow and disgrace a large part of our public does not believe in the scope of God's works revealed to us by the establishment of the kingdom of Israel, and as the lack of faith breeds a lack of joy, this part of the public cannot be obligated to say the blessing. Think of this example: A person who sees his friend and is happy upon seeing him, should greet him. If he is happy – he may greet. If he is not happy, he does not greet.*

*Rabbi Maimon, who was completely devoted to the rebuilding of God's people and land, he was full of the joy of faith and thus determined that the Hallel would be said with a blessing in his synagogue. This is true for other places – the Israeli military and the religious kibbutzim. But the Chief Rabbinate, the inclusive rabbinate, cannot decree that such a blessing be made obligatory for the entire public when this public is not ready for it. In our yeshiva we follow the Rabbinate's decree, because we are not a sectorial school. We belong to the heart of the people of Israel in Jerusalem. Because faith and joy are lacking, to our sorrow and our shame, among the general public the blessing cannot be made obligatory and we should follow the Rabbinate's instructions to the public at large.*

The *Hallel* (literally, "praise!" in the imperative) is a prayer said on holidays commemorating miraculous events that have occurred to the Jews. Such miracles include receiving the Torah at Sinai (Shavuot), the exodus from Egypt (Passover), the victory of the Maccabees over the Seleucid Empire and the temple miracle (Hanukkah) and others. The *Hallel* has two forms: the full prayer said with blessings at its beginning and end and a version lacking blessings. The full version is considered the more festive one, signifying a celebration of redemption and not simply deliverance from evil. The debate over saying the *Hallel* on Israeli Independence Day was a heated one. Religious Zionist rabbis supported saying the prayer, as they considered the establishment of the state to be a sign of redemption. Ultra-orthodox rabbis disagreed, unable to see divine presence in a secular "Jewish" state. Still, the Chief Rabbinate of Israel, an organ of the state, decreed that the *Hallel* should be said without a blessing. This was a political choice, meant to ameliorate the effects of the rabbinical debate.

In 1974, the Chief Rabbinate decreed that the *Hallel* should be said with the blessings, a sign of the waning influence of the ultra-orthodox rabbis on the Israeli state "proper." Still, on Independence Day of 1967, Rabbi Tzvi Yehuda was referring to a state of affairs in which the *Hallel* was said without a blessing.

For Rabbi Tzvi Yehuda, this is a sorry state. His faith in redemption, necessitating a full *Hallel*, seems to have two sides. Faith is justified by the objective nature of redemption, the truth of God's direct involvement in the salvation of the Jews as expressed by the establishment of Israel. Faith is validated by the will of the believer to believe, to see the scope of God's works. The truth of redemption is not sufficient to trump a lack of believing will. The inherent tension between "objectivity" and "subjectivity" is addressed politically. Rabbi Tzvi Yehuda's faith, in practice, is not exclusively theological or moral/ethical because it is not a matter for an individual, alone or with respect to God. Faith in redemption lives in and through the body politic. The determination of the *Hallel* and its format is a political gauntlet, lying before those who would be political leaders.

### E. There is no "My strength (has delivered me)" in the Independence Day parade

*This same person argued another point with me. Why should not the Rabbinate forbid the public to watch the military parade? After all, it may evoke the argument that "my strength (has delivered me)."[23] Still, there is nothing wrong with watching the parade because when we remember that it is God who gives us the strength to win then it is not "my strength" in the negative sense, but the study and the upholding of Torah: We learn that we must carry out the instruction imposed upon us through this strength – to take our land. Not everybody fulfills this instruction with full intentions, with the desire to celebrate the oneness and unity of god. Still, the instruction, the mitzvah, is ultimately fulfilled. It is an instruction meant for the entire people of Israel, imposed upon us all. For this reason, everything that pertains to it, including all the weapons made by us and by the gentiles, everything that belongs to this day of resurrecting the kingdom of Israel – It is all holy!*

How is the body politic established? It begins through physical presence. Attendance at the Independence Day parade reflects the general commitment to the physical instruction incumbent upon the entire people: to take the land that is rightfully theirs. Redemption, God's active role in

---

[23] Deuteronomy 8:17. The chapter, which describes the positive rewards that will come to those who obey God's instructions, also warns the believer not to succumb to the temptation ascribing his or her worldly success to their own strength. They must remember that they were delivered through God's strength.

human events, is an ongoing process. It does not require adoption on the part of the redeemed in order to be validated. Conversely, people are people. They cannot be expected to demonstrate a unity of faith and purpose. Both truths are real and undeniable. Their realness makes their fusion into a physical political entity a difficult undertaking. Can you embrace one without detracting from the other?

Then again, this difficulty is truly difficult only if one seeks to strike a balance, a reasonable interaction between God's will (and works) and the propensities of actual people. The most major challenge for a politics of balance would be its definition of political sovereignty. If the two realities, the two truths, occur simultaneously and of their own volition, who can be considered in charge? In a political framework, power is divided and order maintained through an acceptable authority. Once one recognizes two truths, valid independently of each other, how can sovereign authority be asserted in a meaningful, effective way?

Rabbi Tzvi Yehuda's solution is not based on balance. His integration of the divine and the human is based on expansion. If you lack in faith as an individual, the collective will compensate for your lack. If the state is incapable of producing the weapons required in order to reach its divinely decreed size, it is legitimate to draw upon gentile-made weapons. The parade on Independence Day is permissible, desirable even, because it allows for a coming together. General attendance merges the individual and the state into a union pointed forward. The dynamic of redemption moves ever upward and outward with no need for equilibrium. Redemption is total and whole, the truth to top all truths. This knowledge liberates and constrains the body politic. Totality offers a constant horizon, an incentive for striving to expand. Simultaneously, totality undermines political attempts to "get it right." Sovereignty is inherently fragile in the face of totality, whether such sovereignty arises from the purity of a religious community or the military strength of the state. With the complete truth both constantly occurring and just beyond one's grasp, it is difficult to establish authority, or to distinguish the mundane from the miraculous.

### F. The value of Independence Day as an initial demonstration of redemption – As revealed in the holy texts

*There are some sages who view the value of our state's day in its demonstration of deliverance, but consider the day's redemptive qualities to belong to the realms of divine mysteries. When confronted with such explanations, we should make it clear that this is not the case. The redemption inherent in our state's day are not mysteries, but clear and overt. In the Talmud (Sanhedrin, 97–98), Rabbi Yehoshua deduces that redemption need not come only after the complete repentance of the people. Rabbi Eliezer, who disagrees with him, remained quiet ... The explanation is simple. Rabbi Eliezer's silence is an acceptance (of Rabbi Yehoshua's statement). No one disagrees. It is clearly written: "Repent, o Israel, for I have redeemed you." Repentance will come after redemption.*

*Following this debate we find the words of Rabbi Abba: "And Rabbi Abba said: There is no clearer demonstration of the final times than the following verse: 'And you, mountains of Israel, your branches shall bud and you shall bear fruit for Israel, my people, for they will soon return'" (Ezekiel 36). What are the marks of redemption – the settlement of Eretz Yisrael (the land of Israel) and the return of the Jews from exile. Let us engage with the details. Why does the text say "**and** Rabbi Abba said"? Rabbi Yehoshua and Rabbi Eliezer argued long decades before Rabbi Abba, so how are the two statements related? We must assume that the relation is based on content. As the earlier rabbis deduce that redemption is not conditional upon repentance – this is their conclusion – how can we know redemption? We know when the land of Israel bears bountiful fruit. With God's blessings, our land is bearing exceedingly bountiful fruit ...*

This display of rabbinical interpretative technique demonstrates the effect of expansion as political rationale. Rabbi Tzvi Yehuda begins with the downplaying of repentance as a harbinger and engine of redemption. Human[24] instinct links redemption to repentance, assuming that redemption is the ultimate prize for complete repentance. Repentance means ultimate submission, the human (Jewish human, of course) acknowledgment of God's sovereignty. Rabbi Tzvi Yehuda interprets the Talmudic debate in Sanhedrin as a rejection of this supposed connection. Redemption, divine truth, is total and dynamic. It is not dependent on the human acknowledgment at play in repentance. God's sovereignty does not require human obedience as validation. Once again, this elevates and lowers human potential simultaneously. Humans are allowed to approach divine truth and play their part in its unfolding. On the other hand, humans are not expected to earn redemption by, say, leading a virtuous life in accordance with clear ethical standards.

Rabbi Tzvi Yehuda denies the "mystery" other rabbis see in the truth of redemption. This denial removes the mystery from "faith" as a cornerstone of the relationship between humans and God. They mystery now lies within the political, and particularly within the notion of sovereignty.

---

[24] I use "humans" in order to underscore the broader theological implications of this discussion. Rabbi Tzvi Yehuda, it is worth restating, is referring to Jews.

This new political mystery is driven by silence. If repentance is no longer necessary, what defines authority in redeemed society? His answer, based on hermeneutical prowess, expands authority beyond the human. Rabbi Abba, historically removed from the first debate, suggests that the mark of redemption will be found in nature, tangible and beyond controversy. The Holy Land will bear fruit when the return of the exiles is near. The pattern and timing of redemption are cosmic, or elemental at the very least. There is no need for rabbinical reason or discernment before the immediate impact of nature's verdict. The body politic, the returned exiles, will converge when there is no other choice. The present is relevant as a showcase for these trans-human dynamics. The time is now and the place is here.

### G. The state of Israel as the fulfillment of the positive commandment to settle Eretz Yisrael

*Continuing to look into the textual origins, The words of Nahmanides[25] in his "Book of the Commandments" (Sefer Hamitzvot) ... are clear: "We were commanded to inherit and take the land God gave to our forefather, Abraham, Isaac and Jacob, and was not left for any nation but us ... we shall not forsake the land into their hands ... or the hands of any other nation at any time." This a direct Halacha, a valid religious ruling.*

*Nahmanides continues: "I say that this commandment held so dear by the sages, residing in the land of Israel, it is all a positive commandment, an instruction to act – we were commanded to take the land and settle in it ..." The meaning of this is clear. The main part of the commandment is the institutional, national and all-Israeli occupation of this holy territory. From this general commandment the private instruction incumbent upon every Jews is derived, the instruction to reside in the land of Israel ... the commandment is to occupy and to reside, not simply to reside.*

*Villainous words have been posted on the walls of certain neighborhoods, accusing the "heretic Zionists" who wish to make us into a "fighting people." Does the Torah not command us to carry out religiously justified wars[26] ... Did we not hear of the commandment to fight and occupy from Nahmanides himself? With God's blessings we have been fortunate in the past, and are fortunate even now, to fulfill God's command through the glorious valor of our military. To summarize briefly: Jewish rule in the holy land, that is the state of Israel and its military, are a commandment imposed on all of Israel, important and direct, alongside being a part of an overt redemption.*

---

[25] Rabbi Moshe ben Nahman, known in Hebrew as Ramban, was a prominent Jewish sage and philosopher who lived in thirteenth-century Spain. See https://en.wikipedia.org/wiki/Nahmanides (last accessed on October 18, 2016).

[26] Wars sanctioned in order to take control of the land of Israel, for example.

The body politic, its fighting force but also its institutions and its collectivity, are both a part of direct divine intervention and of an ongoing human effort. The human effort, Rabbi Tzvi Yehuda emphasizes, is an effort of occupation and this occupation is imposed upon the general Jewish public in Israel. Throughout Jewish history, sages presented simple residence within the territorial confines of the Holy Land as a virtue. This is not enough. Individual residence is a derivative of collective occupation. Occupation is a dynamic more than a campaign. It generates convergence and motion. Both are required for the utilization of redemption into politics.

Redemption is a tense process, particularly when it comes to the Jewish state. The state demands authority, as states will, on the merit of its institutional practices. States fight, collect taxes and establish borders. States are not divine endeavors. They are also not communal enterprises in the immediate, almost-familial sense of "communal" that had characterized Jewish existence for long centuries. The Israeli state cannot entrust itself wholly to God, just as it cannot exist as an extension of a ghetto or a North African *Mellah*.[27] In terms of sovereign authority, rabbis are not in charge of the state and neither is God. The temptation to remain passive, according to Rabbi Tzvi Yehuda, is an existential challenge to the sovereignty of the state's institutions. They will withstand this challenge, abstain from sinking into mildness, only if they invest their resources in active expansion.

### H. The holiness of Independence Day

*While discussing matters of law a sage told me that Independence Day, with all of its importance regarding salvation and deliverance, is devoid of holiness. But when we have faith in God's words as we discussed before, the mountains bearing fruit and the commandment to occupy the land which holds for every generation, then we can see the clear validity of the reality of holiness, made apparent when we fulfill the commandment, "he has made us holy with his commandments"! Holiness is a real reality, and not an emotional or a humanistic figure of speech. The reality of holiness is not determined by us; God has determined that we are a holy people, a factual reality of holy souls in holy bodies, becoming individuals out of a general Israelite soul which is all holiness. There is a reality of a holy land, a territory chosen by God ... This is a land the fruit of which is holy, a land the tilling of which amounts to the mitzvah of putting on tefillin (phylacteries) ... So it has been determined: This is the holy land and this is the holy people!*

[27] Jewish quarter in Moroccan cities. See https://en.wikipedia.org/wiki/Mellah (last accessed on October 18, 2016).

*The Rabbi of Chortkov told me once in Vienna that he understood, from my father's work, that all of Israel's corporeality is holy. This is very clear. Everything that belongs to Israel is holy. When one does not take time to study the basic elements of faith, they are forgotten: Every criminal of (the people of) Israel is holy – in spite of his nature! This is the Torah reality that determines: "I have created this people for myself." Thus, it is clear that there is much holiness in the day which established the state of the holy people on the holy land.*

The reality of holiness precedes the goodness of holiness. In fact, even a criminal can be holy if he is a part of God's chosen people. This is clearly what the text says, but it is not a simple point. Equating holiness and goodness is an understandable temptation. If holy is good, one can try to be as good as one can, and assume that these efforts will increase his or her holiness. In other words, the more one is good, the closer one is to God and God's perfect, consoling truth.

Rabbi Tzvi Yehuda describes a different state of affairs. Holiness is, first and foremost, real. The Jewish people and Eretz Yisrael, the land of Israel,[28] are holy because God made them so. God's creation is both true and real. The rejoining of the people and the land, celebrated on Independence Day, is a celebration of holiness, the integration of the true and the real. The undisputed holiness of the day reveals the challenge of other days. Fault lines have already been exposed in the new state and its new society. There are those who want a state above all, one that regulates and fights. Others find it difficult to forgo the communal, diasporic aspects of Jewish existence. The reality of holiness is a challenging reality because within its unfolding people (by definition) are found lacking, perhaps less than real. For Rabbi Tzvi Yehuda, expansion is the only way to transcend the fault lines in order to create a sustainable polity.

## I. The state as a realization of prophetic vision

*And in answer to the question, "Is this the state our prophets foresaw?" I will say: this is indeed the state the prophets foresaw. It is not perfect, of course, but our prophets and rabbis, their heirs, said that the state would be this way. The seed of Abraham, Isaac and Jacob would return and establish communal life and independent political rule. We were not told if they would be righteous or less than righteous. The prophet Ezekiel says: "When I gather the house of Israel ... they will reside on their land ... They will reside safely, build houses and plant vineyards ..." (Ezekiel 28:25–26). He mentions planting vineyards, but not building yeshivas ... It is true that by returning Israel to their land we*

---

[28] That is, "the Promised Land," "the Holy Land," rather than a geographically and legally defined spatial entity. "Eretz" is Hebrew for "Land," rather than "State."

*will increase the glory of Torah, but the first step is to have the people of Israel on their land! Rabbi Eliyahu Gutermacher said: "If 130 families began tilling the holy land, redemption will begin even if the people are not worthy." This sage obviously wants a greater role for Torah and faith, but the order of redemption is agricultural communities, the establishment of the state and from the state, to continue onward, to rise in holiness, to instill and glorify Torah.*

Rabbi Tzvi Yehuda continues his elucidation of expansion as the required dynamic of the Jewish body politic. The biblical prophets were the ones who spoke truth to power. Their prophecies integrated scathing criticism of their current political realities along with soaring visions of just, alternative political orders that will come into being in the future. They were, perhaps, the most actively political protagonists of Jewish scripture. The Israeli proclamation of independence describes the Israeli state as one that "will be based on freedom, justice and peace as envisaged by the prophets of Israel."[29]

The principles these prophets advocated were uncompromising. Their standing before wayward kings or entire kingdoms was based on their solid grounding in divine truth as revealed by God. Rabbi Tzvi Yehuda interprets their vision differently. The borders of the spectrum are known. God created the people of Israel for himself and designated their land holy as well. God will return the people of Israel to their land and their existence will be a model of virtue and justice.[30] Creation and return are real and certain. How can the time and space between these real borders achieve some degree of certitude despite their middling nature?

According to Rabbi Tzvi Yehuda, the political reality of the prophetic vision is one of expansion. One knows redemption through its orderly unfolding but remarkably, there is no predefined end. It begins with physical presence and moves on to establishing institutions. Once these are established, there is necessary, interminable forward motion. The sovereignty of the state, its institutional effectiveness and coherence, is a means for the perpetuation of this forward motion. The liberal nation-state enjoys an institutional coherence that makes the state an end in and of itself. Within Rabbi Tzvi Yehuda's framework of redemption, the

---

[29] See www.knesset.gov.il/docs/eng/megilat_eng.htm.

[30] In the words of the prophet Isaiah: "In the last days, the mountain of the Lord's temple will be established as the highest of the mountains ... Many peoples will come and say: Come, let us go to the mountain of the lord ... He will teach us his ways ... The law will go out from Zion, the word of God from Jerusalem ..." (Isaiah 2:2–4). See www.biblegateway.com/passage/?search=Isaiah+2.

apparatus of the state enjoys no such coherence. The state cannot justify its existence as a manifestation of moral or political truth, because its existence is not bound up in any truth but its own physical realness. The truth of the state lies in keeping up with divine redemption as it unfolds. This can be accomplished only through expansion.

**J. Refuting God's works revealed to us amounts to refuting the written Torah, the oral Torah and the words of the prophets.**

*We have already stated, to our shame and sorrow, that a large part of our public does not believe in the miracles revealed to us. We should speak clearly on this point for once, without wavering. This is a lack of faith, heresy disguising itself in robes of piety and devotion, heretics calling others by that name. This is a case of the pot calling the kettle black! It is heresy against the written Torah, the words of our prophets and the oral Torah, which have all clarified to us how we might know the end – when the land of Israel bears bountiful fruit. How dare they brazenly disrespect the great sages of Israel ... this heresy against God's works and his grace towards us, a heresy dressed as a vicious righteousness, this is what keeps God's word from coming and being revealed in the world. There are even those who hesitate in our circles, fearing the fall into doubt. But we must remember that faith is not doubt ... When Jews subjugate their hearts to their father in heaven – there comes complete redemption.*

Those who do not believe are not the "secular" Zionists, but the ultra-orthodox. Faith is not a function of self-imposed devotion, but of realism. Rabbi Tzvi Yehuda's first demand from his listeners was an active effort to become aware of God's works in the real world. Those who insist on the confines of orthodoxy are the ones who cannot emerge from their cocoon in order to engage (and take part in) reality as it emerges. Their righteousness is a vicious righteousness because it denies them the dilation necessary to believe politically. Their faith falters before the institutional existence of the Israeli state with its wars and secularity. This tension undermines any ultra-orthodox attempt to assert Jewish sovereignty before the world or before God.

With these viciously righteous believers stand those who fear doubt even more than change. Rabbi Tzvi Yehuda identifies them as belonging to "our circles," and most likely means religious Zionists. Their see their faith as "correct"' rather than simply "ordained." To opt for struggle and uncertainty, even for drama, is to reject this correctness. This view limits the political viability of faith because it leaves no leeway for adaptation. The ultra-orthodox mentioned by Rabbi Tzvi Yehuda are, at the very least, combative. They are circling the wagons before the Jewish state and actively defending their beliefs. Those who fear doubt oppose the amplification of awareness required for redemption by opting out of redemption's unfolding. Their politics prize stability above all. Rabbi Tzvi Yehuda rejects this stability. His vision of political sovereignty is based on propulsive motion.

**K. Israel's redemption is a continuous, realistic fact, even if it is not acknowledged with utter faith.**

*There has been constant development for 19 years now. Each day leads onward to the next. We are privileged to witness God's wonders and mysteries – in construction, agriculture, policy, security, corporeality and spirituality. The realness of this divine affair does not change or fade, whether those who engage in it acknowledge this through utter faith or they show no acknowledgment. (The people of) Israel preceded the world, standing in the middle of the heavens and proclaiming "may the name of his glory and kingdom be blessed forever." Israel received the Torah, the "hidden jewel" Moses brought down to us – the people of Israel have left a great impression in all the worlds. True Israel is redeemed Israel, in state and military, a people complete without diasporas. Therefore, when Israel was exiled all the worlds shook. The same occurs with redemption. The shock went through all the worlds, stage by stage, until it reached us, just like Torah went through all the worlds until it reached us. This passage, this linking of worlds, is gradual and ongoing, every year is another psalm, divine and glorious, added as a link to the chain. This year, we recite the 19th psalm.*

So far, we have dealt mostly with the implications and manifestations of redemption in this world, the human world, and the relationship between redemption and the axis of history. Now we are presented with a cosmology of redemption. This cosmos is defined by the two natures of redemption. At the grand, divine level, redemption is the return to the pristine stability of the divine presence. At the worldly level, redemption is a dynamic which links and drives all the worlds. Redemption is constant motion and holistic glory, each carrying the promise of the other.

Of course, we can replace "redemption" with "Israel," used by Rabbi Tzvi Yehuda to mean "the Jewish people." The Jewish people are the embodiment of redemption. They celebrate divine perfection at the heart of creation and they are the ones connecting the worlds, moving only forward. This strikes me as an important point. "Israel" is not just an object of redemption, its status a sign of divine success or failure. The Jewish people *are* redemption.

While there is a wholeness here, there is also a strain that is borne particularly by a Jewish state. Only one face of redemption, according to this description, is sovereign: redemption-that-is-motion, redemption that expands until it includes all the worlds. This is the redemption that demands awareness from the redeemed. The other redemption,

redemption-that-is-glory, is a willfully subservient celebration of perfection. The second redemption has no need for a division of power, because power within it emanates exclusively from God. Awareness is the means for discovering order and meaning in constant motion. Such order and meaning are the bedrock of politics that are truly possible in a world based on faith.

The cost of this actuality, the real politics of faith, is the imperative of expansion. This is not just a geographical necessity, a result of the Jewish state's perilous existence in a hostile neighborhood. The shock sent by Israel's exile contracted all the worlds. The shock sent by their return will expand them. It is useful to remember the still presence that preceded the world, at the heart of all the worlds. That presence is not an attainable goal for the further progression of redemption. It is, at best, a horizon.

**L. The 19th psalm: We begin in earthly nature and come to the spiritual and the celestial**

*The 19th psalm has two parts. In the first part we see the wonders of God in nature and his revelation in creation: "The heavens tell the glory of God and the sky speaks his works." The second part of the psalm describes the Torah, the commandments and devotion to God, all pure and illuminating. This relation has been clarified before ... God's power is revealed in the wondrous world of nature, but holiness always increases, and the force of his revelation through Torah and devotion given to Israel is even greater ... This is the psalm we sing on the 19th year. We will come to the spiritual and the celestial out of earthly nature – we build in the mundane and then we sanctify. We are commanded to reveal the holy from within the earthly element and to aid God in the act of creation ...*

Holiness always increases. Rabbi Tzvi Yehuda's words refer to a rule of Halakha, religious Jewish law, which states that one should always increase holiness rather than decrease it. The Talmudic discussion often cited as the source of this rule was held between two of the greatest Jewish sages, Hillel and Shamai, regarding the lighting order of Hanukkah candles. The Hanukkah menorah holds eight candles, and Shamai suggested that on the first night of the holiday all eight will be lit with one less candle lit every subsequent day. This was in resemblance to another Jewish holiday, Sukkot, during which bulls in decreasing numbers were sacrificed daily at the temple in Jerusalem. Hillel suggested that one candle be lit on the first night, with one more candle added on each day of the holiday. On the final day, eight candles would be lit. Hillel's reasoning – holiness must be increased, not decreased.

This story demonstrates the dualism of holiness in Rabbi Tzvi Yehuda's words. The state of Israel and the Jewish people are holy. This holiness is real and undisputed, guaranteed by God's self-declared bond to the Jews. This holiness cannot even be thought of as status. It is the origin. There is also holiness as a goal, a totality that lies beyond any conscious attempt to grasp it. There is no end to the Torah or to devotion to God.

The divine nature of the end and the beginning are common monotheistic themes. One of the maxims of Islam is "From him, to him," suggesting that the motion of human life is from God (before birth) and to God (after death). They frame a single, divinely inspired continuum. But where does this leave an Israeli Jew in 1967, eager for context and meaning in daily life? In terms we have already used, this framework makes it difficult for an actual Jew to locate himself with regard to the divine through triangulation. There is no third point allowing for a particular human existence, but only motion between the two faces of holiness. Israel and the Jews play a role in the divine drama, but they have no internal coherence of their own outside (or in relation) to this drama.

The actual existence of Jews in Israel, then, can be justified only by expansive, expanding motion. Ariel Sharon escaped the persuasive pull of totality and infinity by placing faith in drawn lines defining (and limiting) the Israeli state. Rabbi Tzvi Yehuda is not interested in achieving escape velocity. Jewish life is rooted in a holiness imposed by God. The Israeli narrative in this holy mode is a story of striving to meet the absolute truths of holiness. Such striving requires the ongoing enhancement of awareness, awe and commitment. These are necessary in ever-increasing quantity, because the state's order cannot validate or justify itself.

**M. There are painful things in the state of Israel with much blasphemy, but this does not remove the sanctification of God that exists in the state and its Independence Day.**

*We have no intention of flattering unbelievers, heaven forbid. There are painful things in the state of Israel with much blasphemy. (I am referring) especially (to) the two horrible menaces: the state's judicial system which applies Roman, Ottoman and British law – perhaps even Hottentot law – but does not base itself upon the true law of Israel … and the spiritual weakness and impotence towards those soul hunters, may their name and memory be erased … who fight us from within. Still, with all the horror of blasphemy, the great sanctification of God will in no way be removed from the matter of the state and its Independence Day.*

The judicial system is the greatest menace to Israeli holiness because it does not apply Jewish law in the daily life of the state. Rabbi Tzvi Yehuda, whose rabbinical authority is an authority vested in Jewish law,[31]

---

[31] A rabbi's title marks one's mastery of Jewish law.

understandably considers the reliance on non-Jewish law to be a source of constant personal sorrow to himself. Still, what he does not say is more important. Earlier he called ultra-orthodox criticism of the Israeli state and its sovereignty (as expressed in Independence Day and its military parade) a heretical impediment to revelation. He does not use such strong language when he considers the law of the new Jewish state. In fact, Rabbi Tzvi Yehuda can live with the tension.

The sovereignty of the Israeli state does not lie in its law, the epitome of the state's institutional spirit. Those who have faith can withstand the contradiction. What sort of faith is needed for this challenge? It should be faith in a divine truth that exceeds and supersedes the truth of the world. Jews should not rationally attempt to adapt to the way of the world (the political opinions of non-Jews, for example), but they should also refrain from rejecting the world (like those ultra-orthodox Jews who criticize the redemption inherent in the Israeli state). The world and its truths can reflect aspects of the divine dynamic, but no more.

The world traps faith, forcing it to reconcile or recede. A faith that exists in the world but not through it is faith as expansion. A particularly effective formulation of this faith appears in the work of Rabbi Nahman of Breslau, a Hassidic sage of the late eighteenth century known for his radical, mystically oriented work. He is particularly known for his direct exploration of the Jewish psyche, both individual and communal. Rabbi Nahman describes the dynamic of ideal Jewish faith in the following words:

Only Israel transcends all wisdom by its faith, even the heresy originating in the void. They believe in God with no intellectual inquiry, only with complete faith that God "fills all the worlds and surrounds all the worlds." Therefore, God is supposedly to be found in all the worlds and around all the worlds. But there must be some space between each type of his presence because otherwise, all would be one.

God created all of creation inside the void, that void which was created when he initially withdrew his presence. Therefore, we can say that the void surrounds the world. And God, which surrounds all the worlds, can thus be said to surround the void. This way, God can be said to be both in the world and surrounding the world. The void separates both of God's presences according to this scheme. However, faith suggests that God is both in all the worlds and surrounds them. And since he surrounds all the worlds, the void must have been created by his wisdom. After all, his divinity must exist there, only it cannot be grasped and he cannot be found in the void. Therefore, Israel transcends all questions, heresies and wisdoms originating in the void, because they know all of these cannot be answered. If an answer could be found, if God were present in the void, it would not be a void and creation could not have taken place.

Still, in truth they must have an answer, and God must actually reside in the supposed void.

But philosophical thinking will cause a person to sink into the void, because God cannot be found there (by philosophical thought). One only needs to believe that God surrounds the void, and that his divine presence actually infuses the void. For this reason Israel are called *'Ivrim* (those who transcend or cross over), because by their faith they transcend all wisdom, even that wisdom which is not wisdom, that is the heresy which emanates from the void.[32]

Rabbi Nahman refers to one of the basic Jewish mystical dilemmas. If God created everything and his presence fills everything, how is it that not everything is one being? How can there be human beings, who are born and die, within that eternal presence? The only answer possible is that God vacated his presence from some part of creation, and then created our world in that void.

This void is a paradox. Any attempt to explain it philosophically, embracing one aspect of the void over another[33] leads to an almost necessary heresy. The only way to transcend this void is to believe, simply and profoundly, in the possibility of having your cake and eating it, too. Particular cosmological machinations notwithstanding, Jews are called *'ivrim* (The Modern Hebrew term for "Hebrews") because their faith is capable of crossing over the conceptual obstacle of the paradox. Described by Rabbi Nahman as a river, the obstacle is what separates the purely divine (all presence) from the purely human (all void). Ideal faith is capable of expanding its presence and holding to both riverbanks.

This is the faith Rabbi Tzvi Yehuda places at the heart of Jewish political life in Israel. His faith cannot sit still and reconcile the opposing strands of redemption. The state of Israel is a challenge because it is the worldliest endeavor Jews have undertaken in millennia while being, according to Rabbi Tzvi Yehuda, the most direct encounter Jews have had with direct divine presence during the same period. In order to thrive, the state must strive outward and upward, in territory and in spirit, its politics driven by the simple faith of Israel that is beyond wisdom.

---

[32] See my translation of Rabbi Nahman's 64th teaching in his *Likutei Moharan* (Gleanings from our Teacher), appearing in *Shi'i Theology in Iran: The Challenge of Religious Experience* (Routledge, 2011), p. 162.

[33] For example, "if God created it, then it must exist" over "God is present in all of creation and, therefore, the void cannot exist."

**N. The order of redemption in the book of Ezekiel: Gathering and returning the Diasporas followed by complete repentance.**

*The order of redemption appears in Ezekiel 36: "I will sanctify my name" from "I shall take you from among the Gentiles and collect you from all the nations, and bring you to your land" and only later "I shall douse you with pure water and you shall be purified from all your sins ... and you shall follow my laws." The complete repentance and observance of the people will come only after the Diasporas are gathered and returned ...*

The institutional life of following laws, the stability of a functional social order, is part of a plan beginning with the gathering and returning of the diasporas. This gathering and return is the initial expansion, the defragmentation of the Jews. The heart of expansion is change brought about by motion. Holiness in the divine, absolute sense, the holiness that is perfection, can come only after the generation of motion. Redemption has God on the move, and the ritual of purification is a sign of this ongoing movement rather than vice versa.

**O. When there is, on the same matter, a side of sanctification and a side of blasphemy – the side sanctifying God is the decisive and obligatory of the two.**

*Seemingly one might say: there is a sanctification of God in the construction of the kingdom of Israel on the one hand, but there is blasphemy on the other. The Talmud, in the tractate "Kiddushin," has instructed us that "the sanctification of God is greater than blasphemy." This instruction, obviously, does not teach us that sanctification is always greater than blasphemy, but this is true when they are found together, when there are both sanctification and blasphemy on the same matter. One cannot simply grow inert at this state. The side of sanctification is greater, more decisive and obligatory. This is certainly true when it comes to this great, divine sanctification of God through the rejuvenation of all Israel. The more we continue to settle the land of Israel, by gathering the multitudes of (the people of) Israel into it, from a wholeness and greatness of faith in the realization of God's great work for us – so shall we be blessed by the various blasphemies disappearing. "Every valley shall be raised up, every mountain and hill made low; the rough ground shall become level, the rugged places a plain. And the glory of the Lord will be revealed, and all people will see it together.*

*For the mouth of the Lord has spoken." (Isaiah 40:4–5)*[34]

The sovereignty of a Jewish "kingdom," the authority and viability of the state, is greater than any accusations of blasphemy, but only because neither side can be discounted or ignored. The state wins the day because of its composite tensions and not despite them. This victory is not theoretical

---

[34] See www.biblegateway.com/passage/?search=Isaiah+40.

or abstract. Sanctification is a dynamic and must be enhanced in order to function. It is different from the static quality of "holiness," which will be achieved once the required motion has taken place.

Jews must settle their land by returning to it. They must then settle it, work it and from it constantly increase their spiritual awareness of God's redemption. Redemption needs to be acknowledged as it is enacted. Acknowledgment, awareness of redemption, is redemption is well. Rabbi Tzvi Yehuda begins his talk by establishing physical coordinates for redemption, benchmarks for completion. When we have every inch of the promised land, we may consider our mission accomplished, he says. But the prosperity of (the people of) Israel is not a function of their meeting divinely ordained goals. The cities of the patriarchs must and will be retaken, but Rabbi Tzvi Yehuda does not name them again or call actively for a retaking. The sovereignty of the Israeli state will not be handed down by God, and it will not be settled simply by attaining prescribed borders. Sovereignty is derived from conscious sanctification. The only way to do this, to live in awareness of God's emerging works, is to expand.

The world and its truths constrain the irresistible drive of the divine flow. Jews living in the world who wish to take part in redemption cannot allow themselves to be shaped by the world. Both embrace and rejection of the world are wishes for stability. Redemption, God's direct presence, constantly turns the world on its head. Rabbi Tzvi Yehuda's national narrative for Israel, his "Jewish" narrative, emerges from this tension.

Israel is a holy people, always-already chosen by God. This choice, however, cannot be the pillar of a political existence because it is static. Redemption, God's commitment to the Jews, begins with their return to their land. This return creates a new situation, a "shock" that runs throughout creation. The return of the Jews is not followed by an immediate coming of the messiah and an establishment of certain, divine rule. Returning Jews must establish a political order. They need to establish political sovereignty in order to expand their awareness of holiness in this world. Claiming (and/or taking) what they consider their ancestral land amounts to establishing a platform for this constant expansion.

Should Israeli Jews take their promised land, they will not be shaping redemption, says Rabbi Tzvi Yehuda. Redemption is ongoing and it is God's to shape and carry out. It is exhilarating, but it is also stressful because it threatens to undermine any attempt to manage the gathering of diasporas, to establish a "kingdom," to create a polity. This polity needs to be aware of the part it plays in redemption, but it also needs to be a means for the constant expansion of awareness that is the dynamic of redemption. Redemption grows as it is revealed. The blurring of lines and borders is the clearest political imperative. An order based on lines and borders either embraces the world or rejects the world. But the blurring of lines is a constant challenge, more constant than the desired expansion, to the viability of politics. Rabbi Tzvi Yehuda sees moral, absolute holiness as the very final stage of redemption. The state, the presence in the world of the Jews returned, multiple and lacking in nature, can be justified only as a constant striving toward that perfection.

## A Sort of Conclusion: Two Narratives, No Real

Ariel Sharon mistrusted an environment he saw as a lair of hostility and uncertainty. Sharon believed only in what he could snatch from such an environment. His ultimate act of sovereignty was drawing lines. Sharon's Israel would interact with the world, but only on its own terms and behind a buffer. He used a rhetoric of modernity, equating responsibility and duty with rationality and progress. Still, he offered a progression that was all regression, an Israel forever curling into itself, preserving as its most sovereign right the ability to limit its existence to what it could manage. Sharon did not present this as a concrete plan for a specific situation, but as a principle. This, according to him, is how a sovereign Israeli state should define itself.

Rabbi Tzvi Yehuda's political narrative for the Israeli state anchors sovereignty in an active faith, a faith that seeks awareness. A polity built on faith really exists only as it expands. If the Israeli state seeks a stable space, it rejects the ultimate real: divine redemption. Rabbi Tzvi Yehuda sees and feels it around him as he speaks. Those who call for worldliness, such as the use of non-Jewish law as the law of the state, are ignorant of redemption. Those who advocate purity actively impede redemption, because they claim they know God's intentions and plans. Redemption, however, continues to unfold. Politics in the mode of redemption, a sustainable order in the midst of divine drama, cannot be based on lines. The sovereignty of a faith-based Israeli polity depends on the ability of that polity to expand. No means of expansion should be forsaken, from territory to the individual soul.

Both narratives seem to be anchored in space, but both countermand their spatiality. Sharon wants space only to the extent it can be limited.

His state relies on rationality and sobriety, not on its territory. Rabbi Tzvi Yehuda longs for his ancestral space, the promised Holy Land of the patriarchs. But he longs more for a politics ameliorating the pressure of a prophecy coming true. He wants expansion as a means of remaining within redemption, rather than rejecting or repealing it. Space is important to him only as a platform for constant motion forward and beyond in order to preserve an awareness of redemption. Gershon Hacohen's theology of the real, which we shall now consider, begins and ends in real space.

# 4

## Gershon Hacohen's Theology of the Real

### *Subversive Mediation*

Disengagement was a puzzle. Many Israelis still consider it a puzzle. Ariel Sharon seemed as hawkish as any Israeli politician ever was. In Israel, being a hawk means rejecting the formation of a Palestinian state on territory occupied by Israel after the 1967 Six-Day War. How could one explain Sharon's willingness not just to give the Palestinians territory, but to do so unilaterally? How could Sharon, the epitome of the military man turned politician, agree not just to the removal of civilian settlements but also to the removal of Israeli military presence in the Gaza Strip?

The puzzle is not limited to Sharon's personal decisions and motives. He was a prime minister, an executive leader known for his propensity for solitary action and his mistrust in elected politicians. Sharon broke a promise to abide by a vote of Likud (Sharon's governing party) members in favor or against disengagement. He was a relatively unique presence in a collectively run political system. Many explanations have been offered for his behavior, including an impending criminal investigation into his personal finances (mentioned at the beginning of this part of the book). His campaign for disengagement was, as I tried to show, uncommon at many levels of Israeli consciousness. He attempted nothing less than the creation of a new narrative of Israeli sovereignty.

Perhaps an even bigger puzzle was the behavior of the main opposition to Sharon, the leadership of the settler movement. The core of their national narrative had been articulated in 1967 by Rabbi Tzvi Yehuda Kook. This narrative of sovereignty as faith was not par for the course of Israeli ideological discourse. Israeli ideologies grew from fear for the country's existence, regardless of justifications for that fear. Israelis thought of the wars they fought for the first 25 years of the country's existence as wars over their personal, physical security against an enemy out to "throw them into the sea." Even though, historically, this has not always proven to be the case,[1] Israeli wars forged the worldviews that have shaped Israeli public discourse. By 2005, the nature of Israel's wars and their influence on the country had both changed. Israel was no longer profoundly threatened by the armies of neighboring states. It had been investing most of its military efforts in the maintenance of its occupation of the territories it had won in 1967.

The occupation, perceived by a majority of Israelis as necessary for the security of the Israeli state, has always been a less convenient growth matter for ideologies. An element of denial is always involved in "overt" political discussions of the occupation, constricting an attempt at comprehensive visions. The Israeli mainstream has not accepted civilian and military presence in the territories as organically Israeli. Despite attempts to foster and encourage domestic tourism, for example, the territories are seldom visited by Israeli Jews who do not live there.[2] A trip to "the territories," even for the sake of visiting relatives, is an adventure not lightly undertaken. Israelis are, naturally, aware of the occupation. Still, many have not seen it at first hand. Many others do not like to talk about it.

The settler movement, the ideological spearhead of Israeli civilian presence in the territories, denies the very existence of the occupation. They employ two main arguments. The first is that Jewish presence is legitimized by divine promise and a victor's entitlement. The second argument is that there was no occupation because there was nothing to occupy: the land taken had not been sovereignly controlled by any nation and it was not home to a recognized state.[3] In both cases, the term "occupation" is denied with a vigor sufficient to ground an ideological vision. In 2005,

---

[1] See, for example, the following paper by Israeli journalist Ehud Ya'ari, acknowledging that the Egyptian offensive of 1973 was meant to jumpstart a diplomatic process ending in a settlement with Israel: www.washingtoninstitute.org/policy-analysis/view/israeli-egyptian-peace-forty-years-after-the-1973-war-and-holding (last accessed on October 18, 2016).

[2] For example, the website www.myheartland.ac.il, is the English version of a website describing the regional council administering a central part of the West Bank. The very name of the site demonstrates the eagerness to belong. The American "heartland" describes not only geography, but a certain, romantic authenticity of identity.

[3] For a highly critical (yet informative) overview of this legal argument, formulated most prominently by the Levy Commission (whose recommendations were made public in 2012), see www.btselem.org/settlements/20120711_levy_committee_report (last accessed on October 18, 2016).

the settler movement remained one of few ideologically motivated elements within the Israeli polity.

This ideological movement was also heavily invested in the perpetuation of the occupation. It had become a powerful lobby for a state-sponsored industry producing homes, infrastructure and security for the Jewish population of the West Bank and the Gaza Strip. The combination of practical clout and ideological potency has made the political and executive standard bearers of the settler movement quite powerful in Israeli policy- and decision-making circles. In 2005, after more than for years of violence in the territories, the inevitability of their influence was, perhaps, even greater that it is today.

If this was the state of affairs, how was it that the settler leadership failed to prevent the execution of disengagement? Their failure was multifaceted. A nationwide resistance movement did not succeed in gaining popular support for the rejection of disengagement. The settler supporters tried everything from preaching on the street and passing out of leaflets to strewing nails on highways in order to cause mayhem and press their point. These acts, and others, were to no avail. Sharon maintained solid approval ratings before, during and after disengagement. The settler leadership also failed in its attempts to impede the evacuation itself. They set out to march into the Gaza Strip but failed to cross the perimeter established by the police and the military. Their failure was not a physical one. They were not turned back forcibly. Their mass rally at Kfar Maimon, on the edge of the Gaza Strip, fizzled due to a lack of consensus on the way forward.

A third aspect of their failure, and the one which is of most interest to my discussion, is the expectation-exceeding rapidity of the evacuation itself. The Israeli population of the Gaza Strip – nearly 10,000 Jews who had debated their position toward its Jewish evacuators until the actual arrival of the latter – was removed within a week. Expectations and plans for the duration of the evacuation ranged between several weeks and several months. How did this happen? How did the force created for this unprecedented mission dismantle a presence that had been decades in the making and had enjoyed the full support of the Israeli state?

## Gershon Hacohen: Background and Context

I would like to suggest that this final failure, seemingly the most technical and contextual, originated in an Israeli theology of the real. This theology was formulated and realized by the military force charged with the strategic planning and execution of the evacuation. The commander of that force was Brigadier General (as he then was) Gershon Hacohen. Hacohen was not the only commander who planned or participated in disengagement. He was, however, unique in both his personal background and his view of the mission.

Hacohen, who retired from military service in 2014, comes from an illustrious religious Zionist family of pioneer farmers, scholars and rabbis. Four of his brothers are religious Zionist rabbis. His family played a prominent role in the establishment of *Gush Emunim*, the first and most intense progenitor of the settler movement. Hacohen himself, who spent 41 years in uniform, does not wear the *kippa* (the Jewish skullcap), but has described himself as "sporting a transparent *kippa* on his head."[4] He holds a master's degree in philosophy and comparative literature, another rarity among senior military leaders. Hacohen has been a prolific contributor to the Israeli press, from the national tabloids to children's weeklies. Amir Oren, one of Israel's topmost military commentators, described him in *Ha'aretz* as "one of the most talented and controversial officers in the IDF," and said that he "tries to be involved in a scandal once a decade."[5] Oren was referring to Hacohen's support for the resignation of Eli Geva, an IDF colonel who refused to serve during Israel's First Lebanon War in protest over the war's conception and management. As I mentioned previously, Hacohen published an anonymous article in support of Geva. He was dismissed from the IDF by Refael Eitan, then IDF Chief of Staff, in 1982 and was reinstated to full service in 1987.

Hacohen was the commander of the IDF's 36th Division when he was selected to command disengagement. In his article, Oren suggests that his selection was related to his division's deployment in the Golan Heights, on Israel's northern border, where no conflict was expected. Oren also mentions the diverse composition of the division, including within it units known for their heterogeneity. Such heterogeneity would prevent attempts to brand the evacuating forces as agents of a sectorial agenda.

While Oren does not refer directly to Hacohen's personal background, I believe it played a major role in his selection by his military superiors. Hacohen's religious Zionist credentials and his reputation as a firebrand made him ideal for an operation that generated unparalleled

---

[4] For all biographical references on Hacohen, see https://he.wikipedia.org/wiki/%D7%92% D7%A8%D7%A9%D7%95%D7%9F_%D7%94%D7%9B%D7%94%D7%9F (last accessed on October 18, 2016).

[5] See (in Hebrew) www.haaretz.co.il/misc/1.1558461 (last accessed on October 18, 2016).

tension, attention and ire from all sides of Israeli society. Hacohen had proven to be his own man and had spoken in the 1980s of his faith in democracy, faith that would allow him to fight in a war which he did not support. There was no love lost between Hacohen and Ariel Sharon, the prime minister. In a series of anonymous missives he penned from the First Lebanon War, where he served as the deputy commander of an armored battalion, Hacohen spoke of Sharon as a deceitful bully. During his civilian hiatus, he joined the protests against Sharon, comparing him to Douglas Macarthur. Hacohen was Sharon's choice, most likely, so he might serve as a lightning rod should the evacuation itself backfire.

Hacohen's success – the completion of the evacuation in one week with no serious opposition – won him the silent treatment from the religious Zionist leadership and public.[6] In a remarkable gesture, Ariel Sharon failed to shake his hand at the military ceremony marking the end of the operation despite having shaken the hand of all senior military commanders. While disengagement and its aftermath remain hotly debated in Israel,[7] the operation itself has remained relatively untouched. A few Israeli scholars have considered the IDF's deportment from perspectives grounded in military sociology.[8] These scholarly analyses fail to register the theologically subversive dimension inherent in Hacohen's actions and decisions.

I would like to focus precisely on this dimension. Hacohen, in conversation with Dr. Asaf Hazani,[9] presented his thoughts on the practical side of planning and executing disengagement. This text reflects a theology of the real at stark contrast with the narratives of both Ariel Sharon and Rabbi Tzvi Yehuda Kook. These two narratives make an exclusive case for the either the "democratic" or the "Jewish" sides of the Israeli state,

---

[6] He has continuously been referred to as the commander of "the deportation," the standard term for disengagement among the religious Zionist public. Hacohen was not invited to participate or speak at religious Zionist forums for a decade after disengagement, and he continues to be the recipient of intense disdain and criticism from opponents of the plan and the operation.

[7] For example, critics of disengagement claim that the operation delivered Gaza into the hands of Hamas, the Islamic movement that took control of the Strip in 2007. Proponents of disengagement counter with the argument that continued Israeli presence in Gaza would have involved constant armed conflict, while the Strip and its Hamas rulers can now be effectively blockaded and isolated. And so on, ad nauseam.

[8] See, for example, the chapter by Yagil Levy (in Hebrew) analyzing the IDF's success in the operation as a result of its being an "embedded army," reflecting the negotiated division of power in Israeli society, at www.jiis.org.il/.upload/publications/heb/diseng2009_heb.pdf.

[9] An anthropologist, a lieutenant colonel in the IDF reserves and one of the most original military thinkers on the Israeli scene.

effectively rejecting the fusion of the two so prominent in self-reflective Israeli rhetoric. This preference for exclusivity is accompanied by the rejection of space as a medium of sovereignty. Sharon sees sovereignty as the limitation of Israeli space. Rabbi Tzvi Yehuda fixes sovereignty in the constant expansion of "Israel" – individuals, collective, state and community. Neither narrative has any use for a real space in which the Israeli state can and should exercise its sovereignty in stable fashion. Hacohen's theology of the real envisions and realizes precisely this space.

## Hacohen and Hazani: Space and Disengagement[10]

### *The Uniqueness of Disengagement*

> Hazani: *Before the IDF began to prepare for and act on disengagement, there was a discussion regarding the role of the military in missions of this type. There were those who claimed that this was not a military mission, and those who argued that any mission imposed on the military by the political leadership is a military mission. Both sides considered disengagement to be a unique mission, something the military does not face regularly. But the truth is that a mission of evacuation is not so unusual. The IDF withdrew in organized fashion from extensive territory in Lebanon – in 1985 and then in 2000. The IDF evacuated settlements in the Sinai ... following the peace agreement with Egypt, and was also involved in withdrawals and evacuations after the Oslo accords. How unique was disengagement? Should the IDF establish a formal framework for a maneuver called "evacuation and disengagement," just like one carries out a "withdrawal"[11]?*

> Hacohen: *There is no way to define and determine formal regimens of action for the operational and strategic levels as one would determine forms of battle at the tactical level. Forms of battle, like the one called "withdrawal," are categorically defined actions which are applicable only at the tactical level. At the operational and strategic level, forms such as withdrawal have a dimension of uniqueness. The structure of the operational concept can include many tactical forms, but withdrawal at the strategic level is a unique event, changing significantly each time it takes place. I mean to say that every time the IDF performed a withdrawal during the last few decades, the IDF engaged in a unique event. Every withdrawal was singularly expressed in an operational and strategic logic particularly suited to the unique event. When one talks about such an event at the level of senior command, which was where I operated ... one talks about the strategic concept, not about forms of battle. When it comes to strategic concepts, you certainly can't replicate*

---

[10] The interview was conducted on November 8, 2009.

[11] That is, a type of military operation, generally meaning retreating forces back while maintaining contact with the enemy. See https://en.wikipedia.org/wiki/Withdrawal_(military) (last accessed on October 18, 2016).

*previous events. At this level, the nature of the event depends on its unique-
ness, on its full dependence on the unique context, the political, cultural,
social and geostrategic concept, all unique. The event always takes place in
a unique environment and there is not option of generalization. An attempt
to develop a general or generic mode of action is meaningless. There are no
rules or principles. Every unique system and every unique campaign create
their own rules and principles. The only basic rule may be: plan each case
separately and study each case separately. Anyone seeking to initiate a strategic discussion by observing a given, unique problem as the potential platform for universal rules, will simply lead himself to failure.*

Hacohen's political theology, the potential third point of the Israeli triangle, begins with creation. Strategic campaigns are created by those who
lead them. Creation implies both reality and response. Once these campaigns are, once their necessity brings them into being, they need to be
realized with painstaking thought and execution. Strategic campaigns are
not means or ends of manipulation. They are created in the initial sense
of becoming, addressing a need or a concern or a (political) decision that
demands action. Once they are acknowledged as real, related as they are
to a desirable outcome, such campaigns are planned and performed.

Creation and uniqueness are closely related. Creation involves both
dynamic emergence and static, unavoidable limitations. When God created the world, as we saw before, divine presence needed to be curtailed
for life to burst forth. The basic relationship between the emerging and
the withheld is tension. No set of generic rules can contain or subdue this
tension. The physics of creation imposes this necessity. But this uniqueness is not arbitrary. It can and should be observed, analyzed and developed. The uniqueness of a created campaign is a point of strength. It
carries nearly unlimited potential for emerging and becoming, precisely
because the acknowledgment of unique tension rejects a "rational" quest
for certainty. The leader willing to embrace uniqueness (who is also willing to relinquish the safety of generics) is a leader who accepts faith as a
rational principle. This leader can, literally, perform miracles.

*Hazani: During one of the scenes documented by Israeli television, one of the
evacuees curses you. He tells you that for your work on disengagement you
will be remembered in history as the master of disengagement. You accept
his words, but then you fill them a professional significance. How did you see
your place in the campaign's design? How did you see your role in terms of
designing a campaign that would fulfill a military mission?*

*Hacohen: First of all, a military mission must be connected to the circumstan-
tial logic of its context. This is the role of the systemic leader perched on a
ladder set in the ground with its top in the heavens. From this perspective,
the division commander occupies a middle position, mediating between two*

*dimensions connected in a way that is not mechanical, technical or instru-
mental. This is the connection between the strategic purpose and the tactical forms of execution. These forms, physically aggregated, are supposed to
realize the strategic purpose. That strategic purpose is always given within
unique circumstances. The one who defines this purpose can never define the
always-tactical, concrete forms of realization. Someone else needs to erect
forms of action that express the overall realization of the strategic purpose.
This middle position should be occupied by the military leader at the appropriate level, who is very often the division commander ...*

The stress of creation is not to produce something out of nothing. That
is a divine prerogative. The stress lies in mediation. In terms with which
we are already familiar, creation is not about expansion or reduction.
Hacohen refers to the patriarch Jacob's dream of a ladder set in the
ground with its top in the heavens, upon which angels run continuously
up and down. The dream, coming to Jacob on his way to his uncle's
house and the love of his life, illustrates the connection between leadership and mediation. Creation is motion between absolutes. The leader,
the mediator, enables this motion.

*(Hacohen): ... The tactical form, however, must reach the executing forces for-
mulated clearly and concretely, in significant detail, and containing structured
action patterns that can be measured with benchmarks. One should be able to
drill and train personnel in execution. These patterns, or forms, are meant to be
assimilated. Mediating between these two dimensions – the first which is in the
strategic stratosphere and the second, which is located in a tactical, replicable
consciousness – when the strategic aspect is always unique and the second is
expressed in procedures, techniques and force-building forms, this is precisely
the task of the leader who constructs these campaigns. This needs to be carried
out in constant, demanding discourse with the senior leadership and the decision makers. The mediator needs to coordinate his efforts at both levels with
what the decision makers want. What is required is a point of equilibrium that
is not a mathematical derivative. This point is a creative product of the encounter between the levels, the desires and the constraints. Equilibrium comes about
through a process of study, some of it in discussion and some of it through trial
and error, including tactical friction in the field. Such friction can teach you
about potential difficulties that may arise as the event unfolds. Friction teaches
you, in detail, about areas of incompetence that need to be covered in detail
before the mediator finally considers what is going to be done.*

Mediation, leadership as creation, is a pursuit. The mediator needs to
keep both the strategic and the tactical in clear sight. These are absolute in their internal coherence, but nothing will come of them if they
are not fused. Mediating leadership is concerned with the event and the
consequences of such fusion. Mechanisms must be put in place in order

to carry out decision and to deal with the implications of these decisions. It may be useful to think of a reflection-based dynamic. The means reflect the desired outcome and the possible ends. The ends reflect the means and the constraints of applying them. No side is simply "real" on its own, self-enclosed terms. Ends, means and outcomes stage engagements and encounters. The mediating leader enables these engagements and encounters by creating – in thought and action, friction and analysis – an emerging, evolving environment which is the *sine qua non* for a successful strategic campaign.

> *Hazani: I would like to use your image of Jacob's ladder and think about the angel of God running up and down, maintaining balance by running.*
>
> *Hacohen: Walking on a wire, a thin wire.*
>
> *Hazani: Walking on the wire is mediation, but if I understand you correctly your mediating angel is also creating a space for mediation. The angel is walking on the wire and creates the wire through his walking ...*
>
> *Hacohen: Precisely. This is how the intensity of action is determined. That is, space is not just about acreage, but it is also structured around the presence and actions of objects in space. This, alongside the decision about what should be done in a space, these create the significance of space. I can say that with regard to disengagement, we sought the point of equilibrium between what was desirable at the policy level and the appropriate means for achieving that end. We needed a point of equilibrium connecting form and purpose. In this case, uniquely, we needed a form that could realize a forceful encounter between brothers, This was an encounter where Jews wearing military and police uniforms in the name of the Israeli state will encounter – we called it an "encounter of eyes" – brothers who are Jews forcefully removed from their homes in the land of Israel, the land of their forefathers.*

The true creation of the mediator as leader is the creation of space for mediation. There is no room to maneuver at the strategic heights or the tactical lows. Both draw their coherence from their self-enclosure. Strategy seems to be "universal," while tactics are "technical." For the mediating leader, strategy is unique while tactics are feasible. Both reflect each other, and through this reflection deepen and embolden each other. The challenge, once again, is to create a space in which these processes can occur. Absolutes have no free space. In the case of disengagement, the required space needed to include, and to hold, both force and fraternity.

> *Hazani: That's one version of an encounter. You could have created other encounters. But assuming that this is a campaign, action carried out on a stage and intensely observed by others, and that there is preceding friction enabling learning, how do you prepare? How do you design the arena in advance? What was the space in which you acted and what qualities did you try to inject into that space?*

> *Hacohen: The form of action in space is defined, among other things, by very concrete elements like roadblocks. We built the Kisufim roadblock [the terminus which, in preparation for disengagement, was the only point of entry and exit from the Gush Katif, the Jewish settlement bloc in the Gaza Strip – OG] three weeks before the actual operation took place, the removal of people from their homes. The roadblock needed to look as though it created a different physical presence from other roadblocks, like the one in Khawara.[12] This was supposed to be a roadblock that created the conscious indication that something was changing within physical space – that from now on you need to pass through a roadblock in order to get to Gush Katif, and this roadblock served as a shock to the crosser's consciousness. The first night after the roadblock began to operate was horrible. On the other hand, it needed to look human, to encapsulate the terrible shock it created for people, because it was the first encounter with the understanding that deportation was coming. We allowed a protest tent to be set up next to the roadblock. This way, the space contained all the tensions around the event.*
>
> *Hazani: Three weeks in advance?*
>
> *Hacohen: Yes! And that is why I sat with Eli Armon, the architect, to see how we can make a roadblock that does not have so many sharp points. I wanted something that, how should I call it, could contain the pain. For example, we decided that there will always be a general on duty. People from the general staff were on a roster there. That made it possible to make decisions on the spot,[13] and whenever someone needed to enter they could. Otherwise, the IDF would have been perceived as insensitive. The actual encounter with the roadblock created the impression of an idea expressed physically, something very powerful but not impermeable. It expressed the motto of disengagement, coined by the Chief of Staff – "sensitivity and conviction."*

Physical space is shaped as a conduit for crossing between spaces, but also as a receptacle for emotion. A thing created is, but it also becomes. Creation involves faith, but can it serve as a platform for a political theology? Can creation breed sovereignty? For Sharon, Israel's sovereignty was drawn from an Israeli core, an essence of "statehood" that could be accessed and asserted even at the cost of territorial withdrawals. Creation would serve, according to this narrative, to refine and distinguish the core. For Rabbi Tzvi Yehuda, that core could only be divine and the only feasible politics at the human, Israeli level were politics of expansion. Jews were created and chosen to strive toward the divine, their origin and ultimate destination.

---

[12] Other roadblocks are, of course, directed at controlling the movement of Palestinians in the occupied territories or in in the Gaza Strip. The *Kisufim* roadblock was meant to regulate the movement of Jews.

[13] Without the need to call for a decision to be made at IDF GHQ, in Tel Aviv.

Hacohen understands himself as an agent of Israeli sovereignty. For him, that sovereignty lies in the duality of creation. The state is power, demarcating and separating, but it is also brotherhood. The state can curtail the rush of life, but it can also ensure its flow. This, however, is true only if one treats the act of shaping the space of the state as an act of creation. The creative drive and responsibility are the elements that allow for uniqueness, a uniqueness founded on duality. Sovereignty erupts from this uniqueness. Without creation, the body politic contracts urges incompatible with life, such as self-reduction and self-negation.

*Hazani: You spoke, previously, about a "lower" Gush Katif and a "higher" Gush Katif, using both designations as qualities of space. Is this related to what you're saying here?*

*Hacohen: Right from the start, it was clear that we are operating within an event loaded with symbols, as well as layers of meaning and faith. It was clear that we were acting on widely observed stage, that every step we made reverberated. Everything we did was like a statue in a town square, functioning not simply through physical presence. In this context, the big question was how do we express and realize infinite metaphysical ideas within a finite, physical space. This is where I drew the line between the higher and the lower Gush Katif. As I saw it, our mission consisted of destroying the lower Gush Katif. This was Gush Katif as it existed physically, its homes, settlements, gardens. Everything else, everything that had to do with the supernatural being of Gush Katif, the idea and the symbol, the vision, the values, the dream and the Zionist yearning that was expressed in the physical space of Gush Katif, we tried not to harm all that. The necessity of this distinction was made clear by voices demanding that our action be seen as a historic turn, "the Zionist river turned back" ... Prominent public figures expected that our actions, the destruction of the lower Gush Katif, would mark the beginning of the end for the ideological foundations of the higher Gush Katif. "Settlements would no longer equal Zionism." In stark contrast, we attempted to design our entire array of activities in a way that would color the evacuation as a Zionist event. That was my main message when I presented the plan to (Major General Dan Harel) the chief of IDF Southern Command. We wanted our actions to convey the message that despite the full implications of the evacuation, the Zionist river would keep flowing, would not turn back, would deal with an obstacle, detour around it, and continue in its known, familiar direction.*

*In order to express this we needed to understand that we were going to destroy the lower Gush Katif, the houses, the trees, the infrastructure, get the people out, all of this because we were ordered to do so. But we were going to preserve the system of values, the beliefs, the link to the place. That was why we made a real effort to neutralize any potential for a "religious war." We wanted to avoid anything that Michel Foucault might have described as "anti-religious chauvinism." We intended to express an ongoing age of redemption. The story I tried to tell was one that we, the evacuators, shared*

*with the Jews who lived there. I wanted our actions to show that we shared
the ideas that were the reason for their presence there – the ideas that allowed
them to hold on throughout years of attacks. In fact, we wanted not only to
preserve these ideas but to demonstrate the deep respect we had for them.
We needed forms of action that would make it clear that we were not there
to destroy what I'm calling the higher Gush Katif. We needed actions that
would drive this message home, not declarations. We knew that whoever
controlled the cultural space would control physical space. For that reason,
we created a cultural space that fostered a bond between the forces, the
"evil" forces of the evacuation, and the evacuees themselves.*

Hacohen's goal cannot be formulated, much less accomplished without
extensive, expansive faith. The soldiers carrying out the evacuation do
not have to share his faith, because they are in charge of the tactical,
concrete forms of action. Such forms are effective if they are solid and
replicable. They do not require faith. Sharon, the grand strategist of disengagement, does not need faith as well (despite the final words of his
speech). He trusts in his authority and the might of the state, as well as
in an indisputable "Israeliness" that is a measure of effectiveness and
relevance. Faith is required from the leader in Hacohen's position, the
mediator.

Faith is a necessary component of sovereign mediation, because
events in mediating space are uncertain almost by definition. Friction
between two absolute, holistic concepts (Jewish and democratic, state
power and divine mandate), regulated as it might be, can result in successful synthesis as much as in an irreversible conflagration. The planning and thought that are invested in the creation of a mediating space
certainly have a vision in mind, and they are also devoted to the creation of means for realizing this end. Still, the realness of the encounter between vision and practice is a generated, emerging realness. The
uniqueness that is a measure of emergence accentuates the theological
dimension of this realness.

In the case of disengagement, Hacohen's plan is doubly dualistic. The
first dualism lies in his conceptualization of the challenge at hand as a
mission involving action in both lower and higher realms. The second
dualism is located in the use of state power to both determine and destroy
the physical space of the state. The tension inherent in these dualisms is
the source of the energy that generates the uncertain, emerging encounter
between evacuators and evacuees. Hacohen's true creation is not the plan
for disengagement, nor is it the successful removal of settlers from their
homes. His sovereign creation is the space that can contain, and foster, an
emerging encounter.

In this political theology, creation amounts to the erection of a space and the generation of an event, planned and thought through, within that space. Realness has dimensions of being alongside dimensions of materialization. It is and it becomes, both occurring in actual space. Hacohen's ability to wed vision and action depends on his faith in the occurrence of these entwined qualities of realness.

> *Hazani: If initially you were the creator of the rope that enabled mediation, now you talking about roping both sides into this idea, into a common space. You have created a new space. I thought of it at first as a question regarding the vectors you were facing. In the northern part of the Gaza Strip you did not always have this space. The idea was that the evacuating forces, military and police, stay outside the settlement's perimeter with all of the implied implications. In Amona[14] we saw a very different operational concept. Can you formulate other operational concepts that might have been enacted? I ask because it seems that your job as a commander would have been easier with other concepts in play, concepts of struggle and fighting that are more in line with the nature of the military organization.*
>
> *Hacohen: The other ideas produce a front line. You are creating a frontal vector that pushes forward, and you are facing resistance. Our operation, "Brotherly hand," included the handing over of the official letters (to each family) demanding their evacuation as well as help with the packing and other logistics. The chief of IDF Southern Command, MG Harel, wanted to create a space in which our forces mingled with the local inhabitants. This mixture, the encounter created at each and every home – the evacuating forces stood before the people about to be removed from their homes outside each and every house – with all the anger and the pain, the eyes of Jews sharing the pain met (across what would have been a divide). Even if the intensity of the pain was not identical, the feeling was. We spread the forces throughout the physical space in a way that created points of friction over nearly all the space. We undid the linear order and transformed it into a nearly chaotic mix.*

The space of mediation is the space of creation, but this is not creation *ex nihilo*. Only God can create something from nothing. Mediating creation, creative, faith-based leadership, depends on friction. This creation takes place in a middle ground between absolute truths, but this is not an ameliorative middle ground. Differences are not smoothed away or downplayed. The middle ground is an arena, intentionally defined as a site for encounters.

---

[14] Amona was the largest settlement outpost in the West Bank. Settlement outposts are unauthorized "mini-settlements" extending from an established settlement. The Israeli national police demolished several structures in Amona, on February 1, 2006, following a Supreme Court order to that effect. The evacuation and demolition were met with violent resistance. The violence stood in stark contrast to the evacuation of Gush Katif.

The distinction between what Hacohen calls "higher" and "lower" with regard to Gush Katif is not a separation. When he spoke earlier of demolishing the one but maintaining the other, he was not voicing an expectation that the evacuees take heart in keeping a part of what they stood for while they lost another part. Their loss was real. The history and values they represented, as well as their sense of fraternity with their evacuators, were also real. Full-fledged confrontation between two realities cannot achieve creation. One reality wins while the other loses, and the loser is consigned to oblivion. Several levels of the real can coexist, but if they confront each other head-on, the losers become unreal almost by definition.

Oblivion is not an acceptable state when attempting to maintain the integrity of a body politic. For Hacohen, unreality is not an option when he creates the mediating space for disengagement. His theology of the real is a political theology. Neither the state nor the evacuees can walk away defeated from disengagement. If they do, the implosion of the historical, social and political order is at stake. Strategies of expansion or retraction are not useful before this challenge, because such strategies are willing to pay enormous costs to ensure the victory of one truth over another.

Hacohen is determined to re-create the integrity of the body politic. He will not achieve this goal by asserting the validity of one truth at the expense of another. Politics can and should acknowledge loss, pain, conflict and struggle, according to Hacohen, because they are all real. Acknowledgment and realness can be appropriated and used for creation if they are approached within a middle ground and through friction. Encounters ensure that neither side is able to claim or take the upper hand. Occupying a common space may be unpleasant, but unpleasantness reeks of realness. When the situation becomes real, notions of zero-sum games lose their relevance and their appeal.

The Israeli Jewish body politic is a created being. According to Hacohen, it does not have the inviolable core Sharon saw as the source of Israeli sovereignty and of his own personal authority as leader.[15] Alternatively, the state of Israel cannot be exclusively invested in expansion, a forward motion that ignores or bulldozes through complexity. Both narratives

---

[15] As leader, Sharon was the one charged with (and capable of) identifying the necessary withdrawals and the lines that could and could not be crossed around the Israeli core. He was, in a way, adapting Karl Schmitt's classical formula of sovereignty, "sovereign is he who decides on the exception." See Karl Schmitt, *Political Theology: Four Chapters on the Concept of Sovereignty*, trans. George Schwab (University of Chicago Press, 2005), p. 5.

separate being from becoming. Hacohen's theology of the real rejects this separation. His plan for disengagement envisioned creation as an ongoing work, generated in space and by friction.

The year preceding disengagement was marked by a discourse of impending doom by both settlers and the Israeli establishment. Settler rabbis discussed their "nuclear option" of protest and resistance, the possibility that religious Zionist IDF officers and soldiers would disobey orders to evacuate settlements.[16] The mainstream Israeli press, along with Sharon's closest advisors, warned of violence that would tear Israeli society apart from the inside.[17] This discourse of doom was built on premises of inviolable, primal truth. Israel (Jewish Israel, to be more accurate) was what it was and that "wasness" could not be existentially threatened. Hacohen's theology of the real considered creation to be the epitome of the Jewish real. Creation took place in a negotiated, mediated space. It was, in itself, an act of mediation.

Political faith, according to Hacohen, was placed in the creation of a space that existed and emerged. This realness of this space was established through friction, the immediate contact between evacuators and evacuees across the entirety of Gush Katif. These encounters established commonalities – origins, values, pain. Friction also established the urgency of motion. Settlers and police officers cannot simply engage in a staring contest. Once they found themselves sharing the same space, even if simply through physical proximity, they discovered they could not cancel each other out through faith or force. Something real needed to happen, something involving both motion and decision.

> *Hazani: I'd like to ask you a professional question about space. You describe a conflict between what we called, in earlier conversations, "Russian thinking" and "German thinking." I am reminded of (French) thinkers like Virilio, Deleuze and Guattari. What are these forms of thinking, and how have you concluded that they assist you?*
>
> *Hacohen: Simply put, we consciously disrupted the linear structure. The Germans, with all their notions of deep penetration, when they set out on their Blitzkrieg they were simply acting linearly in space. A force penetrates the strategic depth of the enemy and waits for other forces to join it quickly. Then they set out to regulate space in unitary, sequential fashion.*

---

[16] See, for example, the following rabbinic debate between a proponent and an opponent of the proposal to refuse: http://traditionarchive.org/news/_pdfs/Lichtenstein1.pdf (last accessed on October 18, 2016).

[17] See, for example, the following report of a public warning delivered by Shaul Mofaz, Sharon's minister of defense: www.voanews.com/a/a-13-2005-07-12-voa15-67536567/387202.html (last accessed on October 18, 2016).

*The Russian approach allows for operational entities to act, over time, when they are detached from each other. That is why they don't have a problem with Koenigsberg, beyond Lithuania, which is a part of today's Russia. It is not necessary to maintain a geographical continuum. A nation of islands, like Greece, that maintains a unity even though there is no common dryland space between the islands.*

*We could have carried out an evacuation with linear logic: Tackling Kfar Darom on the first day, Ganei Tal on the second and Katif on the third. Something else each day. We would have gathered steam, flattening every-thing in our path, and we would also have intensified the resistance, every day, in places we had not yet evacuated*

*What we did was establish a bridging campaign, a median event between the initial campaign to isolate Gush Katif and the final campaign, the six days of the evacuation itself. This median campaign included the weeks before actual disengagement. The two-day operation "Brotherly Hand" dispersed the forces throughout the entire space of Gush Katif. Once we embarked on the median campaign, our rationale was no longer linear. It was simultaneous and multidimensional. Additionally, since each commander was allowed to make particular arrangements in his sector, our rationale was realized in identical fashion all over Gush Katif. There was some autonomy for the commanders on the ground, and the forms of action for each settle-ment were quite unique.*

*Regarding command, I can say that during the post-operational debrief-ing, when I heard the dilemmas of the commanders and what they did, I said, "it was great that I did not hear about all of these dilemmas in real time." I could never have given them a solution better than the one they worked out in their particular sector, a solution suitable for their operational con-text. What I mean is that from the moment they embraced their context they assimilated the unique elements of the unique environment in which they operated. Each settlement was different, of course, and the command-ers then had a compass that let them adjust to the dynamics of emergence in their respective sectors. This was an action that scattered the forces as far as command and control were concerned. Things emerged, we did not control everything all the time.*

The strategist, the creating commander has faith in emergence. The local commanders also need faith, and theirs is a faith in context. They need to embrace their environment and accept that, as it really is, it is unique. The temptation of generics (planning and execution) is avoided through friction and contact. A sector commander standing before a succession of soon-to-be evacuated families would find it difficult to stick to a script prepared beforehand. Each instance of friction is unique, and this sequence of instances makes each operational environment unique. The only repetitive element is the recurring friction, but each time that friction generates a becoming, an event in the making.

When Hacohen talks about *Blitzkrieg*, the German "rapid war," he highlights its dependence on a principle of unity. A force penetrates the enemy's territory quickly and deeply, but this is simply a means to a pre-conceived end, the unitary regulation of space. The military action facilitates, rather than generates. The action is successful if the enemy's space is ultimately harnessed and shaped according to the interests and needs of the penetrating force. The incredible danger and potential cost of deep, rapid penetration is offset by the necessity of success. The other forces will come, enemy space will be won over, and stability will be restored. All military efforts are variations on a theme, and the structure of the theme is indestructible.

Hacohen knows the price of this unity. The drawing of a line across space, even if this line unites the penetrating force, creates an immediate confrontation between those on one side of the line and those on the other. The dynamic of this confrontation is an escalating one, because as the line grows longer the stakes grow higher. Once the line becomes the axis of the divided space, its one constant, the very existence of an "other side" existentially threatens both sides of the line. A penetrating force steamrolling a line through Gush Katif would leave the locals no real option but resistance.

When each commander operates in context, however, resistance soon becomes futile. There is no separating, inflammatory line. Instead, there is an ecological awareness of context. The evacuees are not allowed to forget their proximity to the evacuators. They are in "this" together, be "this" what it may. Every autonomous subspace is respected and created within this proximity. If the commander stares at the settler across a line, each representing an exclusive narrative, there is no space between them. In such a state, they are raring for confrontation that can only end in defeat or victory. But if there is no line a mediating space opens up, a space that can be occupied jointly by both settler and commander. A willingness to encounter, even if the encounter is initiated by one side (evacuators) and not the other, acknowledges the possibility of a mediating space and generates this space at the same time.

This ongoing chain of encounters and their emerging outcomes are held together by the faith of strategic commander, the creator of the campaign. What Hacohen refers to as "Russian" thought is, in the Israeli context, a demonstration of creation as faith. The two narratives we read in detail, the secure minimalism of Sharon and the raging maximalism of Rabbi Tzvi Yehuda, saw the source of Israeli sovereignty in either "higher" or "lower" Israel. For Sharon, the Israeli state was a model of resilience and savviness. The institutions of the state, its military and technological/economic prowess and, most of all, his leadership, were the assets Israelis could rely on when facing threats or crises. For Rabbi Tzvi Yehuda, the Israeli state reflected the divine, ahistorical process of redemption. A devout Jew could accept the less than perfect Israeli state's role within this process, but only if the state expanded with every breath it took. The major asset of the state of Israel, according to Rabbi Tzvi Yehuda, was the unshakable knowledge of the centrality of Jews in the broadest sense of divine creation.

As Hacohen defines his own sovereignty as the strategic commander, his theology of the real defines Israeli sovereignty differently. As commander, Hacohen does not see himself as capable of answering every dilemma encountered by the sectorial commanders. He is not simply the most senior commander in the field and thus the most knowledgeable or capable. His sovereignty comes from his commitment to dynamic creation. His plan (and its tactical execution) establishes a physical, immediate Israeliness shared by soldiers/police officers and settlers. Conflict is to be expected when two absolutist narratives clash. The transformation of the front line into a mediating space, the imagination and actual carving of this space within an impending faceoff, is a feat of faith.

> Hazani: *In an earlier conversation, we referred to this as "making space dynamic," "an intensification of space," "the life of a space." Can you formulate this as a rule? Perhaps a recommendation for action?*
>
> Hacohen: *Not as a rule! I would say, "idea, not rule." Because a military action usually needs to be regulated, coordinated and synchronized, it has the logic of an assembly line. Each part goes into action at the precise time and completes its defined task. A military action is, thus, a hermetically sealed system when you define who does what. If it was built and planned properly, everyone does exactly what they were planned to do in synchronized fashion.*
>
> *The system we created was an open system, allowing for synchronization through emergence. This is the synchronization of a complex system. In a way, rather than reduce a complex system into a simple system,[18] we empowered space into a complex system. We were willing to merge with the complexity that the other side already possessed, to create entities with an independent space, a space that allows for maneuvering and autonomous emergence. What this actually creates is an adjustment to acting within a complex environment that appears chaotic from afar. What regulates this complex environment is an idea as one's internal compass. This complex environment is enriched by a broad diversity of activities with a similar, ideational core logic that is manifested in different physical structures.*

[18] Which, Hacohen is saying, is the essence of assembly line logic.

Creation as a feat of faith involves the complication of space. Execution regulates and orders the existing world. Creation, in contrast, adds something to the world. I insist on Hacohen's thoughts comprising a theology, rather than a manual of sound management, because what his plan adds to the world are additional dimensions of space. Hacohen's mediating space is the most real element of the narrative clash he encounters. The two absolutist narratives, Sharon's retraction and Rabbi Tzvi Yehuda's expansion, do not tolerate space well. Space, for them, is a hindrance that must be traversed on the way to their minimalist or maximalist goals. Hacohen does not simply tell a story with a predetermined ending.

Instead, Hacohen produces Rabbi Nahman's vacant space, the space vacated by the absolute so that creation might take place. Neither of the grand narratives we've read in such detail is capable of vacating space. They are both holistic and self-enclosed. Their existence is justified through their negation of the other. Conflict, as I suggested earlier, is almost a necessary outcome of their facing off against each other. Hacohen accepts both of them, but does not consider them objects of faith. He believes in an absolute truth that is absolute enough to suspend its own existence: God.

"Jewish" and "democratic" Israel are both real only insofar as they positively exist. They are not engines of creation, but of regulation and maintenance. According to them, Israeli needs to be as fully "Jewish" or "democratic"[19] as it can be in order to fulfill its potential. Stick to the first principle, they seem to say, and all will be well. Hacohen stunts these narratives' pretended absolutism by forcing them to encounter each other. He creates this encounter in a constructed space in which neither narrative is absolute. The organizing principle of this space is faith in the most absolute: God.

Only God is absolute enough to be real in absence. Put differently, vacant space is a medium for creation only if God was the one who vacated it. God is the realest of the real. His realness may be suspended, but it cannot be undone. Carving out a space for mediation, Hacohen provides the conflicting narratives with a truth that can soundly hold both of them in engagement mode.

*Hazani: Just as you described the angel's role, producing the rope that can bridge the gap or mediate it, the space you are talking about produces itself through space. That is, we are not talking about a space that is defined in*

---

[19] Some of Sharon's opponents would undoubtedly argue with my use of this term, suggesting that he was anything but democratic in his behavior.

*advance, a space that just presents itself for action. But I want to ask if you didn't feel like you were doing something dangerous. After all, this could get out of control. You think you are producing a rope, a binding vision, but picture a scenario in which you haven't yet produced anything but the people on the ground have already done something. They've moved forward and you have no rope or mediating space. Did you think about the possibility of different logics and different structures scattered throughout your non-space, with you losing control? Could the compass simply be lost?*

Hacohen: *A year later, (during the) Lebanon War, people were spoken to in a way they did not understand.*[20] *We took great pains to make sure everyone understood exactly what they were doing. It is important to say that we also had time to prepare them, and that was essential. Simulations allowed them to enter their designated locations when they understand their environment. They did not need to be fed by a senior, external source, who would tell them what was happening. They understood it for themselves.*

Hazani: *But are you not introducing an unnecessary complication? You could have told a different story, one about a military mission and clear orders.*

Hacohen: *Let me give an example by describing an internal flow chart that we put together with (national police) Major General Franco. The squad commander understood exactly what was expected of him. We put together a flow chart a person could understand. After the abstract ideas, the tactical action is concretized in a very systematic way, as decision-making of a "zero or one" type. The tactical level operates in an environment that was clearly constructed and guided. But the operational level does not know what might happen, because it assumes that "either this or that" could occur all the time. The accrual of all the "either this or that" situations, extrapolated to the level of complexity involving all the uncertain variables, that is a problem. This was the reason we demanded that they (the tactical commanders) do not define the required achievement for each evening beforehand. We wanted room to maneuver, to say that what was accomplished was what we wanted in the first place.*

Hazani presses Hacohen on the political rationale of the operation. Why did Hacohen not rely on a clear-cut military narrative, "this is our mission and we need to accomplish it within the predefined time"? Hacohen's answer seems to include two competing arguments. The first is that a great deal of effort was put into preparation and simulation

---

[20] Hacohen is referring to an intense public discussion in Israel regarding orders written by several senior military officers during the Second Lebanon War, fought in July and August of 2006. The officers were graduates of OTRI, the Operational Theory Research Institute of the IDF. OTRI, headed by Dr. (and retired Brigadier) Shimon Naveh, attempted to introduce systems theory into the operational thought of the IDF, and remains the subject of high controversy within the Israeli defense establishment. For a critical yet informative examination of OTRI, see www.haaretz.com/israel-news/dr-naveh-or-how-i-learned-to-stop-worrying-and-walk-through-walls-1.231912 (last accessed on October 18, 2016).

as an enhancement of certainty. The tactical commanders had the privilege, not enjoyed by their superiors, of making concrete choices between well-defined options. These choices gave shape to the actual evacuation of the settlers. The second argument is that the operational level had to deal with continuous uncertainty and could therefore not issue a clear narrative.

When considering the way we've traveled so far, however, there is no competition between Hacohen's arguments. Both levels of the operation enjoy different types of sovereignty. The tactical commanders have their mission broken down for them into components that can be put together into a structure satisfying the demands of reality in the field. For their purposes, the tactical commanders are ideally equipped with an arsenal of intermeshing parts that can be joined in a broad variety of ways. The sole prerequisite is the sovereign authority of the tactical commanders to decide on the proper way for the parts to be joined in each context.

The sovereignty of the operational leadership is quite different. They have the authority to continue weaving the abstract strands of mediating space. That is, Hacohen himself does not need to justify his decision by "proving" that "zero" was better than "one." His sovereign reality is one in which zeros and ones can occur constantly, perhaps even simultaneously. Still, he is free from the need for "objective" justification. His is a conceptual clarity that allows definitions of sequence and achievement to emerge from an extremely complex reality. Hacohen is sovereign to see, and thereby to create, a reality from the constant onrush of "eithers" and "ors."

The integration of both sovereignty types into a single vision is an act of faith. A third principle is at play, one that retains its meaningfulness in presence and absence, certainty and uncertainty. The sovereignty that underlies the political order Hacohen enacts and envisions is the sovereignty of the divine. Invoking it entails believing in it.

*Hazani: I'm going to insist once more, because you have been describing the conditions necessary for success – preparation well in advance and simulation. I still think that if you had told a story of "us and them" – we are the agents of the state, the forces of goodness and they, the settlers, the redemption junkies, are the bad guys – two spaces would have been created. You created three spaces: the state, the settlers and the space between the spaces that holds everybody. Could this not be an unnecessary complication? A simpler story would not require all the lengthy preparation, the simulation which was difficult as it was, and the intense dilemmas within the new mediating space.*
*Hacohen: What happened at the synagogue, for example, is an emergence that took place because we entered a shared space of shared destiny. In the*

synagogue at Neve Dkalim²¹ at the end of the evacuation, they spontaneously began to pray when the Torah scrolls were taken out. On the dais stood (police) Major General Bar Lev, (police) Major General Franco, Hanan Porat, Tzviki Bar Hai and others.²² The end of this event was one of the most moving and terrible I have ever experienced, but it was a shared experience. Who did we assign to the evacuation of the two synagogues? Non-commissioned officers from a military brigade, older career men, and not young hotshots from the police riot squad. They were mostly Jews, the evacuators, but there were also Druze NCOs there. The Druze understood precisely what was involved. They knew about the holiness of their operational environment, they knew the meaning of a Torah scroll and what it means to remove a scroll from the Holy Ark. Suddenly you see a single group of people, and the removal of the scrolls ends with them all singing Hatikva, the national anthem. Everyone had tears in their eyes. This is what happens when you throw a group of people into the fire and they unite.

Hazani: Were there people who did not understand?

Hacohen: All those who weren't there and did not experience it.

Hazani: Were there people who were present and did not understand?

Hacohen: You didn't need to understand! This is not an event for understanding. What activates the person in the event is not their cognitive consciousness. That is not how you design the event. This is an experience that unfolds in an emotional environment. For example, we played "mood music." We played a religious song asking God to have mercy on Israel, his people. We prepared the speakers in advance on the roofs of cars parked outside.

Hazani: On the one hand, you are saying that it is all about feeling and sensing. On the other hand, you designed what they were going to sense?

Hacohen: I tried to work, consciously, with a space that would include the music, not just the physics. My space was meant to include the story and the possible demeanors of people in the middle of this thing.

Hazani: I want to ask you about the commander's position. Can the person who designed the stage perform on that very stage? If this is the case, where is the look from above?

Hacohen: I can answer that. I operated like a general of the ancient world, at the head of the troops and in the center of emergence. My ability to control everything the division did from that position was not great. But my situational assessments and the decisions that were made in them, like my assessment that the evacuation of the synagogues should be postponed by 24 hours, they all came from my personal contact with events on the ground. I was at the focal point of emerging reality ...

²¹ One of the largest settlements in Gush Katif, the evacuation of which provided for some of the more public and dramatic scenes of disengagement. For filmed testimony from the evacuation of the synagogue, see www.youtube.com/watch?v=hW-07Q1C3Xk (last accessed on October 18, 2016).

²² Hanan Porat was one of the most significant ideological leaders of the settler movement from its first days in the late 1970s. Tzviki Bar Hai was a settler politician. Generals Franco and Bar Lev were the senior police officers in command of the evacuation.

## Final Words in lieu of Conclusion

The mark of creation is not understanding. Understanding is an external dynamic, a position outside the dance. God does not reside in the Torah scrolls or the holy ark, but in the forging of a shared consciousness in joint, mediating space. Hacohen invests real effort in the cerebral construction of this space, from devising detailed tactical plans to the musical soundtrack of the evacuation. Having done so, he prefers real presence to micromanagement. The latter would, by definition, place him outside the event and its emergence.

Hacohen's theology of the real is a political theology. His words and actions reveal an articulation of sovereignty that rejects the models offered by Sharon and Rabbi Tzvi Yehuda. Both of the narratives we examined closely in the preceding chapters were focused on an assertion of realness. For Sharon, real Israel was the state, known by its institutional coherence (in his case, by the effectiveness of his personal leadership), its economic prosperity and, most of all, the security of its borders. For Rabbi Tzvi Yehuda, real Israel was a manifestation of divine redemption, an ahistorical (or, perhaps, both supra- and infra-historical) drama ending in a divine truth that supersedes all human truths. In both cases, sovereignty was grounded in a preconceived notion of the real. In both, sovereignty was exercised through the excision of redundancy and superfluity in an attempt to align political reality with this broader concept of the real.

Hacohen has no use for this dynamic. His concept of the real hinges on creation. His conscious efforts are expended toward enabling and facilitating creation, and not toward the validation of an existing reality. When pressed against the line distinguishing the "authentic" from the "manufactured" he refuses to acknowledge the line's existence. Something created exists and becomes, and the distinction between what it "really" is and what it "currently" is serves no purpose. Creation is real precisely because it occurs in both essence and context. Moreover, creation is real because it requires faith. Mediating space can hold conflicting, would-be absolutes only if this space originates in realness that exists in presence and in absence. Mediating space first takes form as a void, willfully evacuated by an omnipresent God. The absolute narratives of Sharon and Rabbi Tzvi Yehuda do not require faith, because they just are, whole and complete. Hacohen's mediating space is a creature of faith because it generates a synergy that could not exist on the merits of its single components. Minutely detailed plans are wedded to an emergent presence and produce an understanding that exceeds understanding. This excess comes into being as faith.

Hacohen's earlier remarks about the coexistence of the higher and lower Gush Katif take on an added significance as he clarifies his theology of the real. Sharon's national narrative is focused on the "lower." His insistence on the defensible territorial integrity of the state originates in an intense commitment to the preservation of Jewish lives and their ensured tangible prosperity. In Rabbi Tzvi Yehuda's narrative the "higher" dominates the "lower." The Israeli state is coherent in its capacity as a reflection of divine presence increasingly, inexorably revealed. Just as both narratives exclude each other when confronted, so they are incapable of fostering real engagement between the higher and the lower dimensions of Israeli consciousness.

For Sharon, Gush Katif was perfect for his experiments with unilateralism. The number of Israeli settlers in the Gaza Strip was much lower than in the West Bank. Additionally, the Gush was geographically removed from the densest parts of Israel "proper," located as it was on the southern periphery of Israel. For the settler leadership, hailing mostly from the West Bank, Gush Katif was a favored battleground for similar reasons. Itzik Tzur, a settler from Ganei Tal, spoke of a difference between the "mountain people" and the "sand people" in the midst of disengagement. The mountain people were the West Bank settlers, who lived on high, rocky ground, traveling narrow, circuitous roads in order to get home. The sand people were the Gaza settlers, in close proximity to the Mediterranean Sea, and leading a simpler and easier life.

The mountain people were mostly of *Ashkenazi* (European) origin, emphasizing their strict commitment to the settler ideology. Many of the sand people were of *Mizrahi* (oriental, the Arabic-speaking world) origins and had moved to the Gush from the underdeveloped towns of Israel's periphery.[23] The settler leadership, consisting mainly of mountain men, saw the fate of Gush Katif as a bellwether for the grand struggle still awaiting the settler movement over the collective Israeli soul. As I understand it, disengagement was a containable experiment for the settler leadership, allowing it to test mobilization and protest capabilities while losing as little as possible even in the worst case (and ultimately real) scenario. For Sharon and for the settler leadership, Gush Katif was an exception to most rules regulating public life in Israel.

---

[23] See the following *Ha'aretz* article (in Hebrew) by Nir Hasson, analyzing ethnic and other differences between West Bank and Gush Katif settlers. Itzik Tzur is quoted in the article, published in August 2005: www.haaretz.co.il/misc/1.1032861 (last accessed on October 18, 2016).

For Hacohen, the basic dilemma of the state with regard to Gush Katif, the need to act separately with regard to its higher and lower levels, was the basic dilemma of the Israeli state itself. That is, Hacohen saw disengagement as a chance to reassert the coherence of what he saw as the Israeli national narrative. He did so by recognizing and enabling the theological reality of his mediating space. Why theological? Because his mediating space is not an empty, nihilistic space. It requires the presence and absence of a sovereign absolute that can maintain its coherence in direct friction with conflict and contradiction. That sovereign absolute is God.

From God's sovereignty, Hacohen draws his own. Rabbi Tzvi Yehuda was a sovereign guardian of the one truth, regardless of observable reality and its consequences. Sharon was the Schmittian sovereign, the one drawing the line between the exigent and the mundane. Hacohen is sovereign when he stands at the center of emerging reality, having planned the setting for the emergence to the tiniest detail, and actively relinquishes the "authority" of execution.

The last section of the conversation between Hacohen and Hazani deals with lessons from the Second Lebanon War, fought one year after the summer of disengagement. The war's outcome remains a subject of debate in Israel. Still, there is general consensus that the war did not represent the finest hour of Israel's military and political leadership. As such, it was the radical opposite of disengagement, which ended almost miraculously early, with no casualties or serious damage. I did not include the final section in its entirety, because it focuses mostly on technical military definitions and distinctions. Still, I would like to end our Israeli discussion with Hazani's question and Hacohen's answer on two critical elements of his theology of the real, its practice and its transmission:

> *Hazani: I would like to … ask about the tension between the unique event and the ability to extrapolate from disengagement to other events. What can you learn about the shaping and design of space as the cognitive effort of the strategic commander? What can be applied to different missions in the future? How should commanders study these issues during their training? Our conversations reveal that you have used, in your career, what we've called the "Soviet Method" on numerous occasions. The realization is different each time, but the idea remains.*
> *Hacohen: It is remarkably difficult to teach! …*
> *Hazani: Still, I insist. (I understand some things about) your own learning, but you are charged with the training of senior officers,*[24] *some of whom will*

---

[24] At the time, Hacohen was the commander of the IDF colleges, including staff and command college, as well the national defense college, the most prestigious training program for senior military personnel and civil servants.

*likely advance further. How can you make sure that future division commanders get a feel for space?*

Hacohen: *I would like to speak as simply as I can. You take a place like Red Square and the Kremlin, or the Temple in Jerusalem and its gathering space, the "Azarah," or perhaps Tiananmen Square in China – the combination between an empty space and a monument accentuated and empowered by the space. This is the starting point of my operational thought. It means that you don't just operate over the entire space, but that you use the emptiness as a part of your operational space. If you had buildings in Red Square, you couldn't see the Kremlin. That is how the square empowers the Kremlin. It is a combination between the present and the absent. Emptiness is meaningful.*

*When I use military power, I always have to frame a space in a way that places an event within that space, an event that is enhanced and empowered (by that space). I create the framework which serves as the background for the enhancement of the event. This is a difficult message to convey. I'm talking about aesthetic matters. Issues of design. The relation between space and power is like the relation between space and what is constructed on it. Any concept – in defense and an offense – deals with operations on space that produce the emergence of a different form for that space.*

Hazani: *That is not the way they teach in courses for battalion and regiment commanders. How do you make the transition from commanding units at the tactical level, where the greatest emphasis is placed on the exact fulfillment of pre-planned processes?*

Hacohen: *They really should not be learning this. Not even in the regimental commanders course. This is the point of the operational story, it is extremely complicated and you shouldn't confuse the men.*

Emptiness is meaningful if the leader venturing into emptiness has faith. The tactical commander places his faith in the validity of the replicable process. The strategic commander, the creator, places his faith in the enhancement of the event by the space surrounding it. The relationship between the present and the absent is complicated. They may be "naturally" inclined to annihilate each other. But the creation Hacohen has in mind is not "natural," in the sense of being an innate quality applied at will. His creation requires faith in the potential for overcoming the "natural" in favor of the real.

The real involves a present that is not a simple derivative of past events or preparation for future necessities. Action in the real requires preparation because reality is known by its emergence. Thought, conceptualization and planning are essential for acting in reality. They are all real in and of themselves, not only if they manage to deliver a predetermined end. They are too confusing to teach because teaching, like understanding, places the teacher outside (or beyond) emergence. The teacher takes on a static stability, an immutability that easily succumbs to the lure of a known past or a desirable future. As an actor in the Israeli real, Hacohen cannot afford the luxury of stability. Both Sharon and Rabbi Tzvi Yehuda tell stories focused on increasing stability (cosmic or territorial, faith-based or security-oriented) and decreasing uncertainty.

Hacohen embraces uncertainty as the superior systemic strategy for operation, and his words are corroborated by his accomplishments. He completed the ordeal of disengagement much more rapidly than expected. The mediating space he designed allowed Israeli society, confronted with a nearly certain rupture between Jewish and democratic, to emerge relatively unscathed.[25] His faith in God shapes his strategy as a theology of the real.

God's presence is a necessity, even if there is no direct mention of the presence or of God in the text. God serves as a horizon for the enhancement of the event by its surrounding space. God serves to anchor a present away from the pre- and post-conceptions of "rationally" planning humans. Psalm 127 says: "Unless the Lord builds the house, the builders labor in vain. Unless the Lord watches over the city, the guards stand watch in vain."[26] Even if we were not aware of Hacohen's personal faith and upbringing, it is clear that the psalm echoes his sentiment.

In his embrace of the present Hacohen is dependent on an anchoring principle to countermand the vanity of the dominant Israeli narratives. This principle is the notion of a mediating space, but such space cannot exist as a vacuum. Mediating space must expand and contract in counterpoint to both narratives. It must, in poker parlance, "see them and raise them." This counterpoint cannot be exclusively abstract or purely practical. It must enhance and contain, subtract and add. The required fullness (and emptiness) can be real only if it is divine. Hacohen's God stands before Rabbi Tzvi Yehuda's "redemption" and Sharon's "security" as a sovereign being, connecting emergence and fullness as divine truth.

Hacohen's sovereignty emerges from this quality of the divine. If God can enhance through presence and absence, Hacohen can design and command by relinquishing linearity for emergence. Hacohen creates from and with faith, embracing uncertainty as a manifestation of divine perfection. The tactical commander must decide between one and zero at

[25] Hacohen was not, of course, the sole authority when planning and executing disengagement. He worked under Major General Dan Harel, the commander of IDF Southern Command, and cooperated with national police generals and other senior officers. Still, Hacohen was continuously the odd man out. His military superiors likely considered him useful for his settler contacts and the settler leadership would have sought his military connections. Both sides saw him as a messenger for their ulterior agenda. His insistence on the creation of mediating space ultimately subverted both efforts.

[26] See http://biblehub.com/psalms/127-1.htm (last accessed on October 18, 2016).

every junction. For Hacohen, ones and zeros occur constantly and simultaneously. He creates by refusing to focus on the outcome – one or zero. Outcomes belong to the tactical commander and to God.

Hacohen's theology of the real is not philosophical. It prefers action to wisdom. A political theology, it creates a narrative of power and belonging that subverts the structure imposed by the grand narratives of Sharon and Rabbi Tzvi Yehuda. Hacohen's Israeli sovereignty comes from a commitment to participation rather than from the reflection of an ulterior ideal. This sovereignty views Israeli society's propensity for internal friction as an asset, if it can muster the faith necessary for sustaining mediation such friction requires. Many Israelis would consider Hacohen's theology of the real escapist at best and delusional at worst, for its rejection of clear-cut decisions. For Hacohen, binary choices are not real. They cannot be the platform from which grows a virtuous society. Growth is inspired by the elaborate dance he performs as a leader, moving between faith and action, creation and execution, affirming their bonds in his very movement.

## Interlude II

Gershon Hacohen's theology of the real is formulated (and can exist) only in the context of constraining absolutes. Hacohen's politics are committed to subversive affirmation. His faith drives him to act in the lower realms so that the higher realms might stir. He sees no direct contact between the two, of course, but an obligation to act incumbent on the true believer. This action is the only claim of the here and now can make to the holiness and perfection of the grand divine truth, precisely because this perfection is forever out of the here and now's grasp.

The emerging politics are devoted to mediation that is as incendiary as it is loyal. Hacohen is driven to change and challenge, to take away from the pretense to truth at the level of flawed, ongoing emergence. At the same time, his passion realizes the highest in the lowest, the life in the midst of death. His faith is grounded in constant revolution.

III

# THE URGENCY OF THE REAL

# 5

# ISIS and the Establishment of the Caliphate

## Redemption and Hollowness

On November 13, 2015, several groups of terrorists attacked, with some simultaneity, several sites chosen in advance across Paris. Explosions, suicide bombings and shootings occurred at the Bataclan concert hall, at the Stade De France national stadium and around various popular restaurants at the very center of the city.[1] Nearly 130 people died. The Islamic State (IS), known also as ISIS, ISIL and Daesh,[2] took responsibility for the bombings. In a report published one week after the bombing, *The Economist* spoke of "Jihad at the Heart of Europe."[3]

Will McCants, one of the foremost scholars and analysts of IS and the jihadi movement, published an article in *The Atlantic* entitled "Why did ISIS attack Paris?" The article appeared on November 16, three days after the bombing. In answer to the question posed by his title, McCants suggests "... A range of theories, some of which could overlap, some of them

---

[1] For a timeline of the attacks, see www.bbc.com/news/world-europe-34818994 (last accessed on October 18, 2016).

[2] Islamic State in Iraq and Al-Sham, Islamic State in Iraq and the Levant and *Al-Dawla Al-Islamiyah fi Al-Iraq wa Al-Sham*, respectively. The *Sham*, the area encompassing what are today Syria, Lebanon, Israel and Jordan, is known in Western languages as the Levant. Daesh is the Arab acronym of ISIS. The choice of name often reflects nuances of the political agenda adopted with respect to the phenomenon. For example, few official Western sources would refer to the group as IS, so as not to reinforce the perception that the organization has established an actual "state." For an informative review of the names, see the Wikipedia entry: https://en.wikipedia.org/wiki/Names_of_the_Islamic_State_of_Iraq_and_the_Levant (last accessed on October 18, 2016). For an analysis of several nuances expressed by the choice of name, see www.bbc.com/news/world-middle-east-27994277 (last accessed on October 18, 2016).

[3] See www.economist.com/news/briefing/21678840-brussels-not-just-europes-political-and-military-capitalit-also-centre-its (last accessed on October 18, 2016).

mutually contradictory." His list of theories ranges from the notion that Jihadists cannot but engage in terrorist attacks to a complex plan seeking to draw the international community into Syria in order to exhaust the West's strength.[4] McCants then goes on to say that it may take years until we understand what drove IS to attack Paris, just as it took years to understand what Al-Qaeda hoped to achieve when it planned and executed 9/11. Still, he says, "why" is the most important question for any effective campaign against IS as well. It is also, says McCants, the most difficult question to answer.

In his book, *The ISIS Apocalypse*,[5] McCants explores the apocalyptic aspects of IS theology at some length. Beginning with his analytical biography of IS founder, Abu Mus'ab al-Zarqawi, McCants stresses the constitutive role of a future foretold in the growth of the Islamic State. The future plays a key part in classical Islamic theology, particularly the uncompromising resolution of all earthly affairs which will occur on Judgment Day. To have faith, in the words of the most quoted Islamic traditions (ascribed to the prophet Muhammad himself), is to believe "... in the Last Day and ... in the measuring out, both its good and its evil ..."[6] Judgment Day will involve the imposition of perfect, divine standards and the resulting negation of human desires and machinations. But as McCants points out, Islam also carries a powerful messianic strain, awaiting a future of just rewards and intimate engagement with divine truth and order.

Shi'a Islam, the Islamic school of the largest religious minority in the Muslim world, is overtly messianic. Shi'a Muslims await the return of the Mahdi, the 12th ruler (*Imam*) of a dynasty beginning with Ali, the prophet Muhammad's cousin and son-in-law. The Mahdi's return will bring with it expressly political change, restoring the Shi'a to their proper place at the vanguard of Islamic society in contrast to their perennial persecution by the Sunni majority. Belief in a politically charged Judgment Day is more difficult for Sunnis, precisely because it potentially undermines

---

[4] See www.theatlantic.com/international/archive/2015/11/isis-paris-attack-why/416277/ (last accessed on October 18, 2016).

[5] Will McCants, *The ISIS Apocalypse: The History, Strategy and Doomsday Vision of the Islamic State* (St. Martin's Press, 2015).

[6] These words are taken from the Gabriel Hadith, a tradition describing a meeting between the prophet Muhammad and the angel Gabriel during which the angel had the prophet explain the three levels of religious life. The translation, by Sachiko Murata and William Chittick, is accessible online at www.islamicity.org/5740/the-hadith-of-gabriel/ (last accessed on October 18, 2016).

the achievements of Sunni politics in this imperfect world. Leading the expansion and prosperity of Islam over long centuries, the Sunni political tradition[7] is heavily invested in what a Western reader might think of as "Law and Order." Theologically and practically, divine perfection is a foil for human politicking. One of the radical innovations of the jihadi movement is its framing of a political program in terms of a future worldly dominion of Islam.

McCants suggests that even within the global jihad, IS is and was particularly radical. Al-Qaeda saw itself as a political entity, its worldliness invested and expressed in constant, real-time engagement with the world at large. McCants acknowledges the interest of Al-Qaeda in the establishment of an Islamic state. Still, he describes Bin Laden's agenda as focused on the incremental accumulation of political, military and financial strength and capital which should culminate in the creation of such a state. For IS, beginning with its founder (Zarqawi), the world mattered mostly as the setting for the ultimate victory of Islam in the last battle and the final day.

McCants describes Zarqawi, for example, as extremely fanatical in his hatred for Shi'a Islam. There were many valid reasons for Zarqawi, as a radical Sunni activist, to hate the Shi'a. He was building an Al-Qaeda sponsored network in Iraq, in 2003, when the United States invaded the country. As an independent nation, Iraq has always been torn between Sunni and Shi'a Muslims. It has been ruled by Sunnis since its establishment, in the early 1920s. It is also home to the holy Shi'a cities of Najaf and Karbalah, and to a sizable Shi'a population. The American invasion quickly dispensed with the regime of (the Sunni) Saddam Hussein and found natural allies in Iraq's Shi'a who had been repressively disenfranchised by Saddam. In the aftermath of the occupation, Iraqi Sunnis often felt unjustly treated by the newly installed Shi'a national leadership. McCants describes Zarqawi's feelings in the following words:

Zarqawi's hatred of the Shi'a was all-consuming. To his mind, the Shi'a were not just fifth columnists, selling out the Sunnis to the Americans. They were servants of the Antichrist, who will appear at the end of time to fight against the Muslims. The Americans served the same master.[8]

---

[7] I am aware of the gross generalizations expressed in this phrase. Still, for the purposes of our discussion I believe it best reflects the inherent tensions that gave birth to the political theology of IS.

[8] See McCants, *The ISIS Apocalypse*, p. 10.

McCants also adds a lengthy series of appendices in which he translates the eschatological prophecies inspiring IS in what he sees as the organization's commitment to the present fulfillment of a foretold future.

In March 2015, Graeme Wood published a lengthy piece in *The Atlantic*, entitled "What ISIS Wants."[9] His article set the standard for journalistic coverage of IS, combining ideological and historical analysis with personal interviews revealing the motivations and aspirations of IS soldiers and supporters. He describes two main misapprehensions of IS by the West. The first is the understanding of the jihadi movement as "monolithic," lumping together Al-Qaeda, IS and other organizations. The second misapprehension, in Wood's words, has to do with "a well-intentioned but dishonest campaign to deny the Islamic State's medieval religious nature." Wood ascribes this dishonesty to the conventions established by Al-Qaeda with regard to the nature of the global jihad. Al-Qaeda senior leaders, from Bin Laden to Muhammad Atta, were worldly in both interests and life habits. They saw themselves as players on a global stage and as consumers of global culture. As a player, Al-Qaeda needed others with which to play. The organization's actions were undertaken with an audience and with visions of influence in mind.

The Islamic State was significantly different, Wood said. It was, in his words, "... (of a) medieval religious nature ... Islamic. Very Islamic." Al-Qaeda was thoroughly modern, conversant with the language of power and interests. Wood did not doubt the inspiration Al-Qaeda drew from Islam. Still, he seemed to suggest that Bin Laden and his supporters could, ultimately, define their desires in terms of *realpolitik*. When it comes to IS, however, "much of what the group does looks nonsensical except in light of a sincere, carefully considered commitment to returning civilization to a seventh-century legal environment, and ultimately to bringing about the apocalypse." In another piece, published in *New Republic* in September 2014, Wood concludes that "These beliefs would be merely peculiar, if the punctilious nature of ISIS did not suggest that its leaders believe in the literal truth of prophecy and will act accordingly." Earlier in the piece, he refers to IS plans and beliefs as "a little more predictable than those of a spry, global-reach organization like Al Qaeda."[10]

9   See www.theatlantic.com/magazine/archive/2015/03/what-isis-really-wants/384980/ (last accessed on October 18, 2016).
10  See https://newrepublic.com/article/119259/isis-history-islamic-states-new-caliphate-syria-and-iraq (last accessed on October 18, 2016).

McCants and Wood represent two ways of engaging IS. I use the "engage" rather than "examine" or "consider" because both McCants and Wood assume active engagement of IS is a necessity. Furthermore, they assume that IS wishes to engage the world. Their approaches share a fascination with the religiosity of IS. For both McCants and Wood, what makes IS unique even among other jihadi organizations is the realness of IS religious faith. This faith is strong enough to shape "real world" considerations. Religious faith offers, we might say, a realness that is alternative (and even competitive) to that of the tangible world. As an example of this otherworldliness, McCants and Wood describe IS in the context of Al-Qaeda. They seem to suggest that in its wrath against the world created by secular Arab leaderships and the West, Al-Qaeda located itself firmly within that world. The Islamic State, however, has detached itself from this world by the power of its faith. It does not follow the rules, even if for the purpose of inflicting a greater defeat upon infidels.

McCants and Wood are both drawn to this religiosity, but they do so from different directions. Wood is fascinated by what he repeatedly calls the "medieval" nature of IS. In his lengthy *Atlantic* piece, he devotes plenty of column inches to a discussion of the apocalypse, but approaches it mostly in a personal context. The subject comes up mainly when he interviews Westerners who have either fought with or are actively supporting IS. It is as if the apocalypse were the "alternative" component of IS faith, the aspect most elusive for an engaged Western observer. The past and its dictates, however, are perfectly rational to Wood, in the sense of laying down a clear logic that demands clear obedience. He can relate to the strictures of faith as laid down in scripture or by the prophet Muhammad himself, or at the very least recognize and acknowledge their authority and legitimacy. Reading Wood, I understand him to suggest that the basic allure of religious faith is a belief in God's absolute power and truth. Having had the ultimate truth revealed by the most powerful entity in the universe, strict and particular obedience to the instructions of this truthful power may lead to problematic results, but its basic logic cannot be simply refuted.

If Wood approaches IS through the rationality of the past, McCants does so through the inevitability of the future. Like Wood, he is committed to demonstrating (and, if successful, explaining) the uniqueness of IS faith and the ways in which it shapes the organization's actions and decisions. McCants, conversant with historical scholarship, does not extrapolate from history or assume an indifferent causality. He describes the allure of doomsday prophecies in all religious traditions that possess them and is careful to state several times that most Muslims do not believe in such prophecies or even necessarily know them.[11] Still, he establishes the difference between Al-Qaeda and IS by relating the disdain of Bin Laden and Zawahiri for such beliefs.[12] They are, he suggests, a mark of crudeness among those possessing advanced religious education in the Muslim world. Al-Qaeda, according to McCants' analysis, was led by men who had accepted the perspicuous instrumental rationality of the West as efficient for defeating the West as well as for organizing their own effort. The Islamic State, however, preferred (and prefers) the curious mix of oracular ambivalence and faith-based certainty offered by prophecy. The structure of *The ISIS Apocalypse* is the best demonstration of McCants' conviction to this effect. He translated most of the major prophecies quoted by IS leaders and organized them according to themes reflecting their eclecticism. Prophecies regarding the return of Jesus are adjacent to visions of Islam conquering India. At a casual glance, it is as though McCants was attracted most immediately to the curiosity of the affair, rather than to its attempt at rationality. He does not belittle the seriousness of IS faith in its prophetic sources. Still, his presentation of the prophecies to his readers reflects a degree of incredulity.

The Islamic State's religiosity, then, packs a complicated punch. It is what sets IS apart because the realness of IS faith stands in stark contrast to conventional analytic rationales, from instrumental rationality to historical causality. Still, this very otherness also enables conversation about IS, because it enables clear dichotomies. "We" are not like IS because our behavior is not deterministically shaped by our past, nor is it wholly committed to the realization of a certain future.

This binary fascination with the political theology of IS intentionally disengages from the present tense. This disengagement is not accidental, even if it may be less than conscious. The present, taken on fully, requires an acknowledgment of emergence and uncertainty. Successfully navigating this uncertainty en route to one's rationally defined goals is the mark of a modern, enlightened rationality. The brutality of IS, its remorseless use of violence and stringent enforcement of divine standards at the expense of humanist principles, all these consign IS to the future and/or the past in the eyes of most Western observers.

Nonetheless, IS shapes the world in the present. Let's consider the Paris attack with which we began this chapter. I find the attack too

---

[11] See *The ISIS Apocalypse*, p. 161 (*et passim*).
[12] See ibid., p. 28.

complex simply to reflect obedience to a "medieval" command or fealty to a chaotic vision of the future. The attack was planned and carried out by European Muslims, citizens of France and Belgium who may have received advice and instruction but were mostly left to their own devices. The evolution of these local networks required an acute sensitivity to emerging conditions on the ground, a sensitivity that can only be developed through constant friction and interaction. What can we say about the theology that guides IS through this complicated present?

The question of the present is prominent in the mind of IS itself. Upon occupying a town, IS will gather the inhabitants in the local square and force them to perform the *taqbir*, chanting *allahu akbar* to profess the greatness of God. Having completed the *taqbir*, IS operatives cover the walls of the town with their defining slogan: *baqiyah watatamadad*. The combination, which may be translated as "enduring and expanding" refers to IS itself. It is also a remarkably popular hashtag on the numerous social media accounts devoted to IS. In its own terms, IS exists in the here and now before it exists as an extension of the past or as preparation for the future.

This present, as I've already suggested, is not addressed by most observers and scholars of IS. Commitment to the present dimension requires a reevaluation of the faith underlying IS politics. For Wood and McCants, IS religiosity is what drives the organization but also allows for the clinical, detached examination of the Western expert. It is almost as though IS was the dead butterfly and faith was the pin attaching it to the lepidopterist's viewing board. When considering the theological present of IS, I would like to think differently of its religious faith. Rather than identifying the ways in which faith stabilizes IS from the past and toward the future, I would like to consider the ways in which faith drives IS emergence in the present.

Approaching IS faith, or IS religiosity with anything but vehement condemnations is a challenge. It is difficult to distinguish between intellectual or spiritual constructs and what amounts to a lack of regard for humanity (life and values) demonstrated by IS individual and mass executions, beheadings, graphic media dissemination and general demeanor. Wood and McCants are certainly correct when they emphasize the foreignness, perhaps even the strangeness, of IS and its motivations/aspirations when compared with those of the international community. I would like to think of IS faith as a foreign language, acquirable through immersion in its patterns of speech and meaning production. More specifically, I would like to suggest that this language of faith is articulated most poignantly in IS engagement with reality. We will read the IS text declaring the coming into existence of the caliphate, the Islamic State in its territorial, central-ized form. When we read the declaration, we will focus on the driving, generating capabilities of IS faith in a practical context, the IS theology of the real.

## Leviticus 26: Defining a Life of Redemption

But in order to approach IS faith in this way, I propose a detour that will allow us to acquire (or reacquire) a basic fluency in the faith-imbued language of the IS present. So far, we have encountered narratives of faith from personal perspectives, simultaneously authoritative and subversive. I think it is easier to relate to faith and its dilemmas of political expres-sion at the personal level. The Islamic State is an impersonal carrier of an ideology, an organization occupied with its own coherence and survival. As such, while its messages are as complex as those we saw in the Iranian and Israeli cases, the language of IS is firm and resolute. The personal the-ologies we read openly discussed loss and uncertainty. The Islamic State's theology is concerned with inspiration and victory, adopting a tone of staunch inevitability. It is expressly concerned with the end of days and their effect on political behavior. Our attempt to explore the realness of IS theology, its tensions and uncertainties, requires a refresher course in the ambiguities of messianic language. Otherwise, our close reading of IS truths will seem to present us with nothing but empty superlatives.

And so, before reading the IS declaration of the caliphate (entitled, "This is the Promise of Allah") we will read the 26th chapter of Leviticus. The book of Leviticus devotes itself mostly to the rules and regulations of Jewish life, from ritual worship to sexual behavior. Chapter 26 is some-thing of an exception. It belongs to a sparsely populated genre within Jewish scripture, the listing of blessings and curses.[13] These blessings and curses are actually the rewards and punishments the Jews may expect if they obey or disobey God's commandments, respectively. In Leviticus, the chapter appears at the end of the "Holiness Code," a group of nine chap-ters usually believed to be a separate source incorporated into Leviticus after its composition by the priests of the first temple. The Holiness Code

---

[13] Another chapter belonging to the genre is Deuteronomy 28, where the reading of the blessings and the curses marks the ceremonial entry of the Israelites into the land of Israel.

incorporates laws specifically concerned with leading a holy life, enunciating the immediacy of the relationship between God and the Jews in ordinary, human life.[14] Traditional readings of chapter 26 enforce a basic message of obedience. Blessings are in store for those who obey and curses will plague those who do not. The curses, it is important to note, greatly outnumber the blessings.

I would like to read chapter 26 differently, as a framework of redemption lived within an ordinary human life. What is often seen as a distinction of propriety (do good, be rewarded; do evil, be punished) can also be read as a continuum. Religions based on divine revelation – as are Judaism, Christianity and Islam – also hold within them the inevitability of a second revelation. A religion comes into existence when God reveals himself to a prophet. Time begins to move forward from the moment of revelation as the world enters a new age. But time, in all three religions, also moves backward toward the second revelation. Judgment Day, the coming of the messiah, the rapture, these are all culminations of ordinary human time. They are goals that, when reached, bring with them the stoppage of this ordinary time in favor of a divine stillness, the time of the kingdom of heaven or a just meting out to each person according to their actions. The story of redemption, then, can be read not just as a stable tale of reward and punishment, but as continuum of the time in-between redemptions, the time defined by what it can never be.

The inspiration for my reading is a less-known work by the Italian philosopher, Giorgio Agamben. Agamben is known for his work on biopolitics, the intellectual movement that explores the ways in which political power is used to control the human (and animal) body itself. His *Homo Sacer*,[15] considering the ways in which the Nazis established norms of political control over the body, revolutionized the study of various fields simultaneously. Agamben is also known for his work on religion and its regimentation of social and individual life.[16] The book that shaped my reading of both Leviticus and IS is entitled *The Time that Remains: A Commentary on the Letter to the Romans.*[17] The book is an

---

[14] See, for example, Jan Joosten, *People and Land in the Holiness Code: An Exegetical Study of the Ideational Framework of the Law in Leviticus 17–26* (Brill, 1996).

[15] See Giorgio Agamben, *Homo Sacer: Sovereign Power and Bare Life* (Stanford University Press, 1998).

[16] For example, see Giorgio Agamben, *The Kingdom and the Glory: For a Theological Genealogy of Economy and Government* (Stanford University Press, 2011).

[17] Giorgio Agamben, *The Time that Remains: A Commentary on the Letter to the Romans* (Stanford University Press, 2005).

account of a seminar Agamben gave, purportedly on Paul's Epistle to the Romans but effectively on the very first line of the epistle.

In the book, Agamben suggests that the Catholic Church pulled out all stops in its attempt to remove, in its translation of Paul's epistle, the messianic heart of the text. According to Agamben, Paul's original text in Greek is one of the fundamental messianic texts of the West. He suggests that Paul was less concerned with inventing a new religion than he was with the refutation of Jewish law through an articulation of a messianic time, the time that remains.

Agamben's work allowed me to consider the present dimension of IS in a new light. In what follows, I am not going to ground my work in direct quotes from Agamben's book. He was concerned with the inter-mingled intellectual roots of Judaism and Christianity, connecting these roots to the work of Walter Benjamin and his philosophy of history. An extrapolation of IS theology from his insights would do justice to neither. Still, Agamben's notion of the time that remains, what I've called the "in-between" time, highlights the tension of the faith-based present in remarkably poignant fashion. His deeply learned model demonstrates the difficulty of approaching this present in an a-messianic mode, a Judeo-Christianity seeking stability and linearity. His work will guide us in our reading of Leviticus 26 as well as the IS declaration of the caliphate. The basic principle of the in-between time, that time that moves forward and backward, the time that cannot be fulfilled as it occurs, will be at the foundation of this chapter's take on the theology of the real.

### Leviticus 26: Living In-Between

*Do not make idols or set up an image or a sacred stone for yourselves, and do not place a carved stone in your land to bow down before it. I am the Lord your God.*
*2 Observe my Sabbaths and have reverence for my sanctuary. I am the Lord.*[18]

We begin with the absolutes. God is the epitome of the real. Any other attempt to approximate God amounts to a "stone." The Jews are not told that other gods are inferior to theirs, but that there are no other gods as far as they are concerned. God's presence in the lives of the Jews is another seeming absolute. Observing the Sabbath can be read as a spiritual (or moral) admonition, observing the divinely mandated downtime on the seventh day because of the values this observance celebrated – communal

---

[18] The English text is from the New International Version, accessible online at www.bible-gateway.com/passage/?search=Leviticus+26.

solidarity, free time etc. Still, the observation of the Sabbaths is also about the regularity of time. The instruction to revere the sanctuary, the proto-temple of the desert, emphasizes the stability of Jewish space. The *ur*-place and the *ur*-time, the models of temporality and spatiality in the human world, are those established directly by God.

This structure appears to ground the divine presence firmly in the non-eternal context of human lives. The unassailable power and fixedness of God are the initial principles that regulate, through their stability, the motion that is Jewish life. A life is worth living if it is spent in acknowl-edgment and awe, and later on in observance and reverence. There is seemingly no need for an in-between, because the hierarchy is clear.

*3 If you follow my decrees and are careful to obey my commands, 4 I will send you rain in its season, and the ground will yield its crops and the trees their fruit. 5 Your threshing will continue until grape harvest and the grape harvest will con-tinue until planting, and you will eat all the food you want and live in safety in your land.*

*6 I will grant peace in the land, and you will lie down and no one will make you afraid. I will remove wild beasts from the land, and the sword will not pass through your country. 7 You will pursue your enemies, and they will fall by the sword before you. 8 Five of you will chase a hundred, and a hundred of you will chase ten thousand, and your enemies will fall by the sword before you.*

*9 I will look on you with favor and make you fruitful and increase your numbers, and I will keep my covenant with you. 10 You will still be eating last year's har-vest when you will have to move it out to make room for the new. 11 I will put my dwelling place among you, and I will not abhor you. 12 I will walk among you and be your God, and you will be my people. 13 I am the Lord your God, who brought you out of Egypt so that you would no longer be slaves to the Egyptians; I broke the bars of your yoke and enabled you to walk with heads held high.*

The immediate conclusion from the list of rewards is that should the Jews do everything that is expected from them, enhanced stability and predict-ability will be their greatest rewards. Since observance and obedience are the ultimate virtues of an ordinary life, the more one obeys, the more one has an incentive to obey. What makes God truly God are his power and his truth, and they will simply be enunciated further and further, clearer and clearer. The divine presence will never be disruptive or destabilizing, but will deepen the solidity of a faith based on the expectance of reward.

The integrity of Jewish space will grow in immediate ways. The land will yield more crops. The borders will be safe in peace and in war. In fact, Jewish strength will grow to the point where five Jews could chase a hundred non-Jews, and a hundred Jews could chase ten thousand "others." There will be no need for a second revelation or for Judgment Day because, power-wise, non-Jews will stand in relation to Jews as Jews stand in relation to God. The hierarchy will be clear enough to serve as the organizing principle of Jewish life in the physical space they will occupy.

Time, however, will blur. The agricultural cycle of seasons sets farmers on edge, concerned as they are about the time between the end of last season's crop and the coming season's reaping. It is never certain that food will be sufficient, and everything is at stake and dependent on divine providence. The passing of a year is never more distinct than in this in-between time. The Jewish reward for observance is the trivialization, perhaps even the negation, of this poignant period. There will be such bounty that farmers will not have consumed last year's crop before they haul in the new year's crop. One day will segue into another, a life of such ease that one no longer cares too much what time it is in the day or in the year. This blurring of time also makes Jews more like the God they revere. In this proximity, Jews will be stronger than everyone else because God is the strongest. They will care less and less about time because God, in his eternity, does not care about the passage of linear time.

The reward, then, is to grow ever closer to God. This is a gentle, endless curve. There is no rapture, no measuring out, no judgment. Obedience makes Jews less human and more divine by abolishing the lines traditionally distinguishing between the two. That is not to say that Jews will become godly or even godlike. It is precisely their faith in God's singularity that allows them, according to the model life presented by the list of blessings, to obey as fully as is required of them. I'd like to think of the reward as the avoidance of a second revelation. A revelation cannot but jar and shake. Faith that comes from revelation may be consciously aware of the impending second revelation and appreciate its imminent perspicacity. Once the second revelation comes, every person receives their just comeuppance. Still, at the most human level that faith longs for the solace that the faithful consider a just reward for their perseverance and their obedience. This is the reward offered here.

The list of curses and punishments is significantly longer than the list of blessings. Before we begin to consider it, I think it is important to say two things about it. The first has to do with its end. A bit of a spoiler, but a necessary one – the list of curses also ends in redemption. After a lengthy process of purification and distillation through adversity, God remembers his apparently unbreakable covenant with Israel and returns them to their land, and so on and so forth. The second important thing to say about the list of curses is that it leaves the Jews fully, irrevocably human. The curses, laid and executed because of disobedience, represent a state of affairs much closer to an actual human life than the list of blessings. The rationale for my statement is simple: a life lived according to the blessings model grows constantly less human. The dynamic of human life described in the list of curses follows a very different dynamic. It is bookended by two revelations, running simultaneously forward and backward. The list of curses draws for us an image of a human life lived in the in-between time, craving redemption in a world not-yet-redeemed.

*14 But if you will not listen to me and carry out all these commands, 15 and if you reject my decrees and abhor my laws and fail to carry out all my commands and so violate my covenant, 16 then I will do this to you: I will bring on you sudden terror, wasting diseases and fever that will destroy your sight and sap your strength. You will plant seed in vain, because your enemies will eat it. 17 I will set my face against you so that you will be defeated by your enemies; those who hate you will rule over you, and you will flee even when no one is pursuing you. 18 If after all this you will not listen to me, I will punish you for your sins seven times over. 19 I will break down your stubborn pride and make the sky above you like iron and the ground beneath you like bronze. 20 Your strength will be spent in vain, because your soil will not yield its crops, nor will the trees of your land yield their fruit. 21 If you remain hostile toward me and refuse to listen to me, I will multiply your afflictions seven times over, as your sins deserve. 22 I will send wild animals against you, and they will rob you of your children, destroy your cattle and make you so few in number that your roads will be deserted.*

If we can say one thing about the series of curses, it is that they are unfair. The punishments administered exceed the level of the sins sevenfold (at the least). Despite the words of verse 21, there are no fairness or deserts involved. The sovereign decides the severity of the punishment and it is always greater than the sin, because sovereignty is best expressed by superfluity.

These curses are designed to strip any semblance of sovereignty from the punished Jews. God gradually breaks the chains of necessity and causality, denying the expectations of a rational mind. Still, the mind remains. That is, the curses do not end in death. They may bring about the death of loved ones, and we will consider the implications of this, but the one or the group cursed do not die. Death would be beside the point, because it would nullify God's sovereignty. What is an omnipotent deity without subjects upon whom to wreak his potency? The mind remains to witness how what it once held to be secure and stable, its moorings, become vain, redundant fancies.

The Jews think they are strong but their false strength will be broken. This lesson will not be learned in conventional fashion, through defeat and subjugation. There is no need to subjugate the Jews because they are already God's to command. Their vanity will be demonstrated by the severing of all that grounds the Jews in their reality. Their soil will not bring them crops. Their children will be robbed from them and their roads will be deserted. God will not kill "them" specifically, but he will leave them adrift. The absence of children leaves no link to the future, no real hope for its coming. Deaths are mentioned in passing in verse 22, but I think the real punishment is the limitation on movement. Roads are a mark of civilization. The constant traffic on them drives away wild animals and marks them as exclusively human. This will no longer be the case. The unfairness of the curses is related, then, not simply to the severity of the punishment involved but to the unmoored isolation which they generate. Jews are left alone in their own heads, none of their hopes and aspirations corresponding with emerging reality. They are also left alone in physical space, no safe borders on the one hand and no way to leave their collapsing homes on the other.

*23 If in spite of these things you do not accept my correction but continue to be hostile toward me, 24 I myself will be hostile toward you and will afflict you for your sins seven times over. 25 And I will bring the sword on you to avenge the breaking of the covenant. When you withdraw into your cities, I will send a plague among you, and you will be given into enemy hands. 26 When I cut off your supply of bread, ten women will be able to bake your bread in one oven, and they will dole out the bread by weight. You will eat, but you will not be satisfied. 27 If in spite of this you still do not listen to me but continue to be hostile toward me, 28 then in my anger I will be hostile toward you, and I myself will punish you for your sins seven times over. 29 You will eat the flesh of your sons and the flesh of your daughters. 30 I will destroy your high places, cut down your incense altars and pile your dead bodies on the lifeless forms of your idols, and I will abhor you. 31 I will turn your cities into ruins and lay waste your sanctuaries, and I will take no delight in the pleasing aroma of your offerings. 32 I myself will lay waste the land, so that your enemies who live there will be appalled. 33 I will scatter you among the nations and will draw out my sword and pursue you. Your land will be laid waste, and your cities will lie in ruins. 34 Then the land will enjoy its sabbath years all the time that it lies desolate and you are in the country of your enemies; then the land will rest and enjoy its sabbaths. 35 All the time that it lies desolate, the land will have the rest it did not have during the sabbaths you lived in it.*

The misfortunes of the cursed Jews do not affect the ways of the world. The world is made strange for the Jews. Once again, the punishment is not death. Or rather, as many do actually die, their death carries no significance for its own sake. Having died, one makes one's way out of the greater dynamic of potential redemption. The organized practices of faith are made ridiculous. The destruction of idols is to be expected by a vengeful God, but what about those rejected aromas, burnt and offered for the Lord's pleasure? God's truth is reinforced not simply through the rejection of falsehoods, but through overall, comprehensive rejection. Imagine those steamy vapors, wafting about in an iron sky, unable to make their way into the holiest of holies.

This is the in-between time, after one revelation which has laid down the law in absolute terms, before what is bound to come in the direct presence of God. The world, as it is experienced by Jews, is not destroyed and it is not replaced. It is laid bare so that it may be rejuvenated. God's vengeance does not end in obliteration, and truth, in the words of Psalm 85 (verse 11), "springs forth from the earth."[19] By running both forward and backward, the in-between time reveals the inherent emptiness of linear time and demarcated space. God does not need to win or to demonstrate his truth's superiority to that of human truths. God and humans do not play the same game. This is the point driven home by God's vengeance, the absolute truth of the divine. Redemption is not driven by the logic of reward and punishment.

The Sabbaths that Jews were commanded to observe at the beginning of the chapter established the proper flow of time, the order that should not be questioned in a world of observance and obedience. At the end of this batch of curses, the Sabbaths represent a cleanliness, a starkness at odds with any human pretension to meaning or even to orientation. The Sabbaths have not stopped occurring. The covenant cannot be broken, despite the gallant attempts of the Jews, but its constant violations are also unacceptable. During the in-between time the world cannot cease its daily motion. Judgment Day has not yet come. Nonetheless, the world cannot continue to function under rationales imposed by human agendas. The foundations of humanity itself, the time-space continuum, must be made bare before they can be reclaimed.

*36 "As for those of you who are left, I will make their hearts so fearful in the lands of their enemies that the sound of a windblown leaf will put them to flight. They will run as though fleeing from the sword, and they will fall, even though no one is pursuing them. 37 They will stumble over one another as though fleeing from the sword, even though no one is pursuing them. So you will not be able to stand before your enemies. 38 You will perish among the nations; the land of*

---

[19] See http://biblehub.com/niv/psalms/85.htm (last accessed on October 18, 2016).

*your enemies will devour you. 39 Those of you who are left will waste away in the lands of their enemies because of their sins; also because of their ancestors' sins they will waste away. 40 But if they will confess their sins and the sins of their ancestors – their unfaithfulness and their hostility toward me, 41 which made me hostile toward them so that I sent them into the land of their enemies – then when their uncircumcised hearts are humbled and they pay for their sin, 42 I will remember my covenant with Jacob and my covenant with Isaac and my covenant with Abraham, and I will remember the land. 43 For the land will be deserted by them and will enjoy its sabbaths while it lies desolate without them. They will pay for their sins because they rejected my laws and abhorred my decrees. 44 Yet in spite of this, when they are in the land of their enemies, I will not reject them or abhor them so as to destroy them completely, breaking my covenant with them. I am the Lord their God. 45 But for their sake I will remember the covenant with their ancestors whom I brought out of Egypt in the sight of the nations to be their God. I am the Lord."*

*46 These are the decrees, the laws and the regulations that the Lord established at Mount Sinai between himself and the Israelites through Moses.*

For redemption to emerge, hearts and minds must be made bare as well. Being itself is remade. In *The Time that Remains*, Agamben mentions the biblical term *She'erit Israel* (the remainder of Israel) as reference to a state of mind rather than as a quantitative description.[20] Revelation may open up endless possibilities, but it is also a trauma one must survive. A life worthy of the second revelation – the coming of the messiah, Judgment Day, the final battle – should be a life that acknowledges that trauma, a life that remains. Infinity is not equivalent to goodness. Infinity, when revealed in a finite world, is a never-ending shockwave. The goodness that may ensue from this shock cannot come into being without the shock itself. In order to appreciate the second revelation everyone alive must be remnants, regardless of their actual numbers. This is the obstacle Jews must transcend in order to be worthy of redemption in real life, in contrast to the gradual forgoing of humanity described in the list of blessings.

Convictions should be hollowed from the inside. These convictions, like the world, will not fade or disappear. Those who hold them need to realize that they are depleted, empty shells ready to be filled by the second revelation. The Jews run even when they are not pursued. The passage repeats this state three times, with slightly different nuances. We could read this insistence in reference to the existential fear of the Jews at this stage, the knowledge that God has turned against them and all of

---

[20] See Agamben, *The Time that Remains*, p. 54.

creation with him. I would like to read the passage differently, with an emphasis on the escalating depletion of the Jewish psyche.

A leaf falls and the sound it makes seems threatening, the softest sound bearing the harshest potential consequences. Once again, this could be read as excessively cautious behavior, especially when bearing in mind all the terrors already visited upon the Jews. I understand it to be saying that the first thing to go, the first hollow in the soul of an actively redeemed Jew is a sense of proportion.[21] This strikes me as important even before we continue to the following stages of hollowness. The evacuation of proportion suggests that the "objective" world does not change at all. What changes in the in-between time is one's perception of oneself within the world. One becomes a survivor, a remnant. This is the only proper posture to adopt before the second revelation, the one to come. Vacuity is the proof that a believer has abandoned pretensions to sovereignty that is not derived from the ultimate sovereignty of God. The world remains as it was but the believer's standing in it changes irrevocably.

The second sovereign faculty to be hollowed is the sense of linear progression and coherence. The Jews begin to run as though they are fleeing from the sword. At the end, they fall though no one is pursuing them. There is no longer a stable thread woven through their lives, one that allows for steady expectation that the beginning will occur at the beginning and the end at the end. If their "fall" is meant to evoke death, this death still remains relatively trivial. The main punishment is the loss of sequence.

The third expression of blanked sovereignty, perhaps the most immediate one, is the "simple" loss of sovereign existence in space. When running from the sword, Jews will trip and stumble over each other. Not only will they fall needlessly, but they'll do it in an undignified heap. Even in relation to their own physicality, Jews will not be able to maintain the boundaries that make each person sovereign. Running for one's life, despite the ignominy, is an event that sets every person apart from all others. "My life passed before my eyes," we often hear from people whose lives have been under real threat. Still, while Jewish bodies maintain their physical integrity, they cannot steer a distinct path in physical space. There is no obliteration or destruction, just an emptying out.

The fourth and final loss of sovereignty, the indignity which prepares the Jews for actual redemption, is the emptying of the land. Their

---

[21] The list of curses, after all, draws an interactive image of ongoing redemption; the list of blessings involves no redemption whatsoever.

dispersal into the land of their enemies is important only to the extent
that the land is allowed real rest. The land of the Jews is not taken over
and is not destroyed. It was chosen by God and thus enjoys the solidity
of divine truth. Still. It must be emptied before it can be reclaimed for the
covenant, for God and for his chosen people. This is the sovereignty of
the in-between time, the conscious hollowing of the world. It can occur
only in the present, being an anti-vision and anti-tradition. It is an anti-
vision because aspirations require a positive horizon while in-between
existence negates and is negated. It is anti-tradition for the very same reason. Nothing is passed on from the past. In fact, the heart of the tradition
is gradually removed, leaving an empty shell.

## Interim Conclusion: Not the End, the In-Between

Creation is framed by a beginning and an end. That end could come in
the form of a messiah, a day of reckoning or the exercise of divine judgment. In any case, that end marks a certain departure from conventional,
human wisdom and order. It is a certain end. The time stretching from
the beginning to the end can be seen as a segue, a predetermined motion
merely accentuating the staunch certitude of both beginning and end.
This reading consigns an entire realm – in time and space – to incon-
sequentiality. Because the analytical languages of Western scholarship,
from history to political science, are geared toward the encounters of
"fact" and "interests," they produce linear narratives that cannot accept
the intermediary qualities of the in-between time. These qualities, in turn,
are not relativistic or hedonistic. "Intermediary" does not mean "middling" and it does suggest ambiguity. The in-between time runs between
certainties. Faith in these certainties strongly suggests one's priorities and
potential practices during the in-between time.

Leviticus 26 suggests a political conception of in-between-ness, a
framing of the in-between time in terms of power, loss and sovereignty.
It begins by asserting the realness of the in-between, its motion and
dynamic. This stands in contrast to the growing immutability provided
by an attachment to the absolute. The Jews who obey and observe grow
more and more like God, easily relinquishing uncertainty and movement.
They simply receive more and more, caring less and less for the time and
the space that define realness. The Jews who don't obey enter a shockwave of uncertainty and, perhaps more significantly, depletion. What
prepares them for the second revelation (the renewal of the covenant)
is their gradual stripping from any and all pretensions to a sovereignty

independent from that of God. They are not destroyed, because God is not simply a stronger version of humanity. They are not replaced, because God's selection of them is a part of God's perfect truth. The Jews who do not obey appear to stay in place while their world is made desolate from within. Their social conventions, their ritual, their communal relations and their personalities are hollow husks. The space within them will allow them to witness and accept the second revelation, the coming of God. What was inside them has grown tainted and corrupt. Anything they could hope, personally, to place inside themselves can only be similarly tainted and corrupt. Emptiness is the only state allowing them to partake of redemption.

## IS, the Caliphate and the Empty Present

The hollowing out of the world is the supreme political principle (and goal) of the Islamic State. We took the detour into Leviticus in order to reacquire the language of redemption, of the in-between, as politically potent. The emptying of the world is thrust upon the Jews of Leviticus, even as it is the only true path to meaningful salvation. The Islamic State, in contrast, wants to speak this language affirmatively. This makes IS a radically innovative entity. It also confuses the West immensely, because IS makes overt what the best efforts of the best institutional minds of the religious West have tried to keep under wraps. In-between-ness speaks with a real voice and demands real things, if one truly believes in the certitude of the beginning and the end. The in-between time is not a pale, benign version of perfection. Precisely because they believe in the absoluteness of creation and judgment, the faithful believe in the realness of the in-between time and in its realist, political agendas.

If this is true, it calls into question the attempts we reviewed to present IS as deterministically driven by either a clear-cut past or a foretold future. Specifically, it is the relationship between religiosity and determinism that grows problematic. Leviticus 26 presents us with a model of faith that is, perhaps, anti-deterministic. Believing in the realness of absolute perfection allows no escape from realness that is less than perfect. Still, this imperfect realness cannot stand parallel to the realness of God, his creation and his judgment. Those living in an imperfect realness must undergo, or initiate (or most likely, both) a continuous devaluation of their flawed, contextual reality. They must inhabit it and contradict it simultaneously, asserting their sovereignty in this hollowing out of world and self.

Both McCants and Wood tie the confusing aspect of IS – its ability to connect medieval ideology, mystical prophecy and modern (psychological) warfare – to an intensity the West has not yet discovered. Wood places that intensity in the past, in a revelation that continues to reverberate, growing in strength and impact. McCants identifies the source of intensity in a future that burns brightly, a predestined, inescapable end. The politics of IS, according to both readings, can only be means to one of these two ends. In fact, the two ends – the God of the first revelation and the God of the second revelation – ultimately coalesce into one being.

But what about the intensity of the imperfect present, an intensity without resolution or coalescence? The gap between the elaborate, enlightening readings of Wood and McCants[22] and the restless volatility of this present is perhaps most prominent in the case of the caliphate, the Islamic State "in the flesh."[23] Both Wood and McCants present the caliphate as a demonstration of the faith-inspired determinism of IS. For Wood, the caliphate represents the most literal attempt to restore the Islamic empire of yore. His reading returns to the defining revelations of Islam to the prophet Muhammad, in the early seventh century AD. Those revelations saw nothing less than the entire world as the bed for their realization. The original Arabic for caliph is *khalifa* or "replacement." The caliph was the replacement, the substitute for the prophet Muhammad, the last and greatest of the prophets and the man who held power over all Muslims and an intimate relationship with God simultaneously. There could be no greater political authority, and while the caliph was no prophet, he was meant to be the closest approximation possible. Political authority became a sign of divine favor and a mark of the founding revelation of Islam. For Wood, Islam's relevance to the world in its own eyes has been continuously unpacked since that revelation. Its most potent political form would be, therefore, a caliphate. This train of thought offers one tenable, holistic explanation for the present of IS.

For McCants, the caliphate is the fulfillment of prophecy. One of the most important traditions he quotes (having translated it) says the following:

"Prophethood is among you as long as God will it to be. Then God will take it away when He so wills. Then there will be a caliphate in accordance with the prophetic

---

[22] For the purposes of our discussion – the relationship of IS perceptions of the "past" and the "future" with their understanding and practice in the "present" – Wood and McCants effectively represent the spectrum of learned global readings of IS.

[23] Speaking of the caliphate, I am referring to the actual declaration establishing the Islamic State as the caliphate, the long sought "true" Islamic State.

method. It will be among you as God intends, and then God will take it away when He so wills. Then there will be a mordacious monarchy. It will be among you as long as God intends, and then god will take it away when He so wills. Then there will be a tyrannical monarchy. It will be among you as long as God intends, and then God will take it away when He so wills. Then there will be a caliphate in accordance with the prophetic method." Then he [the prophet] fell silent.[24]

"A caliphate according to the prophetic tradition" (*khilafa 'ala minhaj al-nubuwwa*, in Arabic) is, along with *baqiyah watatamadad*, the second most dominant IS slogan, visible on every IS media from billboards[25] in IS territory to IS films uploaded to the internet. McCants quotes it in an appendix devoted to religious proof that the Mahdi, the messiah who will lead the faithful in the final battle, will be preceded by an Islamic state. McCants describes the issue of the state, the debate over whether to declare a physical caliphate or not, as a major bone of contention between the founders of IS and the leadership of Al-Qaeda. While the caliphate was declared in 2014, an Islamic state was announced in Iraq in October 2006. The founders had sworn fealty to the leadership of Al-Qaeda but they did not consult that leadership before making their announcement. In McCants' words, "the timing of the Islamic State's announcement was based on an apocalyptic schedule."[26]

The leaders of the Islamic State repeatedly earned the disdain and anger of Al-Qaeda leadership for their radical hastiness. Bin Laden wanted a state to be declared once the support of the locals had been won in Iraq. McCants writes that "Bin Laden and Zawahiri's disdain for apocalypticism reflects their generation and class ... [they] grew up in elite Sunni families, who sniffed at messianic speculation as unbecoming, a foolish pastime of the masses."[27] Al-Qaeda was an organization with its own ethos of professionalism, and its plans were not subject to the fluctuation of end-times prophecy. The Islamic State and its supporters, however, saw themselves (according to McCants) as living in the future. He quotes a talk given in Melbourne by Musa Cerantonio,[28] an Australian convert to Islam, in 2012. Cerantonio spoke of the escalating violence in Syria

[24] See McCants, *The ISIS Apocalypse*, p. 178.
[25] See, for example, the following gruesome photo: https://twitter.com/ulil/status/ 574369620766781440 (last accessed on October 18, 2016).
[26] See McCants, *The ISIS Apocalypse*, p. 15. Generally, see pp. 5–45 of McCants' book for a detailed description of IS early history.
[27] See ibid., p. 28.
[28] Also interviewed by Wood. Yet another example of how the past-oriented and future-oriented visions of IS ultimately coalesce into one vision intent on minimizing the importance of the IS present.

and suggested that it was not accidental. Syria, according the some of the prophecies espoused by IS, will be the site of the final battle between the forces of good and evil, with good set to win the day. "God had revealed the future to Muhammad, Cerantonio said," writes McCants, "so the Muslims could prepare themselves for battle. That future had come."[29]

McCants and Wood both present readings emphasizing the unescapable, undeniable force of IS's motivation to establish a state, at least as far as the organization's leadership and believers are concerned. In other words, the theology of IS can only produce a caliphate or a desire for one. This determinism leads seamlessly to talk of plans for world domination, a global Shari'a empire. The human role in the unfolding of the divine plan is negligible, at best, particularly with regard to the political dimension of human life. Human authority is, at best, useful for keeping things orderly until the coming of Judgment Day, somewhat like the lives of the blessed Jews at the beginning of Leviticus 26. There is no in-between-ness in both deterministic understandings of IS theology and politics.

I propose a different reading, focused on the emerging nature of the in-between time. In this reading, there is a pronounced role for humans in IS theology of the real as the agents of the in-between imperative, the hollowing out of the world. The purpose of the in-between time is not the establishment of a new empire. The notion that such an empire can serve, in its own right, as the fulfillment of a religious vision is generally difficult, but it is particularly difficult with regard to the in-between time. An IS formulation of its own political emergence will, I suggest, be significantly grounded in the present rather than in a predestined future or a forgone past. In order to explore this present, we turn now to the IS declaration of the caliphate.

## Announcing the Caliphate: Sovereignty, Resistance and Emptiness

The declaration of the caliphate, on June 29, 2014, followed more than a decade of plans and failed political ventures. Abu Mus'ab al-Zarqawi, the founding father of the Islamic State, established Al-Qaeda in Iraq (AQI) in 2004 and spoke repeatedly of his desire for an Islamic state in the country. As I mentioned previously, Al-Qaeda's central leadership

[29] See McCants, *The ISIS Apocalypse*, p. 99.

did not discourage him, but viewed his messianic agenda and tendency for violence with suspicion and reticence. When he died in 2006 (of an American bombing), his heirs were quick to announce the establishment of an Islamic State in Iraq (ISI). The American surge of troops in Iraq, in 2007, drove ISI from Baghdad and caused it massive losses in personnel and infrastructure. The continued extreme violence of its leaders was also responsible for the loss of public support for the organization. The leadership of ISI did not maintain regular contact with Al-Qaeda's leadership, leading to a loss of trust between the organizations despite their nominal link.

In 2009, Iraq's Shi'i prime minister, Nuri al-Maliki, began to act against Sunni leaders at the national and local level, arousing Sunni anger and renewing support for ISI. The organization, growing stronger, carried out a series of suicide attacks in Baghdad, killing hundreds. In 2010, the two leaders of ISI died in an American–Iraqi operation and Abu Bakr al-Baghdadi assumed leadership of the organization. Baghdadi was more capable and less overtly violent than his predecessors, devoting time and effort to strengthening the organizational prowess of ISI on various fronts. In 2011, he sent ISI operatives to Syria, where one of them established the Nusra Front, which rapidly became one of the prominent rebel organizations fighting the Assad regime.

In March 2013, with the fall of al-Raqqa (a city in northern Syria) to the rebel forces, ISI and the Nusra Front established a presence in the city. Under Baghdadi, who moved to Syria during that year, ISI began relocating personnel and resources from Iraq and attempted (with success) to join the fighting on several Syrian fronts. Baghdadi claimed that ISI and the Nusra Front formed the "Islamic State in Iraq and Syria" (ISIS), but the Nusra Front denied this and reasserted its allegiance to Al-Qaeda. In August 2013, ISIS began fighting with other rebel groups in Syria, including the Nusra Front. During the first months of 2014, ISIS (as it now was) took over Raqqa and formally severed its ties with Al-Qaeda. On June 10, ISIS took over the Iraqi city of Mosul, in the largest offensive it had conducted to that point. Throughout the month of June, ISIS took control of several towns and a border crossing between Syria and Iraq. On June 29, ISIS spokesperson Abu Muhammad al-Adnani[30] declared the establishment of a caliphate and the organization's change of name to IS,

[30] Since killed in an American bombing on August 30, 2016.

the Islamic State. The caliphate abolished the border between Syria and Iraq and was to be ruled by Abu Bakr al-Baghdadi, to be known from that day as the *khalifa* (Caliph) Ibrahim.[31]

The declaration is a formal, eloquent document, composed in high Arabic prose and full of quotations and Quranic references. We will read the translation posted by IS itself, skipping several passages in the case of repetitions unnecessary for our argument.[32] At times, in order to facilitate reading flow, I will not quote the Quranic verses brought in support of IS arguments in full, but the reference to the verses will be provided.

## This Is the Promise of Allah

*Praise be to Allah, the Mighty and Strong. And may peace and blessings be upon the one sent with the sword as a mercy to all creation. As for what follows:*

*Allah (the Exalted) said: {Allah has promised those who have believed among you and done righteous deeds that He will surely grant them succession [to authority] upon the earth just as He granted it to those before them and that He will surely establish for them their religion which He has preferred for them and that He will surely substitute for them, after their fear, security, [for] they worship Me, not associating anything with Me. But whoever disbelieves after that – then those are the defiantly disobedient} [An-Nūr: 55].*

*Succession, establishment, and safety – a promise from Allah reserved for the Muslims, but with a condition. {They worship me [Allah] and do not associate anything with me} [An-Nūr: 55]. Having faith in Allah, keeping far from the gateways to shirk (polytheism) and its various shades, along with submitting to Allah's command in everything big and small, and giving Him the level of obedience that makes your lusts, inclinations, and desires to be in compliance with what the Prophet (peace be upon him) came with – only after this condition is met will the promise be fulfilled. For by fulfilling this condition comes the ability to build, reform, remove oppression, spread justice, and bring about safety and tranquility. Only by meeting this condition, will there be the succession, which Allah informed the angels about.*

---

[31] For the extensive IS timeline, see www.wilsoncenter.org/article/timeline-rise-and-spread-the-islamic-state (last accessed on October 18, 2016). For an interesting integration of ideology and history (still in the mold of Wood and McCants), see Cole Bunzel's paper, "From Paper State to Caliphate: The Ideology of the Islamic State" (The Brookings Project on U.S, Relations with the Islamic World, Analysis Paper No. 19, March 2015), available online at: www.brookings.edu/wp-content/uploads/2016/06/The-ideology-of-the-Islamic-State.pdf (last accessed on October 18, 2016).

[32] The translation, entitled "This Is the Promise of Allah," is available online at https://ia902505.us.archive.org/28/items/poa_25984/EN.pdf (last accessed on October 18, 2016).

Faith is a condition. Without faith, there can be no continuous physical existence or earthly authority,[33] no unifying thread of religion and no security. Without faith, there is fear. But faith is not merely a prerequisite. It is also a quality, a position. With faith, succession and substitution are never far apart, and this is reflected in the language of the Quran. The original Arabic verb, *yastkhlifa*, is constructed on the same root from which the word "caliph" was derived. If you believe, God will provide you with continuity and coherence, but also with the potential for transformation. Humanity's active role in creation is based on accepting its proper place, below God's absolute power. This role is also based on humanity's ability to undergo change. Faith is the hinge that allows humanity to participate in both.

There are mechanisms for the expression and operationalization of faith. Obedience, for example, allows a believer to synchronize his or her most human sides – lusts, inclinations, desires – with the commandments revealed by the prophet. Still, despite the accessibility of perfection, faith must be chosen. Moreover, unbelief always exists. The realization of Islam's vision is not a tale of good vanquishing evil. It is a story of will trouncing passivity. Once the condition of faith is met, it is possible to wield authority properly. That is, faith is necessary in order to bring together the urge and need to change with the desire for the permanent. With faith, these are two sides of one endeavor. For a believer, faith is both a benchmark and a vision.

Politically, then, faith is a generator of constant tension. It is not an ideal of charity or grace, diluting contradictions into a puddle of bliss. Within a political order, the realization of a vision carries subversive potential. If you've done what you set out to do, what commitment do you have toward the apparatus that allowed you to act? Consider the example of post-1967 Israel. If the Israeli state can, after the Six-Day War, claim to be the biblical Holy Land, what justifies the existence of the state's institutions? Benchmarks, on the other hand, are exactly what they are when realized. One either achieves a benchmark or one does not. In the case of the Israeli settler movement, for example, the conceptual breakthrough of Israeli settlements in the West Bank rapidly turned into the ongoing count of Israelis residing there. The sense of achievement one

---

[33] Compare the Sahih International translation used by IS with the Abdel Haleem translation: "God has made a promise to those among you who believe and do good deeds: He will make them successors to the land." Available online at: https://archive.org/stream/ TheQuranKoranenglishEbook-AbdelHaleem-BestTranslationInThe/the_QURAN-abdel-haleem-ebook-english_djvu.txt (last accessed on October 18, 2016).

gets from living in the scope of a vision is different from the accomplishment of benchmarks. An authority dependent on both vision and benchmark as its main driving force is, by definition, an embattled authority.

*Without this condition being met, authority becomes nothing more than kingship, dominance and rule, accompanied with destruction, corruption, oppression, subjugation, fear, and the decadence of the human being and his descent to the level of animals. That is the reality of succession, which Allah created us for. It is not simply kingship, subjugation, dominance, and rule. Rather, succession is to utilize all that for the purpose of compelling the people to do what the Sharia (Allah's law) requires of them concerning their interests in the hereafter and worldly life, which can only be achieved by carrying out the command of Allah, establishing His religion, and referring to His law for judgment.*

*This succession, along with the aforementioned reality, is the purpose for which Allah sent His messengers and revealed His scriptures, and for which the swords of jihad were unsheathed.*

*Indeed, Allah (the Exalted) honored the ummah (nation) of Muhammad and blessed them. He made them the best ummah of all peoples.*

*{You are the best nation produced [as an example] for mankind. You enjoin what is right and forbid what is wrong and believe in Allah} [Āl 'Imrān: 110].*

*And He promised to grant the ummah succession to authority. [An-Nūr: 55].*

*He also made leadership of the world and mastership of the earth for the ummah, as long as it fulfilled the condition: {They worship me [Allah] and do not associate anything with me} [An-Nūr: 55].*

*Allah (the Exalted) also gave honor to the ummah.*

*{And to Allah belongs [all] honor, and to His Messenger, and to the believers, but the hypocrites do not know} [Al-Munāfiqūn: 8].*

Prophecy was performed for the sake of succession and substitution (one and the same). The jihad is still performed for the same purpose. Succession/substitution is reality. God sent his messengers and revealed his books so humans could work in this world. The prize is not heaven and the suspension of the law, but the congruence between the divine commands and human desires. It is good to desire authority if one is capable of using that authority to further the cause of God. But this succession cannot be achieved if there is no faith to begin with. Succession is logical, but it also miraculous, the moment when fear turns to security. Succession is hard, practical work (compelling the people, establishing religion, reforming, changing etc.), but it is also a revelation, something seen and felt only once one has the required faith.

This drama unfolds against the entire world as backdrop. In the words of the Quran, Islam is the best nation (community) produced for humankind. At stake with the Jews of Leviticus was their relationship with God.

Their trials and tribulations were meant to make them fit for a reassertion of the covenant. The case of the Muslims is different. Judgment Day is not a horizon for them, a place they strive to reach and by which they judge themselves. Their standards are grounded in the political here and now – leadership, honor, justice. Their main challenge is the proper wielding of their worldliness. Power is, naturally, constantly present in Muslim reality as temptation but also as inevitable practice. Because they are in the world, they have power and can use it to do both right and wrong. The rightness or the wrongness will not change the realness of the action, and the action can skew the desired duality of faith, between vision and benchmark, in one direction only. Muslims must consider this power carefully in order to discharge it meaningfully.

*Yes, honor is for this ummah. It is from the honor of Allah (the Exalted) – honor that mixes with the faith residing in the believer's heart. Thus, if faith becomes firm in the heart, honor becomes firm along with it. It is honor that does not hunch, soften, or become disgraced regardless of how great the anguish and tribulation become. It is honor befitting the best ummah – the ummah of Muhammad (peace be upon him) – an ummah that does not accept submission to anyone or anything other than Allah. It does not accept transgression nor oppression.*

*This is an honorable and noble ummah, which does not sleep and ignore grievance. It does not accept degradation.*

*{So do not weaken and do not grieve, and you will be superior if you are [true] believers} [Āl ʿImrān: 139].*

*It is a mighty and powerful ummah. How can it not be such, when Allah supports it and grants it victory?*

*{That is because Allah is the protector of those who have believed and because the disbelievers have no protector} [Muhammad: 11].*

*This is the ummah of Muhammad (peace be upon him) which, whenever it is truthful with Allah, He brings about His promise for them.*

*Allah (the Exalted) sent His Prophet (peace be upon him), while the Arabs were in the depths of ignorance and blinding darkness. They were the most naked, the hungriest, and the most backwards of peoples, sinking in depths of lowness. No one cared about them or gave them any regard. They submitted in humiliation to Khosrau and Caesar, yielding to the conqueror.*

God is the source and the epitome of honor, but for the believers, honor is conditioned upon faith. Honor is a quality of God, while faith is the quality of a human being. If you have faith, honor can appear in concrete form. Even then, it is a responsive, engaging quality and not divine and unconditional. In real life, honor carries with it the gap of faith, the gap between concept and criterion. Honor also carries the burdens of history, an existence without honor. The community must be truthful with God, but what is truth?

Politically, truth begins with reaction and not with a principle. The mark of a true ummah is that it does not sleep, ignore or accept. Power for power's sake induces lethargy and numbness. The power of an honorable ummah emerges in that ummah's desire to respond to injustice and grievance. Submission to God is proof of submission to no other. Submission is not a passive recognition of God's superior power, a knee-jerk affirmation of fear or greed. Truthfulness with God involves the active rejection of all attempts to conceive power outside the divine.

*Allah (the Exalted) also said, {And remember when you were few and oppressed in the land, fearing that people might abduct you} [Al-Anfāl: 26].*

*Qatādah (may Allah have mercy upon him) said in explanation of this verse, "These clans of Arabs were the most disgraced, the hungriest, the most ignorant, and the most naked. They were people who were eaten but did not eat. Whoever lived from them lived miserably. And whoever died from them fell into hellfire." His words end here, may Allah have mercy upon him.*

*A group of the Sahābah (companions of the Prophet – peace be upon him) entered upon Khosrau Yazdajard on the day of the battle of al-Qādisiyyah to call him to Islam. He said to them, "I don't know any nation on the earth that was more miserable, fewer in number, and more divided than you. We would entrust the people of the villages in the outskirts to hold you back. Persia did not wage war against you, nor did you ever hope to stand and face it." So they were silenced. Then al-Mughīrah Ibn Shu'bah (may Allah be pleased with him) responded to him, saying, "As for what you've mentioned of our poor condition, then there was no condition poorer than ours. As for our hunger, then it was unlike any hunger. We used to eat scarabs, beetles, scorpions, and snakes. We considered such as food. As for our homes, then they were nothing but the surface of the earth. We did not use to wear anything except what we made from the fur of our camels and sheep. Our religion was to kill each other and oppress each other. One of us would bury his daughter alive, hating the thought that she would eat from his food."*

*This was the condition of the Arabs before Islam. They were in dispute and broken up; they were dispersed and had infighting, striking each other's necks, suffering hunger, lack of unity, and capture. Then, when Allah blessed them with Islam and they believed, Allah unified them, united their ranks, honored them after their humiliation, enriched them after their poverty, and brought their hearts together, all through Islam. Thus, by the grace of Allah, they became brothers.*

The first revelation came to the Arabs when they were empty. They were, in fact, a model of destitution, completely forsaken by God and man. This model status was accepted by the Arabs and their most bitter enemies alike. Khosrau Yazdegerd (as his name is commonly spelled) was the king of Persia, defeated by the Muslims at al-Qadisiyyah at AD 636. His defeat opened the way for the Muslim conquest of Persia. Before the battle, the caliph 'Umar sent a delegation to negotiate and attempt to convert the

Persian king to Islam.[34] His response to the Muslim suggestion indicates the realness of Arab dilapidation before the advent of Islam. Like the Jews of Leviticus, Arabs suffered mental anguish in addition to material adversity. Unlike the Jews of Leviticus, their redemption was immediately and inherently political.

Revelation united the Muslims and located them firmly in history. Honor after humiliation and enrichment after poverty are different from unsolicited grace. Still, revelation came to them when they were empty, not when they had proved themselves worthy. Muslims became worthy after they became Muslims. The realness of revelation was apparent in two dimensions. It was a miracle, because it turned the lowest into the most high. It was also an ongoing process, living up to a challenging, elusive standard.

*Allah (the Exalted) said, {And He brought together their hearts. If you had spent all that is in the earth, you could not have brought their hearts together; but Allah brought them together} [Al-Anfāl: 63].*

*So the animosity and hatred they had for each other vanished from their hearts. They were united by faith, and piety became their measuring scale. They did not differentiate between an Arab and a non-Arab, nor between an easterner and a westerner, nor between a white person and a black person, nor between a poor person and a rich person. They abandoned nationalism and the calls of jāhiliyyah (pre-Islamic ignorance), raised the flag of lā ilāha ill Allāh (there is no god but Allah) and carried out jihad in the path of Allah with truthfulness and sincerity. So Allah raised them through this religion and honored them by having them carry its message. He bestowed His grace on them, and made them the kings and masters of the world.*

The first Islamic empire united the world by emptying it of distinctions. the words of the prophet Isaiah (which we previously encountered) resonate here as well:

> A voice of one calling:
> "In the wilderness prepare
>     the way for the LORD;
> make straight in the desert
>     a highway for our God.
> Every valley shall be raised up,
>     every mountain and hill made low;
> the rough ground shall become level,
>     the rugged places a plain.
> And the glory of the LORD will be revealed,
>     and all people will see it together.
>     For the mouth of the LORD has spoken." (Isaiah 40:3–5)[35]

---

[34] For the classic Muslim text on the battle, see al-Tabari's *The Battle of al-Qādisiyyah and the Conquest of Syria and Palestine*, trans. Yohanan Friedmann (SUNY Press, 1992).

[35] www.biblegateway.com/passage/?search=Isaiah+40 (last accessed on October 18, 2016).

The world, when it is prepared for redemption, becomes a hollow vessel for the glory of God. The purpose of life, for all people, becomes the bearing of witness to that divine glory. The Muslims were raised by God so they might carry his message, a message of faith. That message rings truest in a hollow world. Of course, hollowness does not mean oblivion. The world remains and so do the people in it, but without a sense of exclusive human sovereignty or meaning.

Nonetheless, it is a real world and as such, it must function in an orderly manner. During the in-between time the expected order is different from the order of revelations, the one that came and the one that is to come. The hollowness of Isaiah is not a natural state. Humanity tends toward redundancy and power, always wanting more to command. But the select are also those who remain, the ones who witnessed the harshness of God alongside his munificence. Their message of faith, like their sovereignty, carry both confidence in and a resistance to human divisions of power.

*... Yes, my ummah, those barefoot, naked, shepherds who did not know good from evil, nor truth from falsehood, filled the earth with justice after it had been filled with oppression and tyranny, and ruled the world for centuries. This was neither through any means of strength that they possessed or numbers that they commanded, nor through their wisdom but rather, through their faith in Allah (the Exalted) and their adherence to the guidance of His Messenger (peace be upon him). O ummah of Muhammad (peace be upon him), you continue to be the best ummah and continue to have honor. Leadership will return to you. The God of this ummah yesterday is the same God of the ummah today, and the One who gave it victory yesterday is the One who will give it victory today.*

*The time has come for those generations that were drowning in oceans of disgrace, being nursed on the milk of humiliation, and being ruled by the vilest of all people, after their long slumber in the darkness of neglect – the time has come for them to rise. The time has come for the ummah of Muhammad (peace be upon him) to wake up from its sleep, remove the garments of dishonor, and shake off the dust of humiliation and disgrace, for the era of lamenting and moaning has gone, and the dawn of honor has emerged anew. The sun of jihad has risen. The glad tidings of good are shining. Triumph looms on the horizon. The signs of victory have appeared.*

The shift in this passage is a radical one. First, we read (and hear; this is the transcription of a text delivered live) the story of a rise from rags to riches. Significantly, this was accomplished through a combination of faith and adherence. Faith in itself is not sufficient, because the required vacuity can be achieved only through action. God will raise the valleys or straighten the rugged places. His way must be actively prepared. Suddenly, we find ourselves in the middle of a pep talk. The ummah is assured that it remains the best and most honorable of nations. Leadership "will return to you," the text says, suggesting that it no longer belongs to the Muslims. God remains God, says the text. Faith in his steadfastness will be key, as it was once, to another rise to glory.

How did the Muslims come to their current predicament? No clear reason is given. They may have "slept," but they were also oppressed and humiliated by the "vilest of all people." One can only assume that they lost their faith because with faith they should not have sunk so low. In any case, their emergence from their depravity is not a matter for prophecy. It is happening now, as we speak. The past will not disappear in the future, because it is already gone. It disappeared at the first sign of the second revelation.

The story of the Muslims and of their redemption is one of emergence. Revelation does not appear in causal fashion, at the end of a straight, progressive line. There is nothing gradual about God's presence. The Muslims forgot the in-between-ness of the period between revelations. The inaccessibility of Judgment Day drove them to believe that their religious obligation was one of obedience only, regardless of faith. But once the signs have begun to appear, the Muslims are again capable of realizing that they are living in the in-between time. They are capable of taking up the mission of the in-between time, the hollowing out of the world in preparation for the coming of God.

*Here the flag of the Islamic State, the flag of tawḥīd (monotheism), rises and flutters. Its shade covers land from Aleppo to Diyala. Beneath it, the walls of the tawāghīt (rulers claiming the rights of Allah) have been demolished, their flags have fallen, and their borders have been destroyed. Their soldiers are either killed, imprisoned, or defeated. The Muslims are honored. The kuffār (infidels) are disgraced. Ahlus-Sunnah (the Sunnis) are masters and are esteemed. The people of bid'ah (heresy) are humiliated. The hudūd (Sharia penalties) are implemented – the hudūd of Allah – all of them. The frontlines are defended. Crosses and graves are demolished. Prisoners are released by the edge of the sword. The people in the lands of the State move about for their livelihood and journeys, feeling safe regarding their lives and wealth. Wulāt (plural of wālī or "governors") and judges have been appointed. Jizyah (a tax imposed on kuffār) has been enforced. Fay' (money taken from the kuffār without battle) and zakat (obligatory alms) have been collected. Courts have been established to resolve disputes and complaints. Evil has been removed. Lessons and classes have been held in the masājid (plural of masjid) and, by the grace of Allah, the religion has become completely for Allah. There only remained one matter, a wājib kifā'ī (collective obligation) that the ummah sins by abandoning. It is a forgotten obligation. The ummah has not tasted honor since they lost it. It is a dream that lives in the depths of every*

*Muslim believer. It is a hope that flutters in the heart of every mujāhid muwah-hid (monotheist). It is the khilāfah (caliphate). It is the khilāfah – the abandoned obligation of the era.*

This passage presents a comprehensive description of the Islamic State, but it also presents a broader argument about the relationship between past, present and future in the IS theology of the real. In this relationship, the present is generator of the real, drawing the past and the future into itself. The caliphate, an obligation from the past and a prophecy in wait-ing, is about to be enacted on the strength and comprehensiveness of the present. The present, in terms we have already used, is the epitome of faith. Without faith, honor cannot be experienced by human beings. The realness of the present hinges, then, on its conditional status. It has within it both aspiration and achievement, future and past, with none outdoing the others with regard to strength or integrity.

This seemingly perfect present, the fullness of life in the Islamic State that is, simply, "here," is actually the setting for the establishment of the caliphate, the final obligation. Why does IS need the caliphate if it already functions so well? Perhaps it is because the caliphate offers the world. The Islamic State has done away with superimposed "borders" of nation-states but it remains an entity unto itself. It holds within it the poten-tial for the wrong kind of worldliness, the one that draws moral and political legitimacy from a perception of human supremacy. After all, it does apply "all" of God's criminal punishments just as "the religion has become completely for Allah." The IS present is on the verge of becom-ing too accurate, too self-sufficient. The caliphate brings with it a host of destabilizing experiences, from remembrance (of a forgotten obligation) to disorientation (when faced with the vastness of the entire world).

*Allah (the Exalted) said, {And mention when your Lord said to the angels, "Indeed, I will make upon the earth a khalīfah"} [Al-Baqarah: 30].*

*Imam al-Qurtubī said in his tafsīr (Quranic exegesis), "This verse is a fundamen-tal basis for the appointment of a leader and khalīfah (caliph) who is listened to and obeyed so that the ummah is united by him and his orders are carried out. There is no dispute over this matter between the ummah nor between the schol-ars, except for what has been reported from al-Asamm [the meaning of his name is "the deaf man"], for his deafness prevented him from hearing the Sharia." That ends his words, may Allah have mercy upon him.*

*Therefore, the shūrā (consultation) council of the Islamic State studied this mat-ter after the Islamic State – by Allah's grace – gained the essentials necessary for khilāfah, which the Muslims are sinful for if they do not try to establish. In light of the fact that the Islamic State has no shar'ī (legal) constraint or excuse that can justify delaying or neglecting the establishment of the khilāfah such that it would not be sinful, the Islamic State – represented by ahlul-halli-wal-'aqd (its people of authority), consisting of its senior figures, leaders, and the shūrā council – resolved to announce the establishment of the Islamic khilāfah, the appointment of a khalīfah for the Muslims, and the pledge of allegiance to the shaykh (sheikh), the mujāhid, the scholar who practices what he preaches, the worshipper, the leader, the warrior, the reviver, descendent from the family of the Prophet, the slave of Allah, Ibrāhīm Ibn 'Awwād Ibn Ibrāhīm Ibn 'Alī Ibn Muhammad al-Badrī al-Hāshimī al-Husaynī al-Qurashī by lineage, as-Sāmurrā'ī by birth and upbringing, al-Baghdādī by residence and scholarship. And he has accepted the bay'ah (pledge of allegiance). Thus, he is the imam and khalīfah for the Muslims everywhere. Accordingly, the "Iraq and Shām" in the name of the Islamic State is henceforth removed from all official deliberations and communications, and the official name is the Islamic State from the date of this declaration ...*

The caliphate is its caliph. The unity of the Islamic State is a unity of essentials – schools, security, budgets, roads. Still, the mere essentials cannot serve as a model for the world. The promise inherent in the awakening of IS is the promise of emergence and motion, rather than the promise of autarchic existence. The Islamic State as it now stands, before the caliphate, is a testament to fortitude and devotion. Its transformation into the caliphate is both expansion and countermeasure.

A caliph, and with him the caliphate, adds a degree of realness to the political endeavor of IS. The Islamic State in the previous passage simply *is*. Its very existence is somewhat miraculous, but it does not necessarily force the present to acknowledge the approaching second revelation. A caliph adds the assurance that the process has effectively kicked into gear. While IS exists, the appointment of a caliph reflects the urgency of emerging reality. There can be no reason to refrain from appointing the caliph and announcing the caliphate. If there is no cause to dally, the deed must be done. The political order of Islam, and the world, is now no longer a matter of will and fortitude. The new age is a matter of necessity.

*... So rush O Muslims and gather around your khalīfah, so that you may return as you once were for ages, kings of the earth and knights of war. Come so that you may be honored and esteemed, living as masters with dignity. Know that we fight over a religion that Allah promised to support. We fight for an ummah to which Allah has given honor, esteem, and leadership, promising it with empowerment and strength on the earth. Come O Muslims to your honor, to your victory. By Allah, if you disbelieve in democracy, secularism, nationalism, as well as all the other garbage and ideas from the west, and rush to your religion and creed, then by Allah, you will own the earth, and the east and west will submit to you. This is the promise of Allah to you. This is the promise of Allah to you.*

*{So do not weaken and do not grieve, and you will be superior if you are believers} [Al 'Imrān: 139].*

This is the promise of Allah to you.

*{If Allah should aid you, no one can overcome you} [Al 'Imrān: 160].*

This is the promise of Allah to you.

*{So do not weaken and call for peace while you are superior; and Allah is with you and will never deprive you of [the reward of] your deeds} [Muhammad: 35].*

This is the promise of Allah to you.

*{Allah has promised those who have believed among you and done righteous deeds that He will surely grant them succession [to authority] upon the earth just as He granted it to those before them and that He will surely establish for them [therein] their religion which He has preferred for them} [An-Nūr: 55].*

So come to the promise of your Lord.

*{Indeed, Allah does not fail in His promise} [Al 'Imrān: 9]*

The past and the future blur into each other. You once were what you were and you shall be so again, but what are you now? Muslims are, now, in a state of transition. Perhaps they are in a state of transformation. In any case, they cannot accept the conceit of stability. The Muslims who will flock to the banner of the caliphate are those who remain because they are those who reject. The ideals of the West are renounced wholesale simply by "rushing to religion and creed," but this is almost too easy because Western ideals are "garbage."

We can approach the rejection when we consider the repetition of Quran 24:55, the verse from the Chapter of Light (Surat An-Nur). God promises those who believe the stability of authority, space and religion, the transformation of fear into safety. In the beginning of the declaration, this seemed a vision to fight for. At this stage of the text, the Islamic State is already standing. It is functional in every way, surrounding its inhabitants with everything an Islamic state should and can offer. If so, what is the promise of God that has not yet been fulfilled? The appearance of verse 55 at this stage of the text reasserts the constant conditionality of any vision of authority. The isolated holism of IS is misleading.

The first revelation came to the Arabs when they were the lowest of the low. Consensus on their depravity includes both their own sages and their worst enemies. They lived in mud houses and ate scorpions, oblivious to the world and to themselves. The revelation came when the Arabs were empty enough to be filled by God's religion. The second revelation is as certain as the first. Now, the Muslims are not physically depraved, but they have been continuously oppressed and humiliated. They are low in the esteem of non-believers, and they are low in their own esteem. They will begin to redeem themselves when they remember that God's promise (in Quran 24:55) is not a one-time deal, specific in context and content. The Quranic promise is an exhortation to move. The Muslims who believe are those who relinquish their notion of self and come full circle to emerge as others. They remain in the present because they do not hold fast to the present. Every achievement, even the most whole and perfect, reminds them that the stability they most wish for lies in substitution. There is no core.

*And a message to all the platoons and groups on the face of the earth, consisting of mujahidin and people working to support the religion of Allah and raising the Islamic banners – a message to the heads and leaders of these groups – we say:*

*Fear Allah with regards to yourselves. Fear Allah with regards to your jihad. Fear Allah with regards to your ummah.*

*{O you who have believed, fear Allah as He should be feared and do not die except as Muslims, and hold firmly to the rope of Allah all together and do not become divided.} [Al 'Imrān: 102–103].*

*We – by Allah – do not find any shar'ī (legal) excuse for you justifying your holding back from supporting this state. Take a stance on account of which Allah (the Exalted) will be pleased with you. The veil has been lifted and the truth has become clear. Indeed, it is the State. It is the state for the Muslims – the oppressed of them, the orphans, the widows, and the impoverished. If you support it, then you do so for your own good.*

*Indeed, it is the State. Indeed, it is the khilāfah. It is time for you to end this abhorrent partisanship, dispersion, and division, for this condition is not from the religion of Allah at all. And if you forsake the State or wage war against it, you will not harm it. You will only harm yourselves.*

*It is the State – the state for the Muslims. Sufficient for you should be what al-Bukhārī (may Allah have mercy upon him) reported from Mu'āwiyah (may Allah be pleased with him). He said that he heard Allah's Messenger (peace be upon him) say, "This matter is for Quraysh. No one opposes them regarding it except that Allah throws him down on his face, as long as they establish the religion." ...*

Those who remain are simultaneously the highest and the lowest. That is their claim to realness in the face of hubris and revelation. The Islamic State is the state for the oppressed and the impoverished. It is also the state for those God has selected, the vanguard of the faithful elite. With regard to the other Islamic movements fighting for the cause, those who established IS are akin to Quraysh, the clan of the prophet Muhammad. The disparity between these two extremes is inescapable. The vision of IS is not a realization of the sermon on the mount, full of grace inverting earthly reality in preparation for the kingdom of heaven. It is not the meek who are inheriting, but the real people who are rising to meet the second revelation. In its ascension, realness requires the suspension of divisions and differences. The rugged places must be made into plains and the mountains into valleys. The world, and the jihad, must become a vessel to be filled.

*... Know that your leaders will not find any arguments to keep you away from the jamā'ah (the body of Muslims united behind a Muslim leader), the khilāfah, and this great good, except for two false and weak excuses. The first excuse is the same matter they have accused it with before, that it is a state of khawārij (a sect that excommunicated Muslims for sins that do not warrant excommunication) and other accusations whose falseness has become apparent in the cities that are ruled by the State. Second, your leaders will assure both you and themselves saying, "This is just a gust of wind which will be extinguished, or a temporary whirlwind that will not last, and that the nations of kufr (disbelief) won't allow it to remain, and they will gather against it so that it disappears quickly and soon. Those of its soldiers who survive will end up in mountaintops, caverns, deserts, and clandestine prisons. Thereafter we will have to return to the jihad of the elite. We cannot handle jihad of the elite far away from hotels, conferences, offices, lights, and cameras. We want to lead the ummah in the jihad of the ummah ..."*

*So let those leaders be ruined. And let that "ummah" they want to unite be ruined – an "ummah" of secularists, democrats, and nationalists ... an "ummah" of murji'ah (a sect that excludes deeds from faith), ikhwān (the "Muslim Brotherhood" party), and surūriyyah (a sect influenced by the ikhwān claiming to be Salafi).*

*{Satan promises them and arouses desire in them. But Satan does not promise them except delusion} [An-Nisā': 120].*

*The State will remain, by Allah's permission. Ask the parties in Iraq and their leaders. How much did they reassure themselves by claiming that the state would vanish. They were greater than your parties in power and greater in accumulation of wealth.*

*{Have they not traveled through the earth and observed how was the end of those before them? They were greater than them in power} [Ar-Rūm: 9]*

The allegations of other jihadi leaders ring false because they treat the strengths of IS as its weaknesses. The Khawarij were a group of dissenters during the first century of Islam. They opposed the notion of arbitration to select new rulers after the prophet Muhammad, claiming that God was the only judge and that his authority would be usurped by scheming humans. They also believed that every Muslim could lead the community, not just the members of the Quraysh clan.[36] These tenets reflect

---

[36] See https://en.wikipedia.org/wiki/Khawarij#cite_note-Glasse-255-3 (last accessed on October 18, 2016).

their penchant for the hollow, for faith as a mechanism of motion and openness that undermines human delusions of grandeur. Still, they are excoriated by other jihadi leaders for their excessive zealotry in branding other Muslims as heretics.

Alternatively, they are treated as trifling. The Islamic State will be wiped out by a concentrated Western effort, say the other jihadis, possibly because they are such radicals. Their soldiers, lording it over other movements because of their state, will be dispersed and scattered, forced to fight for their very survival. The Islamic State, however, considers itself a permanent whirlwind rather than a temporary one. Its in-house rivals recognize the gap at the heart of IS, the emptiness that drives a vision encapsulating (but never fully inhabiting) both highest and lowest. These rivals see this gap as a deficiency, because it reflects the lack of a clear ideology accompanied by clear goals. For IS, its breeziness is its anchor. The Islamic State will remain because it is a great wind leveling the world. It will remain because it is remaining. The realness of IS is generated in and by its present.

*As for you, O soldiers of the Islamic State, then congratulations to you. Congratulations on this clear victory, congratulations on this great triumph. Today the kāfirīn (infidels) are infuriated in such a manner after which there will be no similar infuriation. Many of them almost die from anger and sorrow. Today the believers rejoice with victory from Allah, feeling great happiness. Today the hypocrites are degraded. Today the rāfidah (shia), sahwāt (awakening councils), and murtaddīn (apostates) are humiliated. Today the tawāghīt in the east and west are frightened. Today the nations of kufr in the west are terrified. Today the flags of Shaytān (Satan) and his party have fallen. Today the flag of tawhīd rises with its people. Today the Muslims are honored. Today the Muslims are honored. Now the khilāfah has returned, humbling the necks of the enemy. Now the khilāfah has returned in spite of its opponents. Now the khilāfah has returned; we ask Allah (the Exalted) to make it to be upon the methodology of prophethood. Now hope is being actualized. Now the dream has become a reality. Congratulations to you. You spoke and were truthful. You promised and kept to your word.*

*O soldiers of the Islamic State, it is from the great blessings of Allah upon you that He allowed you to reach this day and witness this victory, which did not arrive except by the grace of Allah (the Exalted) and then by the blood and corpses of thousands of your brothers who preceded you from the best of mankind. We consider them such and Allah is their judge, and we do not presume to know better than Him. They are those who carried this banner and under it sacrificed everything. They offered everything generously, even their souls, to pass on this great banner to you. Indeed, they did so. May Allah have mercy upon them and reward them with every good on behalf of Islam. So protect this great trust. Raise this banner with strength. Water it with your blood. Raise it upon your corpses. Die under it, until you pass it on – if Allah wills – to 'Isā (Jesus) the son of Maryam (Mary), peace be upon him.*

*O soldiers of the Islamic State, Allah (the Exalted) ordered us with jihad and promised us with victory but He did not make us responsible for victory. Indeed, Allah (the Exalted) blessed you today with this victory, thus we announced the khilāfah in compliance with the order of Allah (the Exalted). We announced it because – by Allah's grace – we have its essentials. By Allah's permission, we are capable of establishing the khilāfah. So we carry out the order of Allah (the Exalted) and we are justified – if Allah wills – and we do not care thereafter what happens, even if we only remain for one day or one hour, and to Allah belongs the matter before and after. If Allah (the Exalted) causes the khilāfah to remain and gain strength, then such is by His grace and bounty alone, for victory is only from Him. And if it vanishes and weakens, then know that such is from ourselves and because of our deeds.*

*We will defend it – if Allah wills – as long as it exists and as long as one of us remains, and [if it vanishes] we will bring it back – if Allah wills – upon the methodology of prophethood.*

*Whoever has the loftiest height as his own ambition,*
*Then everything he faces will be beloved. [Poetry]*

The tensions of the hollow present grow clearer in this passage. The great triumph is the infuriation of the infidels, rather than their deaths. The ultimate victory, the separation of the righteous from the wicked, will not take place in the present. Here and now, victory consists of reflecting to a heathen world its own emptiness and irrelevance. To be more precise, victory has to do with exposing the vacuity of "the world's" human conventions on power and order. The response of "the world" to such exposure is, rightfully, near-death from anger and sorrow. What could be more fortunate than learning that one's perception of self, at all levels, is false?

The world is emptier in a physical sense as well. The creation of the Islamic State entailed sacrifice. Believers died so that the state may come into real being. Their sacrifice must be remembered and celebrated, and it must become a part of life. Death is a part of life. The presence of every believer at the realization of a political goal is not a necessary condition for this realization. The state, the whirlwind, should be borne up on corpses if necessary, until it reaches the endtimes. Then, it will be passed to Jesus who will command the armies of the faithful.[37] The transition, and the difference, between the present

---

[37] See, for example, the following comprehensive list of signs before the Day of Judgment: www.inter-islam.org/faith/Majorsigns.html (last accessed on October 18, 2016).

and the past could not be clearer. The now is depleted so that the future may be replete.

The present is its own justification. The caliphate was not established deterministically. Previously, the argument was that there was no reason not to establish it ("Why? Why not?"). But the argument has shifted subtly. The caliphate was established because the essentials were in place. The victory necessary for the establishment was God's. Apparently, so was the order to move forward with essentials only. There was no completion and no climax. If the caliphate was an expansion, it was an expansion of the hollowing out. the past and the future of each human act are God's to command. The present is a series of moments, each dedicated to the enhancement of the level, open world. The caliphate introduced this world to the Islamic State. Those who established the caliphate profess their disengagement from it. The real world is driven by faith and faith must preserve its duality, preventing an "ideological" commitment to one side or the other.

*O soldiers of the Islamic State, you will be facing malāhim (fierce battles) that cause the children's hair to become grey. You will be facing fitan (tribulations) and hardships of many different colors. You will be facing tests and quakes. No one will survive them except he whom Allah grants mercy. No one will be firm during these fitan except one whom Allah keeps firm. The worst of these fitan is that of the dunyā (worldly life). So be wary of competing over it. Be wary. Remember the greatest responsibility that is now on your backs. You are now the defenders of the land of Islam and its guards. You will not be able to preserve this trust and defend this land, except by fearing Allah secretly and publically, then by sacrificing, being patient, and offering blood.*

*I am amazed by those who possess the stature of men and the sharpness of arrows,*
*Yet their command is not made nor executed.*
*I am amazed by those who find the path to lofty heights,*
*Yet do not traverse the path, wearing it down until no mounds are left.*
*And I have not found a fault in people like that of those*
*Who are capable of completing their effort, but instead abort it. [Poetry]*

The present is the realm of trials and tribulations. The sorting will continue until the very last moment, just before Judgment Day arrives. Faith is necessary for survival, and the biggest test is the world itself. The world carries the temptation of a sovereignty unrelated to God and to what appears to the human eye as the arbitrariness of divine truth. If one could harness the world, whispers the devil inside us all, one could impose true order and sense on unruly creation. Such behavior would be straying from the proper path. On that path, the sovereign

self should practice awe, forbearance and sacrifice. The borders of the
land of Islam are not specified, and neither is potential expansion. In
order to defend God's religion, the believers need to detract from the
world, not add to it. Abortion in the face of completion is the sign of
true virtue.

*O soldiers of the Islamic State, there is one more matter that I wish to call your
attention to. They will look for something to criticize and will attempt to raise
misconceptions. So if they ask you, "How can you announce the khilāfah when
the ummah has not rallied behind you? For your authority is not accepted by the
groups, factions, detachments, brigades, corps, banners, sects, parties, assemblies,
councils, institutions, coordination teams, leagues, coalitions, armies, fronts,
movements, and organizations." Then say to them,*

*{But they will not cease to differ except whom your Lord has given mercy}
[Hūd: 118–119].*

*They have never united on a single issue, nor will they ever unite on any issue
except for those whom Allah has mercy upon. Furthermore, the Islamic State will
bring together those who want unity.*

*If they tell you, "You have stepped over them and acted on your own judgment.
Why did you not consult the other groups, pardon them, and tolerate them?"
Then say to them, "The issue is too urgent."*

*{And I hastened to You, my Lord, that You be pleased} [Tāhā: 84].*

*And say to them, "Whom would we consult? They never recognized the Islamic
State to begin with, although America, Britain and France acknowledge its existence. Whom would we consult? Should we consult those who have abandoned
us? Those who have betrayed us? Those who have disowned us and incited against
us? Those who have become hostile towards us? Those who wage war against us?
Whom would we consult, and whom did we step over?"*

*Indeed the difference between me and my brothers and cousins is very big.
They do not come to my aid, but if they called me for help I would come to their
    rescue. [Poetry]*

The West may despise the Islamic State, but at least it acknowledges its
existence. The leaders of rival jihadi movements find fault with the realness of IS. The founders of the caliphate did not obtain the approval of
the people or of the militias. The caliphate, according to these jihadis, has
no real presence in the potentially Islamic world. The caliphate is empty,
suggest the accusations, empty of supporters and resources. For IS's leadership, this nitpicking is, quite literally, unreal. The ummah, the Muslim
community, has never been united. The uniting message of IS, in any case,
lies in its motion and emergence. The notion of uniting around an idea,
pretending to a stability that is God's alone, is reprehensible in any case.
The hostility of the entire world to IS is not the result of an ideological

conflict. The world, claiming false fullness, is angry and afraid almost to the point of death when confronted with the prospect of true hollowness.

This, once again, is the definition of IS success. The Islamic state is not in the business of winning or of vindication. It has already been vindicated and it will win. The in-between time is too present, too occurring, too uncertain for such stable amenities. Living and acting in the in-between time, IS is scorned, trivialized and ignored by those who insist on a politics of absolute concepts. The West trumpets its human rights while rival jihadis swear by the collective will of the ummah, but both suffer from an acute lack of realness.

*And if they tell you, "We do not accept your authority." Then say to them, "We had the ability to establish the khilāfah, by the grace of Allah, so it became an obligation for us to do so. Therefore, we hastened in adherence to the command of Allah (the Exalted):*

*{It is not for a believing man or a believing woman, when Allah and His Messenger have decided a matter, that they should [thereafter] have any choice about their affair} [Al-Ahzāb: 36].*

*And say to them, "We spilled rivers of our blood to water the seeds of the khilāfah, laid its foundation with our skulls, and built its tower over our corpses. We were patient for years in the face of being killed, imprisoned, having our bones broken and our limbs severed. We drank all sorts of bitterness, dreaming of this day. Would we delay it for even a moment after having reached it?"*

*And say to them,*

*We took it forcibly at the point of a blade.*
 *We brought it back conquered and compelled.*
*We established it in defiance of many.*
 *And the people's necks were violently struck,*
*With bombings, explosions, and destruction,*
 *And soldiers that do not see hardship as being difficult,*
*And lions that are thirsty in battle,*
 *Having greedily drunk the blood of kufr.*
*Our khilāfah has indeed returned with certainty*
 *And likewise our state, becoming a firm structure.*
*And the breasts of the believers have been healed,*
 *While the hearts of kufr have been filled with terror.*
*[Poetry]*

*In conclusion, we congratulate the Muslims on the advent of the blessed month of Ramadan. We ask Allah (the Exalted) to make it a month of victory, honor, and consolidation for the Muslims, and make its days and its nights a curse for the rāfidah, the sahwāt, and the murtaddīn.*

*{And Allah is predominant over His affair, but most of the people do not know.}*
*[Yūsuf: 21]*

The sovereignty of the caliphate comes from an evolving, diverse interaction. The leaders of IS were obliged to create the caliphate because they had the ability to do so and did so with fortuitous timing. This is not necessarily the causal chain we might expect. The obligation, and divine grace, are usually seen as creating the ability. Timing, certainly in the case of monotheistic visions, is supposed to be relevant for revelations only. In the case of IS, it is an essential part of the realization. Standing in contrast to the fullness of the divine, such realism is distinctly human and profoundly empty of any and all grand aspersions. The violence of the poetic fragment is a part of the pragmatic unfolding, a heady dose of humanity at its most base enabling the most noble truth. Violence is real, and everything that is real has been used in conjunction so that the caliphate may come into being. Once it has, it will embark on its one true mission in the in-between time. Life and death, high and low, can intermingle so effectively only in a growing void, empty enough to receive and hold them all.

## Presenting IS Theology of the Real:
## Concluding Thoughts

Most observers and scholars of IS, including McCants and Wood, end their analyses with a section of recommendations and action items. McCants entitles it, simply and to the point, "what to do."[38] The Islamic State is, first and foremost, a problem. It is extremely violent in thought and practice. It has fought tenaciously to defend its territory against a broad variety of rivals, from Kurds to the forces of an international coalition directed against IS. The Islamic State has proven itself capable of perpetrating genocide on Iraqi Yazidis, a small religious community branded by IS as heretical.[39] Its supporters have demonstrated both will and capability to carry out terrorist attacks all over the world, particularly in the heart of the West, from the United States to the EU. The Islamic State has become attractive to young, angry Muslims from across the world, and particularly from Europe, the Middle East and North Africa. These Muslim youths slip into Syria through its border with Turkey, receive training and participate in the heavy fighting. Some of them later return to their homes, providing security threats for local intelligence and law

---

[38] See McCants, *The ISIS Apocalypse*, pp. 155–159.
[39] See, for example, the following report on the determination by UN investigators that IS is perpetrating a genocide of the Yazidis: www.reuters.com/article/us-mideast-crisis-syria-yazidi-idUSKCN0Z20WR (last accessed on October 18, 2016).

enforcement entities. The Islamic State's theology is actively disseminated online, and its cyber capabilities are constantly increasing and deepening.[40] These are all expressions of the major gauntlets IS has thrown at the feet of the international community.

All of these problems are occurring now, in real time. Even if the actual Islamic State (stretching between Aleppo in Syria and Diyala in Iraq, as we may recall) were to fall to Iraqi/Syrian/Russian/International coalition attacks,[41] its supporters and partisans look set to continue the struggle all over the world, from Bangladesh to Belgium. The expanding subset of those inspired by IS to violently pursue their own agendas, often personal, is in attendance from Florida to Minnesota and from France to China. But despite this expansion and diversification, despite the dynamic and fluid nature of the IS present, the accounts and interpretations of IS activity ground such acts decisively in an absolute vision of the past or an absolute vision of the future.

Those focused on the past understand the resilience and fervor of IS to be the result of a devout belief in a very certain, very specific notion of leading a religious life. This notion, once revealed, has become absolutely obligatory upon all those who consider themselves truly faithful. Faith is a function of obedience to this binding revelation. Notions of political order highlight the unequivocal nature of the religious duty derived from the revelation. They are based on a strict hierarchy and on violent enforcement and purification (of the world).

Those focused on the future understand IS to be driven by an intense desire to reach the end-times and play the role predestined for the believers. That role, usually connected to the final battle between good and evil, will ensure those believers of a final reward. Those who do not seek salvation are nonetheless eager to assist the progress of the divine plan, to hasten the demise of the *dunya*, the daily and physical world. Living in the end-times entails a disregard for human rules of political behavior and order. When faced with the urgency of the second coming, why would a believer care for abstractions like human rights or Muslim unity? One does what one must do when intent on realizing the ultimate destiny.

Both approaches find it difficult to link religious sentiment to an unfolding present. In the age of critical thought, religion can be explained as a cult of the past or future, but not as a driving force of the here and now.

---

[40] See, for example, the following paper on IS cyber capabilities: http://resources.infosecinstitute.com/isis-cyber-capabilities/ (last accessed on October 18, 2016).
[41] Which it has not, at the time these words are written, in October 2016.

Faith is preserved for the unreal, either the long gone or the yet-to-come. This chapter has been an attempt to approach IS conceptions of the present and its realness, on their merits as demonstrations of faith. The difficulty of this approach with analytical languages geared toward ignoring either present or faith (or both) required a conceptual detour. Our reading of Leviticus 26 allowed us to consider the realness and political vitality of messianic redemption in the lives of believers. We could observe how this realness had little to do with morality, how redemption was a political process that constructed a collective consciousness in its wake.

This consciousness evolved in a temporal dimension that was removed from the first revelation (creation) but also from the second revelation (Judgment Day or a growing proximity to God). This was a specifically human time which I called, in deference to Giorgio Agamben, the in-between time. I suggested that this in-between time anchored a theology of the real, flawed and contextual, against the backdrop of certain faith in divine truth and perfection. The in-between time was devoted to the hollowing out of the world, clearing away the corrupted remnants of human reaction to the first revelation in order to allow human hearts to hold the impending revelation.

From Leviticus, we moved on to the IS declaration of the caliphate. Reading the document closely, we saw how focused it was on a present that was anything but absolute. This present was itself an in-between time, stretching limitless between holy history and potent prophecy. The very certitude in the real occurrence of the sacred past and the definite coming-to-be of the predestined future necessitated the utilization of the in-between time for the hollowing out of the world. What was a superimposed fate in Leviticus became a positive political program in the case of IS.

Reading the declaration of the caliphate, we saw how it introduced the world-to-be: hollowed to the self-enclosed virtue of the Islamic State in Iraq and the Sham (ISIS). We gradually drew the contours of the gap defining IS faith. At its heart, IS theology of the real is driven by an unbridgeable gap between its disparate components: high and low, select and rejected. In fact, the presence of this gap constantly subverts any clear-cut ideological conviction. The Islamic State's theology of the real is committed to the hollowing out of the world in preparation for the coming revelation, but also in order to hold within the world its real, albeit contradictory, elements. The Islamic State moves forward to create a world committed to this notion of the real, rather than a world indentured to the unitary promulgation of jihadi Shari'a.

Finally, I see no obligation to engage with questions such as "what to do." The past and the future may be explained or summarized within a linear argument, seemingly progressing from beginning to end. Still, the immutability of IS's past and future, depending on the analytical approach, severely limit the progression crucial to the integrity of such a linear argument. Engagement with the present, however, sets different goals. There is a need to understand, or at the very least to become immersed in the present, and that need precedes the urge for resolution. The present is less coherent and perfect than the future and the past. As such, attempts to approach the present and speak with it require the conceptual equivalent of decent walking shoes much more than an analytical blowtorch.

A present program dedicated to the hollowing out of the world evades endeavors of accurate naming. Words are elusive in this setting, often reflecting opposite meanings in different contexts and at different times of usage. This ambiguity, in the case of IS, is trivialized as the simple expiry of human time from one defining revelation to a second. I suggested a reading locating the primary focal point of IS faith – of IS realness to be exact – in this ambiguity. I proposed that this ambiguity was remarkably useful in directing the realization of the IS commitment to hollow out the world. The definition of IS success – infuriating the West to the point of near-death – has been remarkably poignant because of its grounding in ambiguity and emptiness. This state of affairs demonstrates when considering a proper response to IS, nothing can be more practical than engagement with IS's present, its theology of the real.

## Interlude III

For the Islamic State, the challenge of political faith is simply to keep up with the pace of an emergence almost too quick to behold. There is no eternity, for IS, between the first and the second revelation. There is, more likely, a blink of an eye. The law that must be applied is harsh and one because otherwise the sheer exuberance of redemption would flow over, demolishing reality (and with it duty and obligation) in its wake.

The Islamic State's theology of the real is grounded in the rush, in the necessity of applying the energy of redemption to the hollowing out of the world. Its ethics and its enforcement are born from the commitment of IS to this rush as the real, not its zealotry and not its opportunism. The politics of IS are not just politics on a mission, but politics with a rhythm you can dance to.

# Concluding Repetition

This book was meant as an exercise in engagement. Engagement is a mode of intellectual pursuit suited to my subjects of inquiry: theologies of the real. I refrained as much as possible (and, hopefully, enough) from resolution of the tensions raised. These tensions, I suggested, were the drivers and generators of realness for the theologies we considered. The Islamic State, torn between the certainty of ultimate victory and the ungrateful unfolding of the present; Khomeini, proactive leader and frustrated believer; Gershon Hacohen, soldier of the state and the architect of mediating space – all could locate and apply their faith to guide them through an emerging, uncertain reality. God, who spoke once and will speak again, remained stubbornly absent from this materializing present. Our protagonists all sought (and seek) means to maintain their own engagement with God, through faith, when God's realness is expressed in divine silence.

In a previous book devoted to revolutionary Shi'i theology in Iran,[1] I suggested that repetition is a key dynamic of that theology. I borrowed the term from the Danish philosopher Søren Kierkegaard, who devoted a minor work to the concept.[2] I would like to revisit Kierkegaard's notion of repetition as something of a conclusion for the journey documented in this book. Kierkegaard's concept has much to say about the engagement practiced in this book.

[1] Ori Goldberg, *Shi'i Theology in Iran: The Challenge of Religious Experience* (Routledge, 2011).
[2] Søren Kierkegaard, *Fear and Trembling/Repetition*, trans. Howard and Edna Hong (Princeton University Press, 1983).

For Kierkegaard, "repetition" is a state of being in the world which stands in contrast to the Greek idea of "recollection." In Kierkegaard's words:

Repetition and recollection are the same movement, except in opposite directions, for what is recollected has been, is repeated backward, whereas genuine repetition is recollected forward. Repetition, therefore, if it is possible, makes a person happy, whereas recollection makes him unhappy – assuming, of course, that he gives himself time to live and does not promptly at birth find an excuse to sneak out of life again, for example, that he has forgotten something.[3]

As a mode of investigation, recollection begins with a void. Something actually happened once but it will not happen again. Recollecting, our point of origin is this unbridgeable chasm. Because we know something happened – God spoke to a prophet, The Red Sea was parted, we felt sudden happiness doing nothing in particular – we also know that occurrence cannot be repeated. We can only try to recollect, remember how it once was. We are repeating backwards, as Kierkegaard says, but what we are repeating is our inability to be certain in the moment that once was. That inability gathers momentum and traction, and it becomes the main dynamic with which we approach the world. A person can go an entire lifetime without living, says Kierkegaard, because having forgotten something she might spend her entire life repeating her inability to remember it. Recollection is the opposite of living because it strives for a solid wholeness it can never achieve.

Recollection seems to provide the comfort of linearity, but this is only a superficial impression. Repetition demonstrates this superficiality. Recollecting, one thinks that simply repeating backward steps will lead us to the inevitable point of origin, the one moment that actually occurred. That is the one moment we seek when we recollect. Realizing that we can never experience it again, however, renders our recollection perennially empty. Unlike the in-between time we considered earlier in the book, the present of recollection can never be filled. Repetition is another matter. When we repeat, we do not strive (pretend, more likely) to the perfect accuracy of a single moment. We recollect forward, assuming that the purpose of an occurrence is to galvanize an entire life of action. Memory runs forward in repetition, emanating from the perfection of the moment without wallowing in it. That perfection is a point of origin, not a vision to be actually realized.

Kierkegaard continues:

Recollection's love [*Kjærlighed*], an author has said, is the only happy love. He is perfectly right in that, of course, provided one recollects that initially it makes a person unhappy. Repetition's love is in truth the only happy love. Like

---

[3] Kierkegaard, *Repetition*, p. 131.

recollection's love, it does not have the restlessness of hope, the uneasy adventurousness of discovery, but neither does it have the sadness of recollection – it has the blissful security of the moment. Hope is a new garment, stiff and starched and lustrous, but it has never been tried on, and therefore one does not know how becoming it will be or how it will fit. Recollection is a discarded garment that does not fit, however beautiful it is, for one has outgrown it. Repetition is an indestructible garment that fits closely and tenderly, neither binds nor sags.[4]

The perfection of the moment is not equal to the security of the moment. Security does not lie in the static quality of perfection. Recollection's love seems happy because one can devote oneself to such love forever, doting on the perfect memory that forever remains outside one's grasp. The futility of recollection is the key to its permanence. Repetition accepts the imperviousness of time. What happened has already happened. The moment is secure because it has really occurred, not because there is a possibility of it occurring again in exactly the same way. The realness of the moment, its holism, lies in its completion. Respect for that realness requires forward motion, recollecting forward. Repetition is indestructible because it is the only mode of being that acknowledges the permanence and solidity of other moments, of all moments, without wishing to undo that permanence. Recollection is disrespectful because a person can never fully occupy her present moment, since that moment is always enslaved to a past (or a future). Repetition is the epitome of respect because only when fully occupying the present can one fully appreciate the truth of the past.

Hope is a lovely maiden who slips away between one's fingers; recollection is a beautiful old woman with whom one is never satisfied at the moment; repetition is a beloved wife of whom one never wearies, for one becomes weary only of what is new. One never grows weary of the old, and when one has that, one is happy.[5]

Kierkegaard's articulation of happiness provides our excursion, I think, with a suitable denouement. The theologies of the real which we read and considered are happy in the Kierkegaardian sense, and that may be their most downplayed and misunderstood quality. For these theologies, the real is emergence and uncertainty, but also faith. They are secure in what has happened and in what will happen. Khomeini knows that Iran was defeated, just as he knows that the Mahdi will come to deliver the Shi'a at the end of days. Gershon Hacohen knows that he must enforce

4 Ibid., pp. 131–132.
5 Ibid., p. 132.

the will of the state in order to ensure its continuity and progress. Doing so, he affirms the faith of his Zionist forefathers and rejects the zero-sum game played by the flawed sovereignties of Ariel Sharon and Rabbi Tzvi Yehuda Kook. The Islamic State knows the initial revelation brought by the prophet Muhammad. It knows the oppression and humiliation of the Muslims, but it also knows the assured triumph of the final battle. For all three, what was and what will be impose an imperative to participate fully in what is.

One is never happy with the new because the new throws one for a loop. Newness becomes its own reward, and once that happens the race for the newer never ends. Novelty becomes the only mark of virtue, detached from tradition but also from emotions. Singlehanded pursuit of the new has no room for happiness because happiness is irrelevant. The theologies of the real we've examined have little use for the exclusively new. The realness of these theologies involves both certainty and unfolding. They must have confidence in a beginning and an end in order to effectively progress through the emanating middle. Realness is the integration of all three ingredients. Happiness is a condition of realness, mixing security, expectation and motion.

Our theologies of the real often seem somber, full of loss and sacrifice and never-ending devotion. They are. Nonetheless, they are also full of life and worldliness, repeating rather than recollecting. In fact, their practitioners would be puzzled at an accusation of fanaticism or a lack of realism. They understand their vision of the real to be the richest, fullest vision possible precisely because they do not forgo the security of any moment. Engaging them meaningfully requires that some relinquishing of recollection. The threat of IS, the spirituality of pragmatic Zionism and the messianic belief of Iranian Shi'a – all three can be approached as problems seeking solutions, two-dimensional entities at the mercy of an analytical intellect. In this book, I have attempted to suggest otherwise. Their challenge is their foundational link of faith and realness. Those wishing to engage them cannot do so without asking how and why they themselves believe in the real.

# Select Bibliography

This is, indeed, a select bibliography. The book's style is personal and essayistic, not allowing for much studious reference. The bibliography is meant as a roadmap of sorts through the various fields and disciplines that provided pastures and havens on my path toward engagements with theologies of the real. Other works were consulted as well, but the ones appearing below had significant influence on my thinking and writing. I've attempted to list the newest editions available of the works mentioned.

Abrahamian, Ervand, *A History of Modern Iran* (Cambridge University Press, 2008).
  *Khomeinism: Essays on the Islamic Republic* (University of California Press, 1993).
Adib-Moghaddam, Arshin (ed.), *A Critical Introduction to Khomeini* (Cambridge University Press, 2014).
Agamben, Giorgio, *The Kingdom and the Glory: For a Theological Genealogy of Economy and Government* (Stanford University Press, 2011).
  *Profanations* (Zone Books, 2015).
  *The Time that Remains: A Commentary on the Letter to the Romans* (Stanford University Press, 2005).
Anidjar, Gil, *Blood: A Critique of Christianity* (Columbia University Press, 2016).
  *The Jew, The Arab: A History of the Enemy* (Stanford University Press, 2003).
Ankersmit, Frank, *Aesthetic Politics: Political Philosophy Beyond Fact and Value* (Stanford University Press, 1997).
  *Sublime Historical Experience* (Stanford University Press, 2005).
Arjomand, Said Amir, *The Turban for the Crown: The Islamic Revolution in Iran* (Oxford University Press, 1989).
Axworthy, Michael, *Revolutionary Iran: A History of the Islamic Republic* (Oxford University Press, 2013).
Ayoub, Mahmoud, *Islam: Faith and History* (Oneworld publications, 2005).
Bachelard, Gaston, *The Poetics of Space* (Beacon Press, 1994).
Barth, Karl, *The Epistle to the Romans* (Oxford University Press, 1968).

Brekke, Torkel, *Faithonomics: Religion and the Free Market* (Oxford University Press, 2016).
 *Fundamentalism: Prophecy and Protest in an Age of Globalization* (Cambridge University Press, 2011).
Brumberg, Daniel, *Reinventing Khomeini: The Struggle for Reform in Iran* (University of Chicago Press, 2001).
Buber, Martin, *Two Types of Faith: A Study of the Interpenetration of Judaism and Christianity* (Syracuse University Press, 2003).
Casanova, Jose, *Public Religions in the Modern World* (University of Chicago Press, 1994).
Cockburn, Patrick, *The Rise of Islamic State: ISIS and the New Sunni Revolution* (Verso, 2015).
Cook, Michael, *Ancient Religions, Modern Politics: The Islamic Case in Comparative Perspective* (Princeton University Press, 2016).
Critchley, Simon, *The Faith of the Faithless: Experiments in Political Theology* (Verso, 2014).
Davis, Creston, John Milbank and Slavoj Žižek (eds.), *Theology and the Political: The New Debate* (Duke University Press, 2005).
De Certeau, Michel, *The Practice of Everyday Life* (University of California Press, 2011).
De Vries, Hent, *Philosophy and the Turn to Religion* (Johns Hopkins University Press, 1999).
 (ed.) *Religion: Beyond a Concept* (Fordham University Press, 2000).
De Vries, Hent and Lawrence Sullivan (eds.) *Political Theologies: Public Religions in a Post-Secular World* (Fordham University Press, 2006).
Efrat, Elisha, *The West Bank and the Gaza Strip: A Geography of Occupation and Disengagement* (Routledge, 2006).
Evans, C. Stephen, *Faith Beyond Reason: A Kierkegaardian Account* (Eerdmans, 1998).
 *Kierkegaard on Faith and the Self: Collected Essays* (Baylor University Press, 2011).
Farrin, Raymond, *Structure and Qur'anic Interpretation: A Study of Symmetry and Coherence in Islam's Holy Text* (White Cloud Press, 2014).
Feige, Michael, *Settling in the Hearts: Jewish Fundamentalism in the Occupied Territories* (Wayne State University Press, 2009).
Filiu, Jean-Pierre, *From Deep State to Islamic State: The Arab Counter-Revolution and its Jihadi Legacy* (Oxford University Press, 2015).
Gadamer, Hans Georg, *Philosophical Hermeneutics* (California University Press, 2008).
 *Truth and Method* (Bloomsbury Academic, 2013).
Gerges, Fawaz, *ISIS: A History* (Princeton University Press, 2016).
(Al-)Ghazali, *The Ninety-Nine Beautiful Names of God, translated with Notes by David Burrell and Nazih Daher* (The Islamic Texts Society, 2012).
Gleave, Robert, *Islam and Literalism: Literal Meaning and Interpretation in Islamic Legal Theory* (Edinburgh University Press, 2013).
 *Violence in Islamic thought from the Qur'an to the Mongols* (Edinburgh University Press, 2015).

Gorenberg, Gershon, *The Accidental Empire: Israel and the Birth of the Settlements, 1967–1977* (Holt Paperbacks, 2007).

Görke, Andreas and Johanna Pink (eds.), *Tafsir and Islamic Intellectual History: Exploring the Boundaries of a Genre* (Oxford University Press in Association with the Institute of Ismaili Studies, 2015).

Hamid, Shadi, *Islamic Exceptionalism: How the Struggle over Islam is Shaping the World* (St. Martin's Press, 2016).

Hatina, Meir, *Martyrdom in Modern Islam: Piety, Power, and Politics* (Cambridge University Press, 2015).

Helman, Anat, *Becoming Israeli: National Ideals and Everyday Life in the 1950s* (Brandeis University Press, 2014).

Inbari, Moti, *Messianic Religious Judaism Confronts Israeli Territorial Compromises* (Cambridge University Press, 2012).

Karsh, Efraim, *The Iran–Iraq War, 1980–1988*, Kindle Edition (Osprey Publishing, 2002).

Kierkegaard, Søren, *Eighteen Upbuilding Discourses: Kierkegaard's Writings, Vol. 5* (Princeton University Press, 1992).

*Fear and Trembling/Repetition: Kierkegaard's Writings, Vol. 6* (Princeton University Press, 1983).

*Practice in Christianity: Kierkegaard's Writings, Vol. 20* (Princeton University Press, 1991).

*Upbuilding Discourse in Various Spirits: Kierkegaard's Writings, Vol. 25* (Princeton University Press, 2009).

Khomeini, Ruhollah, *Islam and Revolution: Writings and Declarations of Imam Khomeini*, trans. Hamid Algar (Mizan Press, 1981).

Lambek, Michael (ed.), *A Reader in the Anthropology of Religion* (Wiley-Blackwell, 2008).

Landau, David, *Arik: The Life of Ariel Sharon* (Knopf, 2014).

Lefebvre, Henri, *Critique of Everyday Life* (Verso, 2014).

*The Production of Space* (wiley-Blackwell, 1992).

Lilla, Mark, *The Stillborn God: Religion, Politics and the Modern West* (Vintage, 2008).

Lustick, Ian, *For the Land and the Lord: Jewish Fundamentalism in Israel* (Council on Foreign Relations Press, 1988).

McCants, William, *The ISIS Apocalypse: The History, Strategy and Doomsday Vision of the Islamic State* (St. Martin's Press, 2015).

Medding, Peter, *Mapai in Israel: Political Organization and Government in a New Society* (Cambridge University Press, 2010).

Milbank, John, *Beyond Secular Order: The Representation of Being and the Representation of the People* (Wiley-Blackwell, 2014).

*The Politics of Virtue: Post-Liberalism and the Human Future* (Rowman & Littlefield International, 2016).

*Theology and Social Theory: Beyond Secular Reason* (Wiley-Blackwell, 2006).

*The Word Made Strange: Theology, Language, Culture* (Wiley-Blackwell, 1997).

Mirsky, Yehudah, *Rav Kook: Mystic in a Time of Revolution* (Yale University Press, 2014).

Moin, Baqer, *Khomeini: Life of the Ayatollah* (IB Tauris, 2009).

Momen, Moojan, *An Introduction to Shi'i Islam: The History and Doctrines of Shi'i Islam* (Yale University Press, 1987).

Mottahedeh, Roy, *The Mantle of the Prophet: Religion and Politics in Iran* (Oneworld Publications, 2008).

Murray, Williamson and Kevin Woods, *The Iran–Iraq War: A Military and Strategic History* (Cambridge University Press, 2014).

Ochs, Peter, *Peirce, Pragmatism and the Logic of Scripture* (Cambridge University Press, 2005).

Pals, Daniel, *Nine Theories of Religion* (Oxford University Press, 2014).

Pickstock, Catherine, *After Writing: On the Liturgical Consummation of Philosophy* (Wiley-Blackwell, 1997).

   *Repetition and Identity: The Literary Agenda* (Oxford University Press, 2014).

Razoux, Pierre, *The Iran–Iraq War* (Belknap Press, 2015).

Ricoeur, Paul, *The Conflict of Interpretations* (Northwestern University Press, 1974).

   *Figuring the Sacred: Religion, Narrative and Imagination* (Fortress Press, 1995).

   *Interpretation Theory: Discourse and the Surplus of Meaning* (Texas Christian University Press, 1976).

   *The Rule of Metaphor: The Creation of Meaning in Language* (Routledge, 2003).

Sachedina, Abdulaziz, *Islamic Messianism: The Idea of the Mahdi in Twelver Shi'ism* (State University of New York Press, 1981).

   *The Just Ruler in Shi'ite Islam: The Comprehensive Authority of the Jurist in Imamite Jurisprudence* (Oxford University Press, 1998).

Schmitt, Carl, *Dictatorship* (Polity, 2013).

   *Political Theology: Four Chapters on the Concept of Sovereignty* (University of Chicago Press, 2006).

Sells, Michael, *Approaching the Qur'an: The Early Revelations* (White Cloud Press, 2007).

Silberstein, Laurence, *The Postzionism Debates: Knowledge and Power in Israeli Culture* (Routledge, 1999).

Tanizaki, Junichiro, *In Praise of Shadows* (Leete's Island Books, 1977).

Taub, Gadi, *The Settlers and the Struggle over the meaning of Zionism* (Yale University Press, 2011).

Taylor, Charles, *A Secular Age* (Belknap Press of Harvard University Press, 2007).

   *Sources of the Self: The Making of the Modern Identity* (Harvard University Press, 1992).

Tuan, Yi-Fu, *Space and Place: The Perspective of Experience* (University of Minnesota Press, 2001).

Vahdat, Farzin, *God and Juggernaut: Iran's Intellectual Encounter with Modernity* (Syracuse University Press, 2002).

Warrick, Joby, *Black Flags: The Rise of ISIS* (Anchor, 2016).

Weiss, Michael and Hassan Hassan, *ISIS: Inside the Army of Terror* (Regan Arts, 2015).

Westphal, Merold, *Kierkegaard's Concept of Faith* (Eerdmans, 2014).

Winzeler, Robert, *Anthropology and Religion: What We Know, Think and Question* (AltaMira Press, 2012).

Wistrich, Robert and David Ohana (eds.), *The Shaping of Israeli Identity: Myth, Memory and Trauma* (Routledge, 1995).

Zertal, Idith and Akiva Eldar, *Lords of the Land: The War for Israel's Settlements in the Occupied Territories, 1967–2007* (Nation Books, 2007).

Žižek, Slavoj, *On Belief* (Routledge, 2001).

*The Sublime Object of Ideology* (Verso, 2009).

Žižek, Slavoj and Boris Gunjevich, *God in Pain: Inversions of Apocalypse* (Seven Stories Press, 2012).

# Index